T0214384

Lecture Notes in Computer Science 11284

Commenced Publication in 1973
Founding and Former Series Editors:
Gerhard Goos, Juris Hartmanis, and Jan van Leeuwen

Editorial Board

David Hutchison
  Lancaster University, Lancaster, UK
Takeo Kanade
  Carnegie Mellon University, Pittsburgh, PA, USA
Josef Kittler
  University of Surrey, Guildford, UK
Jon M. Kleinberg
  Cornell University, Ithaca, NY, USA
Friedemann Mattern
  ETH Zurich, Zurich, Switzerland
John C. Mitchell
  Stanford University, Stanford, CA, USA
Moni Naor
  Weizmann Institute of Science, Rehovot, Israel
C. Pandu Rangan
  Indian Institute of Technology Madras, Chennai, India
Bernhard Steffen
  TU Dortmund University, Dortmund, Germany
Demetri Terzopoulos
  University of California, Los Angeles, CA, USA
Doug Tygar
  University of California, Berkeley, CA, USA
Gerhard Weikum
  Max Planck Institute for Informatics, Saarbrücken, Germany

More information about this series at http://www.springer.com/series/7409

Tianyong Hao · Wei Chen
Haoran Xie · Wanvimol Nadee
Rynson Lau (Eds.)

Emerging Technologies for Education

Third International Symposium, SETE 2018
Held in Conjunction with ICWL 2018
Chiang Mai, Thailand, August 22–24, 2018
Revised Selected Papers

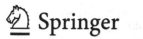
Springer

Editors
Tianyong Hao
South China Normal University
Guangzhou, China

Wanvimol Nadee
Maejo University
Chiang Mai, China

Wei Chen
Chinese Academy of Agricultural Sciences
Beijing, China

Rynson Lau
City University of Hong Kong
Hong Kong, Hong Kong SAR, China

Haoran Xie
Education University of Hong Kong
Hong Kong, Hong Kong SAR, China

ISSN 0302-9743   ISSN 1611-3349 (electronic)
Lecture Notes in Computer Science
ISBN 978-3-030-03579-2   ISBN 978-3-030-03580-8 (eBook)
https://doi.org/10.1007/978-3-030-03580-8

Library of Congress Control Number: 2018960677

LNCS Sublibrary: SL3 – Information Systems and Applications, incl. Internet/Web, and HCI

© Springer Nature Switzerland AG 2018
This work is subject to copyright. All rights are reserved by the Publisher, whether the whole or part of the material is concerned, specifically the rights of translation, reprinting, reuse of illustrations, recitation, broadcasting, reproduction on microfilms or in any other physical way, and transmission or information storage and retrieval, electronic adaptation, computer software, or by similar or dissimilar methodology now known or hereafter developed.
The use of general descriptive names, registered names, trademarks, service marks, etc. in this publication does not imply, even in the absence of a specific statement, that such names are exempt from the relevant protective laws and regulations and therefore free for general use.
The publisher, the authors, and the editors are safe to assume that the advice and information in this book are believed to be true and accurate at the date of publication. Neither the publisher nor the authors or the editors give a warranty, express or implied, with respect to the material contained herein or for any errors or omissions that may have been made. The publisher remains neutral with regard to jurisdictional claims in published maps and institutional affiliations.

This Springer imprint is published by the registered company Springer Nature Switzerland AG
The registered company address is: Gewerbestrasse 11, 6330 Cham, Switzerland

Preface

SETE 2018, the Third Annual International Symposium on Emerging Technologies for Education, was held in conjunction with ICWL 2018 organized by the Hong Kong Web Society. SETE was open to the public for organizing a workshop or track to achieve diversity in the symposium. Fueled by ICT technologies, the e-learning environment in the education sector has become more innovative than ever before. Diversified emerging technologies containing various software and hardware components provide the underlying infrastructure needed to create enormous potential educational applications incorporated by proper learning strategies. Moreover, these prevalent technologies might also lead to changes in the educational environment and thus in learning performance. Moreover, new paradigms are also emerging with the purpose of bringing these innovations to a certain level where they are widely accepted and sustainable. Therefore, this symposium aims at serving as a meeting point for researchers, educationalists, and practitioners to discuss state-of-the-art and in-progress research, exchange ideas, and share experiences about emerging technologies for education. This symposium provides opportunities for the cross-fertilization of knowledge and ideas from researchers in diverse fields that make up this interdisciplinary research area. We hope that the implications of the findings of each work presented at this symposium can be used to improve the development of educational environments.

This year's conference was located in Chiang Mai, the largest city in northern Thailand, which sits astride the Ping River, a major tributary of the Chao Phraya River.

This year we received 51 submissions from eight countries and regions worldwide. After a rigorous double-blind review process, 23 papers were selected as full papers, yielding an acceptance rate of 45%. In addition, three more short papers were selected. These contributions cover the latest findings in areas such as: emerging technologies of design, model and framework of learning systems, emerging technologies support for intelligent tutoring, emerging technologies support for game-based and joyful learning, and emerging technologies of pedagogical issues.

Moreover, SETE 2018 featured keynote presentations and two workshops, covering user modeling and language learning, and educational technology for language and translation learning.

We would like to thank the Organizing Committee and especially the organization co-chairs, Wanvimol Nadee, Tianyong Hao, and Wei Chen, for their efforts and time spent to ensure the success of the conference. We would also like to express our gratitude to the Program Committee members for their timely and helpful reviews. And last but not least, we would like to thank all the authors for their contribution in maintaining a high-quality conference – We count on your continued support in playing a significant role in the Web-based learning community in the future.

August 2018

Tianyong Hao
Wei Chen
Haoran Xie
Wanvimol Nadee
Rynson Lau

Organization

General Co-chairs

Wanvimol Nadee   Maejo University, Thailand
Rynson Lau   City University of Hong Kong, Hong Kong SAR, China

Technical Program Committee Co-chairs

Sarana Y. Nutanong   City University of Hong Kong, Hong Kong SAR, China
Haoran Xie   The Education University of Hong Kong,
         Hong Kong SAR, China

Workshop Co-chairs

Taku Komura   Edinburgh University, UK
Dickson Chiu   The University of Hong Kong, Hong Kong SAR, China
Tianyong Hao   South China Normal University, China

Publication/Media Chair

Wei Chen   Chinese Academy of Agricultural Sciences, China

Doctoral Consortium Chairs

Zuzana Kubincová   Comenius University in Bratislava, Slovakia
Marco Temperini   Sapienza University of Rome, Italy
Preben Hansen   Stockholm University, Sweden

Web Co-chairs

Wanvimol Nadee   Maejo University, Thailand
Nattapon Arjin   Maejo University, Thailand

Program Committee

Xiaojing Weng   The Education University of Hong Kong,
         Hong Kong SAR, China
Yan Huang   The Education University of Hong Kong,
         Hong Kong SAR, China
Zongxi Li   The Education University of Hong Kong,
         Hong Kong SAR, China
Tak-Lam Wong   Douglas College, Canada

Chiu-Lin Lai	National Taiwan University of Science and Technology, Taiwan
Guangliang Chen	TU Delft, The Netherlands
Yun Ma	City University of Hong Kong, Hong Kong SAR, China
Yunhui Zhuang	City University of Hong Kong, Hong Kong SAR, China
Zhenguo Yang	Guangdong University of Technology, China
Ke Niu	Beijing Information Science and Technology University, China
Peipei Gu	Zhengzhou University of Light Industry, China
Xiangyu Zhao	Beijing Research Center of Information Technology in Agriculture, China
Ruoyao Ding	Guangdong University of Foreign Studies, China

Contents

Emerging Technologies of Pedagogical Issues

UMLL (International Symposium on User Modeling and Language Learning)

Emerging Technologies of Design, Model and Framework of Learning Systems

Evaluation of the Use of Mobile Application in Learning English Vocabulary and Phrases – A Case Study

Blanka Klímová[1]([⊠]) and Aleš Berger[2]

[1] Department of Applied Linguistics, University of Hradec Kralove,
Hradec Kralove, Czech Republic
blanka.klimova@uhk.cz

[2] Department of Informatics and Quantitative Methods, Faculty of Informatics
and Management, University of Hradec Kralove,
Hradec Kralove, Czech Republic
ales.berger@uhk.cz

Abstract. At present, there is an increasing trend in the shift from the use of traditional technologies such as a desktop computer towards the use of mobile technologies such as a mobile phone. Nearly all students nowadays own a mobile device and about half of them own more than one. Therefore, students are well equipped for mobile learning. The purpose of this article is to firstly explore the use of mobile learning and its use in English language teaching. Secondly, on the basis of students' needs, the authors aim to exploit and describe a mobile application aimed at learning English vocabulary and phrases among students of Management of Tourism in their third year of study. Finally, on the basis of the results from the final tests, they attempt to analyze and evaluate to what extent the mobile application is effective in their learning of English vocabulary and phrases. The results show that the use of mobile app contributes to the improvement of students' learning, in this case of English vocabulary and phrases relevant to their needs. In addition, the findings also confirm that professional and careful guidance of learning via a mobile app can lead to independent learning, i.e. students' self-study.

Keywords: Traditional learning · Mobile application · English
Students · Benefits · Self-study

1 Introduction

Nowadays, there is an increasing trend in the shift from the use of traditional technologies such as a desktop computer towards the use of mobile technologies such as a mobile phone or a smartphone. Over 90% of people in developed countries now own and use a mobile phone, while the desktop computer enjoys only 40% of popularity [1, 2]. In addition, the number of smartphone ownership is increasing as well. For example, 75% of Americans owned a smartphone in 2016, which is a double number compared to 2011 [3]. In Great Britain, it was 71% and almost the same number is true

© Springer Nature Switzerland AG 2018
T. Hao et al. (Eds.): SETE 2018, LNCS 11284, pp. 3–11, 2018.
https://doi.org/10.1007/978-3-030-03580-8_1

for Central Europe (70% of smartphone owners) [4]. Smartphones are ubiquitous among younger adults, with 92% of 18- to 29-year-olds owning one [3].

Mehdipour and Zerehkafi [5] summarize the key characteristics of mobile technology:

- Portability: The technology is available whenever the user needs to learn.
- Individuality: The technology can be personalized to suit the individual learner's abilities, knowledge and learning style, and is designed to support personal learning rather than general office work.
- Unobtrusiveness: The learner can capture situations and retrieve knowledge without the technology becoming overly noticeable or imposing on the situation.
- Availability: The learner can use the technology anywhere, to enable communication with teachers, experts and peers.
- Adaptability: The technology can be adapted to the context for learning and the learner's evolving skills and knowledge.
- Persistence: The learner can use the technology to manage learning throughout a lifetime, so that the learner's personal accumulation of resources and knowledge will be immediately accessible despite changes in technology.
- Usefulness: The technology is suited to everyday needs for communication, reference, work and learning.
- Usability: The technology is easily comprehended and navigated by people with no previous experience using it.

Therefore, thanks to their ubiquitous nature, mobile phones/smartphones and particularly mobile applications (apps) are nowadays widely exploited in education, including foreign language learning.

The findings from research studies on English language teaching [6–11] show that mobile apps have a primary impact on the development of all four language skills, including their testing. Nevertheless, these apps especially have quite a significant impact on the development and retention of students' vocabulary. For example, Wu [6, 7] states that students using a smartphone app for learning English words, remember more words, approximately about 89 words more, than the students who do not use them. This positive fact is connected with the combination of multiple forms of media, which the apps can offer.

In addition, Teodorescu [8] reports that the language apps also enable students to adapt the practice to their level of knowledge, by choosing between apps for beginners, intermediate or advanced, and the possibility to assess themselves and monitor their progress. In fact, repetition, accessibility and convenience are the key aspects of successful language learning [7]. The research also indicates that students using smartphones and their apps are more motivated to learn both in class and independently outside their classes [8–10]. Furthermore, they exhibit less anxiety [11].

The purpose of this article is to firstly explore the use of mobile learning and its use in English language teaching. Secondly, on the basis of students' needs, the authors aim to exploit and describe a mobile application aimed at learning English vocabulary and phrases among students of Management of Tourism in their third year of study. Finally, on the basis of the results from the final tests, they attempt to analyze and evaluate to what extent the mobile application is effective in their learning of English vocabulary and phrases.

2 Methods

The authors of this article used the following methods in the exploration of the effectiveness of mobile learning and its suitability for their teaching. Firstly, the method of needs analysis was employed. Secondly, the mobile app was designed on the basis of this analysis to meet students' needs.

2.1 Analysis of Students' Needs

As it has been described above, mobile learning has a positive impact on the learning of English. Therefore, the authors of this article decided to implement it in their teaching of English in the winter semester of 2017 among the full-time students of Management of Tourism. However, before the mobile app started to be used, a needs analysis had been carried out among these students at the first lesson of the winter semester. This needs analysis was performed by using a SWOT (strength, weaknesses, opportunities, and threats) analysis. The analysis showed that the most problematic area was the acquisition of English vocabulary.

Therefore, in the winter semester of 2017, the mobile app was developed by a PhD student studying at the Faculty of Informatics and Management in Hradec Kralove, Czech Republic. The app is especially designed for the learning and practicing of new English words and phrases. Altogether 33 students started the course, out of which 23 students also started to use the mobile app. Nevertheless, two students dropped off during the course and thus, 31 students finished the course with the final test and 21 students eventually were using the mobile app.

2.2 Description of the Mobile App

The described mobile app consists of two application parts and one server part. The first application part is designed as a web interface for the teacher (Fig. 2) and the second application part is presented with a mobile application for students (Fig. 3). The server part is responsible for storing information, authenticating users, efficiently collecting large data, processing, distributing messages, and responding to events from both applications.

The main principle of the proposed solution is Firebase technology from Google, Inc. After a thorough analysis of all requirements and possibilities, this technology was identified as the most suitable. Firebase offers a variety of mobile and web application development capabilities, ranging from authentication, efficient data retention to communication.

The web application (Fig. 1) offers a number of features, specifically for the teacher. Each teacher can run several lessons. Each lesson defines individual lessons to which specific words and phrases fall. Teachers can register their students, distribute news or alerts through notifications, and respond to their comments. Using these options, the teacher can make contact with his/her students and draw attention to the upcoming events. The web interface also offers the visualization of the results of all students. Based on the visualization, it is possible to evaluate each student separately, to compare the results between several study courses or to modify the study plan.

Fig. 1. An overview of the teacher's web app with all the functions in the upper part (authors' own processing)

The web application is written in Javascript. A modern ReactJS library from Facebook, Inc. was used for the user interface. Thanks to the strong community around this library, many other add-ons can be used to make it easier for the teacher to make the web environment simple, fast and intuitive.

Students are assigned a mobile application (Fig. 2). Through a mobile application, the student are enrolled into a specific course. The app offers the ability to study and test available vocabulary and phrases. The student chooses the lesson s/he needs to study and tests words and phrases in it. For each phrase or vocabulary, s/he can get a translation, while using TextToSpeech technology, as well as pronunciation. The application enables immediate communication with the teacher. At the same time, the application collects all user data and distributes it to the server part for subsequent research and evaluation by the teacher. The student is advised by his/her teacher by means of notifications, e.g., to study a certain lesson. Via the mobile application, the student is able to contact his/her teacher at any time to make contact and discuss the given problem.

One of the principles of the mobile application is its simplicity. It is very important for the user to concentrate only on the studied issues. Many of the available mobile applications that focus on similar issues also offer possibilities and functionality that the student does not use and unnecessarily complicate the learning process through the

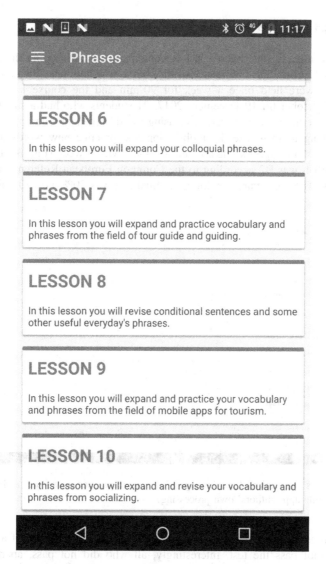

Fig. 2. An overview of available lessons in the student's mobile app (authors' own processing)

application. This mobile application offers only what students really need and is designed to be as simple as possible for their users.

Currently, the proposed solution only offers an Android application, which is available for free at Google Play store. The reason was the ratio of students who use the Android operating system on their smart devices. Java was selected to develop the mobile application. The next step in the development of this mobile application will also include its expansion to the Apple's platform and iOS.

3 Findings and Discussion

As it has been already stated above, 31 students participated in doing the final test in the Course of English. The attendance of the course was optional. The contact classes of the course were held once a week for 90 min and the course lasted from the beginning of October till 19 December 2017. 21 students who had a smartphone and the Android operating system were also using the designed mobile app. The teacher was encouraging them to use the mobile app and practice new words and phrases discussed in class through mobile app notifications twice a week (Fig. 3). The level of students' English was B2 according to the Common European Reference Framework for languages. The pass mark for doing the final test was 50%, i.e., 30 points.

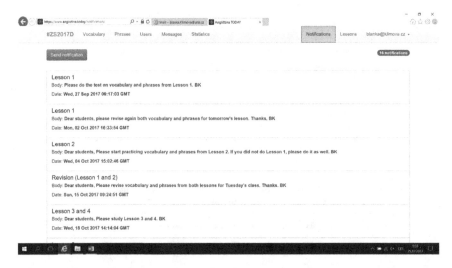

Fig. 3. Teacher's notifications for encouraging students to practice new words and phrases with the help of mobile app (authors' own processing)

The findings in Table 1 below show that only seven students out of a total of 31 students did not pass the test. Interestingly, all who did not pass, apart from one student, did not attend 70% of the seminars and use the mobile app. This means that they attended some lessons, but the number of lessons did not make up 70%. Otherwise, all the students who did not attend 70% of the classes but used the mobile app passed the test. This indicates that the mobile app can be also used for students' self-study. There were also four students who neither attended 70% of classes, nor they used the app, but they successfully passed the test. One can only assume that they might have consulted the materials with those who attended the class. Overall, those who attended the classes and used the app passed the test apart from the only exception discussed above.

Table 1. An overview of the results (authors' own processing)

Student	Result of the final test in points	Attended 70% of the seminars	Used the mobile app
1	21	No	No
2	22.5	No	No
4	26.5	No	No
5	27.5	No	No
3	28	Yes	Yes
6	28.5	No	No
7	29.5	No	No
8	30.5	Yes	No
9	31.5	No	No
10	32.5	No	Yes
11	32.5	No	Yes
12	32.5	Yes	Yes
13	35	No	Yes
14	39	No	No
18	40.5	Yes	Yes
19	40.5	No	No
15	42	No	No
21	42.5	Yes	No
22	42.5	Yes	Yes
23	42.5	Yes	Yes
16	43	Yes	Yes
17	44	Yes	Yes
20	46	No	Yes
26	48.5	Yes	Yes
27	48.5	No	Yes
28	50.5	No	Yes
24	51	Yes	Yes
25	51	No	Yes
30	54.5	Yes	Yes
31	55.5	Yes	Yes
29	56	No	Yes

Explanations: Red color – students who failed; Green color – students who attended the seminars but did not use the mobile app; blue color – students who did not attend 70% of the seminars and did not use the mobile app; yellow color – students who did not attend 70% of the seminars but use the mobile app.

Thus, it can be concluded that the use of mobile app contributes to the improvement of students' learning, in this case of English vocabulary and phrases. The mobile app does not have to be only a support tool for learning, but as this case study indicates, it can be also an independent learning tool and exploited in students' self-study. In fact, it might replace the traditional, face-to-face learning among the learners whose English is comparatively high, at least at B2 level. However, such learning must be pedagogically well-thought of, carefully planned and facilitated by the teacher through notifications via a mobile app in order to encourage students to learn and revise new words [12]. For instance, Celik and Yavuz [13] state that guided and controlled learning via smartphones can improve the effectiveness and quality of language learning process. Moreover, they claim that the whole learning process must be designed by experts.

In addition, during the final lesson students in their reflections on the course and the use of the mobile app expressed their positive attitudes towards the exploitation of the mobile app. They particularly liked its interactivity. They also pointed out that they had been learning faster and more effectively since they could use it at any time and anywhere, on the way home, for example, on the bus or train. Moreover, they appreciated that they were forced to learn and revise new words and phrases by being sent notifications by their teacher twice a week. Generally, they were motivated to study. This in fact confirms the findings described above, as well as those in other research studies [8–10].

The limitation of this case study consists in the small subject sample, which is connected with piloting the mobile app. Nevertheless, as it has been pointed out above, it is in compliance with other research studies on this topic.

4 Conclusion

The findings of this study reveal that mobile apps might be suitable learning tools, which can thanks to their interactivity motivate students to learn. However, such learning requires dedicated teachers who must be ready to assess students' learning needs, design a course syllabus and materials corresponding to these needs and offer learning tools, which would enhance their learning in this respect [14–16]. In this article, the authors showed that such an approach made students' learning effective.

Future research should focus on the effectiveness of mobile apps for learning with bigger sample sizes.

Acknowledgments. This study is supported by the SPEV project 2018/2104, run at the Faculty of Informatics and Management, University of Hradec Kralove, Czech Republic.

References

1. Statista: Percentage of Households with Mobile Phones in the United Kingdom (UK) from 1996 to 2016 (2017). https://www.statista.com/statistics/289167/mobile-phone-penetration-in-the-uk/
2. Pew Research Center: Mobile Fact Sheet (2017). http://www.pewinternet.org/fact-sheet/mobile/
3. Smith, A.: Record Shares of Americans Now Own Smartphones, Have Home Broadband (2017). http://www.pewresearch.org/fact-tank/2017/01/12/evolution-of-technology/
4. eMarketer: Czech Republic Just Tops Russia for Mobile Penetration (2017). https://www.emarketer.com/Article/Czech-Republic-Just-Tops-Russia-Mobile-Penetration/1012047

5. Mehdipour, Y., Zerehkafi, H.: Mobile learning for education: benefits and challenges. Int. J. Comput. Eng. Res. 3(6), 93–101 (2013)
6. Wu, Q.: Learning ESL vocabulary with smartphones. Proc. Soc. Behav. Sci. 143, 302–307 (2014)
7. Wu, Q.: Designing a smartphone app to teach English (L2) vocabulary. Comput. Educ. https://doi.org/10.1016/j.compedu.2015.02.013
8. Teodorescu, A.: Mobile learning and its impact on business English learning. Proc. Soc. Behav. Sci. 180, 1535–1540 (2015)
9. Balula, A., Marques, F., Martins, C.: Bet on top hat – challenges to improve language proficiency. In: Proceedings of EDULEARN15 Conference 6–8 July 2015, pp. 2627–2633, Barcelona, Spain (2015)
10. Tayan, B.M.: Students and teachers' perceptions into the viability of mobile technology implementation to support language learning for first year business students in a Middle Eastern University. Int. J. Educ. Liter. Stud. 5(2), 74–83 (2017)
11. Luo, B.R., Lin, Y.L., Chen, N.S., Fang, W.C.: Using smartphone to facilitate english communication and willingness to communicate in a communicate language teaching classroom. In: Proceedings of the 15th International Conference on Advanced Learning Technologies, pp. 320–322. IEEE Press, New York (2015)
12. Klimova, B.: The role of a teacher in foreign language teaching enhanced by information and communication technologies. Adv. Sci. Lett. 23, 965–967 (2017)
13. Celik, O., Yavuz, F.: The effect of using mobile applications on literal and contextual vocabulary instruction. IJLT 10(2), 126–136 (2017)
14. Pikhart, M.: Managerial communication and its changes in the global intercultural business world. In: SHS Web of Conferences, vol. 37, p. 01013 (2017)
15. Klimova, B.: Mobile phones and/or smartphones and their apps for teaching English as a foreign language. Educ. Inf. Technol. 23(3), 1091–1099 (2017)
16. Klimova, B., Poulova, P.: Mobile learning in higher education. Adv. Sci. Lett. 22(5/6), 1111–1114 (2016)

Adaptive Learning System for Foreign Language Writing Based on Big Data

Wei-Bo Huang, Ling-Xi Ruan, Jiang-Hui Liu$^{(\boxtimes)}$, and Xiao-Dan Li

Guangdong University of Foreign Studies, Guangzhou 510006, Guangdong,
People's Republic of China
247031690@qq.com

Abstract. Innovative education big data can help improve the current learning system framework and implement the analysis and mining mechanism of learning based on the data flow. It is rather hard make accurate analysis possible in the past. The Quantified Self Learning Algorithm (QSLA) will be the key to analyze education big data and realize adaptive learning. The learning process of foreign language writing is a complex system. It is influenced by many factors, such as teachers, textbooks, environments and students. Based on adaptive learning and adaptive control theory, this paper designs and implements adaptive learning system for foreign language writing. This has some theoretical and practical significance to realize personalized and intelligent learning and improve improvement of learning effect.

Keywords: Foreign language writing · Adaptive learning system
Big data · QSLA

1 Introduction

The collection of education big data has stronger real-time, coherence, comprehensiveness and naturalness [1]. Its analysis, process and application services are more diversified, intelligent and personalized. Education big data enables teachers to fully understand students' learning status and promote personalized education. Under the support of education big data, teachers can focus on the individual learning behavior and learning path, forecast learning outcomes, diagnose learning needs and problems and carry out personalized education. Students can learn about their preferences, defects in their knowledge and ability, development goals, etc. Students can obtain learning resources and guidance services which are suitable for them [2]. Adaptive learning is an important form for learners to acquire knowledge and skills through positive thinking and operation in the process of solving problems [3]. The essence of adaptive learning system is to provide students with individualized learning environment support, including learning resources and strategies based on the learners' individualized learning situation.

Based on the study of domestic and foreign research on the present situations and the core concepts, the paper puts forward a foreign language writing intelligent learning system model. It studies the key link to realize the model, including the modeling of foreign language writing knowledge, design of resources and tools, modeling of foreign

© Springer Nature Switzerland AG 2018
T. Hao et al. (Eds.): SETE 2018, LNCS 11284, pp. 12–22, 2018.
https://doi.org/10.1007/978-3-030-03580-8_2

language learners' writing, engine of language writing intelligent learning system, realization mechanism, etc. Finally, it analyses the implementation and application of cases systematically.

2 The Design of Adaptive Learning System for Foreign Language Writing Based on Big Data

2.1 Research Methods and Tools Used in This Paper

The Relevant Research Methods are as Follows. The status of relevant theories, concepts and system tools is studied through literature analysis. The current situation of foreign language writing is studied through investigation. Theoretical approach is used to design learning system model and learner model. And it is also used to study the implementation mechanism of foreign language writing. The system can be realized and the application cases can be analyzed through the empirical research method and statistical analysis method.

The Relevant Technical Tools are as Follows.
UML (Unified Modeling Language) Technology. It is a kind of visual modeling technology. It can help people construct system blueprint to express their imagination in a way that is standard and easy to understand. It can also provide a mechanism, in order to share and communicate design outcomes among different people.

SQL and ADO Database Access Technology. One of indispensable things in database access is ADO, Microsoft's latest technology for accessing databases. It can be applied to any database that supports OBDC relations. SQL is an instruction that enables the database to perform data operations quickly after the data source and data objects are established.

Python Technology. Python is a type of interpretive, objectoriented and dynamic highlevel programming language. Python development environment of its diverse extension libraries are very powerful. Python provides various API (Application programming Interface) and tools. It is convenient to maintain and manage the system.

2.2 System Framework and Model

At present, many universities in China have introduced the network teaching system. But these teaching systems are mainly centered on curriculum management. The utilization rate of learning activities is low. Therefore, it is necessary to improve, innovate and build adaptive learning system and guide learners to learn autonomously. Adaptive learning system is based on the user model, the field model and the adaption model. It provides evaluation information for the learners by the presentation of implementation, navigation and sequence of adaptive engine [4].

The construction and development of adaptive learning model for foreign language writing needs to consider all the factors that may affect the learner's learning. It can carry out the teaching practice and data deduction of the learner's individual model.

Combined with the existing equation, this study attempts to construct an adaptive learning equation, as shown in Eqs. (1) and (2) [5].

$$Adaptive\ coefficient = learning\ pressure/learning\ ability = Y/X = C \qquad (1)$$

$$Position\ vector:\ APi = (Xi, Yi) \qquad (2)$$

The essential idea of adaptive learning equation is that learners' challenges will increase if the learning pressure increases. The increase of learning ability will improve the learners' learning efficiency. When the ratio of Y and X is 1, a Y = X line will be formed. At this time, the learning pressure fits the learning ability, and the learning content fit the learners' expectation. This study names the line "adaptive line". To realize the adaption of learning, the position vector APi falls in surrounding area of adaptive line. This study names the area "adaptive area". The above of boundary and "adaptive line" is "adaptive area with difficulty". When the adaptive coefficient is greater than 1 and less than 1.25, the area is the "active interval" for learners. It means that the learners can achieve basically through efforts. When the adaptive coefficient is greater than 1.25, it means the current difficulty is too high for the learners. The downward part of boundary and "adaptive area with difficulty" is "adaptive area with less difficulty". When adaptive coefficient is greater than 0.75 and less than 1, it is the "easy interval" for learners. It means learners do not need to spend too much time and energy adapting to the intensity of learning. The burden of cognitive load is relatively low. When the adaptive coefficient is less than 0.75, it means the current difficulty is too low for the learners and not worth learning. Accordingly, the adaptive learning model is constructed in this study, as shown in Fig. 1.

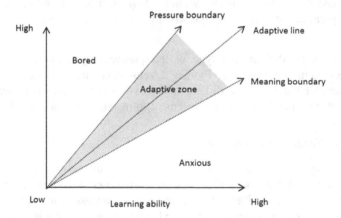

Fig. 1. Adaptive learning model of foreign language writing.

Interpretation of Adaptive Learning Model

The Adaptive Line. In the adaptive line, learning ability completely fits learning pressure. The value of C is 1. The learning environment is comfortable. Learners can be most absorbed in learning activities and have best understanding of learning tasks. To make learners be in this state is the ultimate goal of adaptive learning system.

The Adaptive Zone. The position vector *APi* falls in the surrounding area of the "adaptive line". The above of this line is the "pressure boundary". If it goes beyond the pressure boundary, the pressure will be uncontrollable. The lower part of the line is the "meaning boundary". If it goes beyond the meaning boundary, the learning potential cannot be fully realized. The meaning and value of learning tasks will be low. When the position vector *APi* falls on adaptive zone, learning difficulty fits the learners' knowledge, skills, and ability. Environment variables are in basic and comfortable space. Learners can be highly absorbed in learning activities and have good understanding of learning tasks within a certain time. The value of C between 0.75 and 1.25 can be considered as an adaptive area. In addition, when the adaptive line approaches the pressure boundary, this study is named "active interval", which is suitable to carry out intensive learning. When the adaptive line approaches the meaning boundary, this study is named "easy interval", which is suitable to carry out decentralized study.

"Boring" State. When the position vector *APi* falls under the "adaptive zone" beyond the meaning boundary, that is, when the C value is less than 0.75, the learner's learning ability is strong, while the learning pressure is low. It is easier for students to accept the learning content. But students cannot fully realize their learning potential. They cannot be fully absorbed in the learning activities. When the learning task is highly controlled but the learning task is less difficult than expected, the learners' potential cannot be explored. In the long run, learners will gradually deviate from their learning goals. They may do things unrelated to learning. And they are in the "boring" state of learning.

"Anxious" State. When position vector *APi* falls up the adaptive area beyond the pressure boundary, that is, when the value of C is greater than 1.25, the learners' learning pressure is too high. They cannot have good understanding of learning. The difficulty of the learning task goes beyond their expectations. They cannot get ideal study results. At this time, it is easy for them to escape emotionally and be in an "anxious" state.

The Calculation Equation of Learning Pressure and Data Acquisition. The sources of learning stress include internal and external factors that affect learners' learning status. Internal factors include motivation, emotional factors, learning expectations, etc. External factors include teaching methods, learning environment, etc. Equation (3) can be used to calculate the learning pressure.

$$Y = (i0A0 + i1A1 + i2A2 + \ldots + inAn)/(n+1) \tag{3}$$

In Eq. (3), i_n is the coefficient. A_n is the influence factor of pressure. The initial learning pressure value is generated based on experience. The later learning pressure is generated through test of data. It requires the actual data in the interaction of the learners' status and the system. The value of i_n needs to be adjusted according to the effect of interaction and the subjective experience of the learners.

The Calculation Equation of Learning Ability and Data Acquisition. The influence factors of the learning ability include internal and external factors. Internal factors include learning experience, motivation and emotion, learning expectation, etc. External factors include teaching methods, teachers' experience and the difficulty of learning task, etc. The Eq. (4) can be used to calculate the learning ability.

$$X = (i0B0 + i2B2 \quad i1B1 + \quad + \ldots + inBn/(n+1) \tag{4}$$

In Eq. (4), B_n is the influence factor of learning ability. I_n is the coefficient. To clarify the influence of a certain factor on learning pressure and learning ability, a large number of data tests is also necessary. For example, learning expectation is mainly transformed into learning pressure. But certain learning expectation can also be support of learning ability.

Therefore, the basic working process of adaptive system for foreign language writing is shown in Fig. 2.

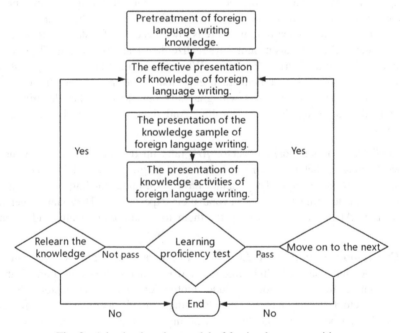

Fig. 2. Adaptive learning model of foreign language writing.

The core modules of personalized adaptive learning system are learners' characteristic model, domain model and adaptive engine. Now the implementation mechanism of these three parts will be discussed.

2.3   The Implementation Mechanism of the Personalized Adaptive Learning System

The Learner Model. The learner model describes the individualized characteristic information of learners. It can reflect the individual difference of learner. It is the basis of personalized service provided by the learning system [6]. According to the requirements of personalized adaptive learning system, this paper gives the following learner models.

(Student Mode 1) = (Basic Information, Knowledge Structure, Cognitive Level, Learning Preferences, Learning History).

Basic Information records the learners' names, genders, ages, classes, schools, contact information and so on. Learning Preference analyzes the preferences for learning resources and tools, learning time, learning sites, common devices and interactive habits. Knowledge Structure includes number of courses, number of knowledge points, performance of knowledge points, etc. It is used to represent the knowledge structure of learners. Cognitive Level is obtained by means of learners' homework and examinations. Learning History records the number of courses, login frequency, login time, login duration, learning location, equipment, learning activity record and so on. From a lot of historical data, learners' learning habits can be further explored. Their learning can be more accurately predicted. And it is convenient to intervene in learning.

Domain Knowledge Model. Domain knowledge model describes the components and their structure in the field of application. It represents the interrelationships among elements in the domain knowledge [7]. The construction of domain model should be conducive to the representation, management, search, evaluation, sharing and inter-action of knowledge resources. It is the basis of adaptive learning system to present knowledge resources. The learners' learning behavior in ubiquitous learning environment is random. The learning demand of knowledge points is situational. The sequence to learn knowledge points has strong autonomy. It does not necessarily follow the framework of knowledge. In the process of learning a certain knowledge point, the presentation and sequence of resources is also strongly personalized. Therefore, the model of domain knowledge cannot be the traditional way of knowledge tree. This paper adopts Yu Shengquan's opinion of "learning cell" [8]. Namely, semantic description information, productive information, format information, learning infor-mation and KNS (Knowledge Network Service) network information are added on the basis of learning content. They can help learners obtain their desired learning resources whenever and wherever. Learners can learn knowledge they want in a relaxed and pleasant learning environment.

Personalized Adaptive Service Engine for Foreign Language Writing. Personal-ized adaptive service engine analyses and diagnoses learners' knowledge level and cognitive ability according to the learner model. It can dynamically arrange learning content and presentation of high fitness degree. It can test and manage the learning process. It can also constantly monitor, modify, maintain the learner model [9]. Per-sonalized adaptive learning engine develops learning strategies, tracks learning status based on learners' models and learning objectives. After the study, it will study the effectiveness of learning strategies. If the learning efficiency is low, it can help to analyze reasons and put forward improvement strategies. In this way, the engine constantly improves and updates itself.

3 Analysis of Study Cases

Intelligent feedback strategies, based on the analysis of network learning behavior, combines with the classification of online learning behavior in cognitive level. It can build a self-learning algorithm QSLA (Quantified Self Learning Algorithm) to quantify big data. Furthermore, it can build an adaptive learning engine [10]. For each learning unit, the current cognitive level of the learners can be obtained and compared by tracking learning behavior. The level of cognitive thinking that needs to achieve is designed by experts according to the relationship and importance of context. In the knowledge map, if {V0, V1,... VN} is the sub-knowledge of V. We believe the rules are as follows.

Rule 1. If a student masters V0, and his cognitive thinking level of V0 is M0, the learning support for V is $S = F(M0) \times S0$. F (M0) is a function about the required cognitive thinking level and the real learning level of the learners. If the learner's current cognitive thinking level of has reached or exceeds the required cognitive thinking level, F (M0) is equal to 1. Therefore, F (M0) is between 0 and 1. The initial value of S0 is worked out based on the relationship between the upper and lower levels of the knowledge points. At this time, S is between 0 and 1.

Rule 2. There are two situations for knowledge point V. If suitable learning degree Min $(1, \sum_{i=0}^{n} F(Mi) \times Si) = 1$, the learners can learn knowledge V. If suitable learning degree Min $(1, \sum_{i=0}^{n} F(Mi) \times Si)$ is greater than or equal to 0.683, and learners learn knowledge point V directly in similar circumstances with similar peers, the education statistical laws show that students' intelligence, including learning ability, practical ability obey is in normal distribution. So when learners finish learning the lower knowledge, the distribution of normal suitable learning degree should be basically obey normal distribution. The area of the place under the normal curve and above X-axis is 1. Under the normal distribution curve $f(x) = \frac{1}{\sqrt{2\pi\sigma}} e^{-\frac{(x-\mu)^2}{2\sigma^2}}$, the area of the horizontal axis $(\mu - \sigma, \mu + \sigma)$ is about 68.3%. The area of the horizontal axis $(\mu - 1.96\sigma, \mu + 1.96\sigma)$ is about 95.4%. The area of the horizontal axis $(\mu - 2.58\sigma, \mu + 2.58\sigma)$ is about 99.7%. The normal distribution curve and area distribution map are composed of three zones: base area, negative area and positive area. Among them, base area accounts for 68.3%. It occupies the dominant position in the area distribution map. When the learner has finished learning the lower level of knowledge, it can be considered that the learners complete the study of the main body of the lower part of knowledge if suitable learning degree reaches 0.683. According to the recent development zone theory and the normal distribution curve of Vergosky, the demarcation point of suitable learning degree is 0.683. At this time, it should refer to the second case of Rule 2 that is Peer Recommend. In the learning process, when the mastering degree of knowledge points change, the system will modify the suitable learning degree of the related knowledge Min $(1, \sum_{i=0}^{n} F(Mi) \times Si)$ and corresponding navigation marks. The system state and corresponding learning status are shown in Table 1.

Table 1. System state and corresponding learning state.

The system state	Learning state
Complete the study	Complete
Recommended learning (according to learners' own suitable learning degree)	SR—Self Recommend
Recommended learning (learning paths of similar peer)	PR—Peer Recommend
Not recommended learning (no prerequisites)	I—Invalid

It can be seen from Table 1 that the learning status of all mastered knowledge points is C, which is used as a marker in the navigation of adaptive learning system for foreign language writing. For all the knowledge points that are recommended to study, it is divided into two situations. The first one is that if suitable learning degree is 1, the learning state is SR. When suitable learning degree is greater than 0.683, and similar peers have reached the cognitive thinking level in similar cases, their learning state is PR. The priority of SR is higher than PR, which is used as a marker in the navigation of adaptive learning system for foreign language writing. For other knowledge points, since the learning premise is not yet available, the mark in the navigation of adaptive learning system for foreign language writing has not been opened. A learning unit includes multiple knowledge points. When learners choose to learn a certain learning unit, the following algorithms are as follows. Step 1: The recommended knowledge points in the learning unit is added to learning module. Step 2: Judgement. If the recommended learning module is not empty, turn to S3. If the recommended learning module is empty, turn to S6. Step3: Learners select knowledge point A from the recommended learning module and start learning. Step 4: if master degree of A changes, it can calculate suitable learning degree of A's superior knowledge B. If suitable learning degree meets one of the following two conditions, B can be added to recommend learning module. (1) If suitable learning degree of B reaches 1, learning state is SR. (2) If suitable learning degree of the upper knowledge reaches 0.683, and master degree of B has reached the set value for similar peers in similar situations, learning state is PR. Step 5: If A is mastered, then A will be removed from the recommended learning module and turn to S2. Step 6: The learning unit task ends.

Implementation of push interface to learning resources in self-adaptive foreign language writing learning systems. According to downloaded keywords to curriculum and personalized priority level of curriculum resources, it recommends learning resources that should be learned first. The key codes are as follows.

/*There are four steps in this method, building the model, calculation of similarity, looking for neighboring collection and foundation of recommended engines. */

```
import MyDataModel as dm
import recommender as rc

def recommend(userID, size):
    try:
        rcder = rc.Recommender( )
        model = dm.myDataModel( ) #building the data model
        similarity = rcder.uncenteredCosineSimilarity(model) #calculate the simi-
larity with Pearson algorithm
        neighborhood = rcder.neighborhood(3, similarity, model)# Calculate the
neighbors of the learners. In programming, the learners whose closet distance is 3 is
considered to be the neighbors of a learner.
        rcder.cachingRecommender(model, neighborhood, similarity)# Use Rec-
ommender to store the Recommendation Item
        recommendations = rcder.recommend(userID, size)# Size Work out the us-
er's recommended result, which is parameter
    except e:
        print(e)
    else:
        return recommendations
```

4   Experimental Results

In order to analyze the learning situation of learners to use adaptive learning system, the system is applied to Class A and Class B of School of English and Education, GDUFS. The experiment designs questionnaire on academic performance, learning interest, learning time and learning satisfaction. All students are required to fill in the questionnaires (154 are actually issued and 150 recovered, the recovery rate is 97.5%). Each question is evaluated at three grades, and the analysis of results is as follows (Table 2).

From the above analysis, most students do think the self-adaptive foreign language writing learning system plays a positive role in academic performance, learning interest, learning time and learning satisfaction, particularly in improving students' learning interest, reducing learning time and improving learning efficiency. And the system can improve academic performance and learning satisfaction.

Table 2. Questionnaire of the effects on using adaptive learning system.

Questions	Strongly agree	Agree	Not agree
Academic performance: students can improve academic performance in adaptive learning system	30 20%	90 60%	30 20%
Learning interest: personalized users' interface and diversified learning objects in adaptive learning system can bring students fun	60 40%	60 40%	30 20%
Learning time: students can reduce learning costs with the help of recommended learning path and learning objects in adaptive learning system	64 42.7%	72 48%	14 9.3%
Learning satisfaction: students are willing to learn in adaptive learning system because it can optimize learning process and meet the needs in learning	20 13.3%	90 60%	40 26.7%

5   Conclusion

The starting point of adaptive learning is to find the comfortable area in learning and build the consistent content and path. Therefore, students can learn more actively and discover their learning potential. Adaptive learning system for foreign language writing tries to match learners' personality characteristics with learning content. The purpose of this study is to improve the learning effect, which is mainly applied to online learning. This study constructs the adaptive learning model and combines with related practice. It puts forward the process of adaptive learning model. At the same time, based on the presupposition of structured data, the model simplifies the data collection and analysis. Concise and intuitive visualization enables people to accurately understand the connotation of the data, and uses it to adjust, intervene and predict learning.

References

1. Xianmin, Y.: Education big data application model and policy recommendations. E-educ. Res. **9**, 54–61 (2015)
2. Qiang, J.: Analysis model and implementation of personalized self-adaptive online learning based on big data. China Educ. Technol. **1**, 85–92 (2015)
3. Huzi, G.: Research status and prospect of learning style model for adaptive learning system learners. E-educ. Res. **2**, 32–38 (2012)
4. Xiaochuan, G.: Strategies for students' adaptive learning and personalized learning in the context of "Internet plus". J. Kaifeng Inst. Educ. **37**(06), 126–127 (2013)
5. Nan, W.: Construction of adaptive learning model and its implementation strategy. Mod. Educ. Technol. **27**(09), 12–18 (2013)
6. Qiang, J.: Design and implementation of adaptive learning system for "service" perspective. China Educ. Technol. **2**, 119–124 (2011)
7. Pingde, C.: Research on Adaptive Learning Support System Based on Web. South China Normal University, Guangzhou (2003)

8. Xianmin, Y.: Construction of learning resource information model in the learning environment. China Educ. Technol. **9**, 72–78 (2010)
9. Jiahua, Z.: Adaptive learning support system: current situation, problems and trends. Mod. Educ. Technol. **2**, 18–20 (2009)
10. Haiguang, G.: Study on self-adaptive learning system based on quantitative self-adaptive MOOCs based on education data. E-educ. Res. **37**(11), 38–42 (2016)

Implementation of Assessment for Learning (AfL) in Blackboard LMS and Its Reflection on Tertiary Students' Second Language Performance

Dagmar El-Hmoudova[✉] and Irena Loudova

University of Hradec Kralove,
Rokitanskeho 62, 50002 Hradec Kralove, Czech Republic
{dagmar.elhmoudova,irena.loudova}@uhk.cz

Abstract. Assessment for learning is assessment that helps both, learner and teacher assess the skills the learner has at present, set objectives for where learning should be directed, and identify ways to gain the educational aim. A cohort of students took a Professional English language course taught by the same instructor in two consecutive semesters. The course instruction uploaded in the university Blackboard LMS made extensive use of blended learning and a variety of other techniques designed to address a broad spectrum of learning styles. This paper describes the performance of the cohort in the English for Tourism course, and examines performance and attitudes in the experimental cohort. The experimental group improved its performance after being provided frequent opportunities to find out about their progress and future targets, where not all AfL assessments need be formal: instructor continually assesses and provides feedback on the progress of students as a matter of course.

Keywords: Assessment for learning · Blackboard · Learning performance
Blended learning

1 Introduction

Assessment is an essential component of education process and the term is very broad and covers plenty of different types of activities with different purposes. In recent years there has been a movement towards Assessment for Learning (AfL) [1]. This teaching strategy that enables personalization of learning, in our case learning of English language as a second language, provides frequent assessment that allow targets to be set for individual learners.

The fundamental principle of AfL approach is that learners should be aware of what they need to learn. Moreover, they should know how far they are progressing towards the anticipated outcomes and what they need to do in order to achieve their targets. This means that teachers – instructors need to be explicit about expected learning outcomes, not only in their lesson plans, but also with learners, and provide frequent opportunities for learners to monitor their progress and future targets. In this respect, we talk about formative assessment, the purpose of which is to give feedback to learners and

© Springer Nature Switzerland AG 2018
T. Hao et al. (Eds.): SETE 2018, LNCS 11284, pp. 23–31, 2018.
https://doi.org/10.1007/978-3-030-03580-8_3

determine the direction of future learning opportunities. Such assessment may take place at any time during the course.

Just about half a century ago, Ausubel [2] suggested that the most important factor influencing learning is what the learner already knows, that teachers should ascertain this, and teach accordingly. In the 1960s, Bloom [3] began to explore the idea that the normal distribution of student outcomes was not a "natural" outcome, but caused by the failure of the instruction to recognize differences in learners.

Individualization is beneficial and of the main reasons is that the tutor is able to identify errors in the student's work immediately, and then to provide clarification, and further follow-up if necessary [4]. Bloom described these two processes as "feedback" and "correctives" and this language has become part of the standard way of talking about assessment ever since.

As noted above, Bloom appeared to conceptualize formative assessment as a combination of feedback and instructional correctives. Black and Wiliam [1] defined formative assessment as follows: We use the general term assessment to refer to all those activities undertaken by teachers—and by their students in assessing themselves —that provide information to be used as feedback to modify teaching and learning activities. Such assessment becomes formative assessment when the evidence is actually used to adapt the teaching to meet student needs".

The term 'formative' itself is open to a variety of interpretations and often means no more than that assessment is carried out frequently and is planned at the same time as teaching. Assessment for learning (formative assessment) is any assessment for which the first priority in its design and practice is to serve the purpose of promoting students' learning. It thus differs from assessment designed primarily to serve the purposes of accountability, or of ranking, or of certifying competence. An assessment activity can help learning if it provides information that teachers and their students can use as feedback in assessing themselves and one another and in modifying the teaching and learning activities in which they are engaged. Such assessment becomes "formative assessment" when the evidence is actually used to adapt the teaching work to meet learning needs [5].

As learning is unpredictable, assessment is necessary to make adaptive adjustments to instruction, but assessment processes themselves impact the learner's willingness, desire, and capacity to learn [6].

For assessment to support learning, it must provide guidance about the next steps in instruction and must be provided in way that encourages the learner to direct energy towards growth, rather than well-being. During the 1990s, a number of studies explored the idea that attention to assessment as an integral part of instruction could improve learning outcomes for students, and at the same time, attempts were made to connect classroom practice to related bodies of research, notably feedback, motivation, attri-bution, and self-regulated learning. For most of this time, the term "formative assessment" was not precisely defined, and, as a result, research studies on one aspect of the use of assessment to improve instruction were used as evidence supporting the efficacy of quite unrelated aspects. Partly in response to this, many authors stopped using the term "formative assessment" preferring instead the phrase "assessment for learning" although again its precise meaning was rarely defined, beyond the idea that assessment should be used during instruction to improve learning outcomes.

2 Research Methods

Ideally, a formal assessment task is constructed by the assessor, bearing in mind the structure and progression of the subject discipline(s) involved, an appreciation of the sequencing of intellectual and moral development progression of students as set out by writers such as Perry [7] and Kohlberg [8] and a knowledge of the current level of intellectual development of his or her students. The students' understanding of the assessment task is enhanced through the specification of assessment criteria. The student interprets and responds to the assessment task according to his or her knowledge of the subject and the level of his or her intellectual development, bearing the assessment criteria in mind. The student's performance is assessed (interpreted) by the assessor against the specified criteria, and feedback is given through grades and/or commentary. At this point there is potential for dialogue between student and assessor. How the student interprets the assessment, together with his or her psychological state and disposition regarding subsequent action are key influences on learning (Fig. 1).

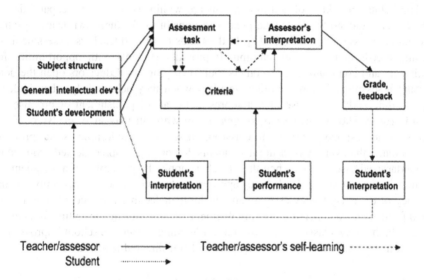

Fig. 1. The process of formative assessment in respect of a formal task (Source: Sadler [9])

We tend to think of students as passive participants in assessment rather than engaged users of the information that assessment can produce. What we should be asking is, how students can use assessment to take responsibility for and improve their own learning? Student involvement in assessment doesn't mean that students control decisions regarding what will or won't be learned or tested. It doesn't mean that they assign their own grades. Instead, student involvement means that students learn to use assessment information to manage their own learning so that they understand how they learn best, know exactly where they are in relation to the defined learning targets, and plan and take the next steps in their learning. Students engage in the assessment for learning process when they use assessment information to set goals, make learning decisions related to their own improvement, develop an understanding of what quality work looks like, self-assess, and communicate their status and progress toward established learning goals.

Eventually, we want students to be able to direct their own learning. Yet it often seems unclear just how students will achieve this goal. Assessment for learning helps students become self-directed learners by developing their self-assessment skills. The principles of assessment for learning are interrelated: Just as involving students in the assessment process helps make assessment more like instruction, students need to learn to self-assess so that they can use the descriptive feedback from the teacher to its best advantage. Sadler [9] and Atkin, Black, and Coffey [10] describe a model of formative assessment in which learners continually ask themselves three questions as they self-assess.

- Where Am I Trying to Go?
- Where Am I Now?
- How Do I Close the Gap?

The habits and skills of self-assessment are within the grasp and capabilities of almost every student. Students take greater responsibility for their own learning when they regularly assess themselves [11]. In the hands of trained teachers, assessment for learning breeds confidence in learning. It provides students with opportunities for monitoring and communicating to others their own progress. Educators open the door to using assessment in more productive ways when they acknowledge that students respond differently to the use of test scores as threats of punishment or promises of reward. Those who succeed keep striving; those who fail may give up. By contrast, most students respond positively to classroom assessment environments that promote success rather than simply measure it. Students demonstrate unprecedented score gains on standardized assessments when their teachers apply the principles of assessment for learning in the classroom [12]. With appropriate training, teachers can improve the accuracy of their day-to-day assessments, make their feedback to students descriptive and informative, and increase the involvement of students in the entire assessment process. In this way, classroom assessment for learning becomes a school improvement tool that helps create responsible, engaged, and self-directed learners.

2.1 Administering Assessments in Blackboard

By using the Assignments tool, any task can become a gradable item. Assignments, especially in the form of partial tests, were added to an online course in Blackboard as a content item. Instructors created Assignments that list the name, point value and clear instruction, including learning objectives and criteria upon which are the students evaluated, see Figs. 2 and 3. After an Assignment was added to a content area, students were able to access the Assignment, and complete it by submitting their answers from their local computer. The instructor could respond to each student with comments about their individual assignment and by attaching files, if necessary. The Discussion Board was often used as the place where students could not only interact with the instructor and with other students, but also rate one another's Discussion Board items providing another platform for stimulating participation and further discourse.

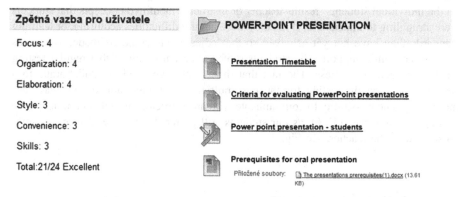

CAJ1 - Unit 2 - g	CAJ1 - Unit 2 - l	CAJ1 - Unit 2 - v	CAJ1 - Unit 1 - l	CAJ1 - Unit 2 - l	CAJ1 - Unit 3 - l
11.00	17.00	35.00	42.00	50.00	18.00
10.00	19.00	31.00	48.00	48.00	20.00
9.00	19.00	25.00	39.00	26.00	--
--	--	--	45.00	46.00	--
--	--	--	--	--	--
8.00	19.00	25.00	40.00	34.00	17.00
--	--	--	--	--	--
3.00	15.00	17.00	34.00	26.00	15.00
11.00	15.00	22.00	41.00	29.00	18.00
4.00	19.00	12.00	32.00	11.00	10.00
7.00	19.00	25.00	42.00	46.00	18.00
7.00	19.00	28.00	41.00	42.00	20.00
--	--	19.00		--	--
7.00	19.00	27.00	41.00	44.00	20.00

Fig. 2. Overview of students' tests results in Professional English in Blackboard course. (Source: university Blackboard)

Zpětná vazba pro uživatele	POWER-POINT PRESENTATION
Focus: 4	
Organization: 4	Presentation Timetable
Elaboration: 4	Criteria for evaluating PowerPoint presentations
Style: 3	
Convenience: 3	Power point presentation - students
Skills: 3	
Total:21/24 Excellent	Prerequisites for oral presentation
	Přiložené soubory: The presentations prerequisites(1).docx (13.61 KB)

Fig. 3. Feedback and criteria for evaluation where detailed explanation of points is provided. (Source: university Blackboard)

Tests created in Blackboard had many options for grading and security, ensuring that instructors had control over the way the tests were administered and evaluated. Self-assessment options were also available, wherein scores could have been excluded from a student's overall grade, and even hidden from the instructor. Tests were released at a predetermined date and time, being password protected to prevent backtracking if needed. All tests had the additional feature of being able to present randomized sets of questions. Any question in a Test could be designated as extra credit.

Feedback to students after taking the test was customized, and the number of attempts that a student was allowed could have been specified. There were many ways to create questions for online Tests in Blackboard. Instructors created their own questions based on course objectives, reading assignments, discussions, or other course materials. Lots of different types of questions were used in the Tests within Blackboard including multiple matching tests, true-false tests, multiple-choice tests and many more.

3 Research Findings

A total of 365 second year bachelor students of Management (186; 136 female, 50 male) and Economics (179; 95 female, 84 male) participated in a study that followed the correlation between the principles of AfL teaching and learning methods and students' learning success in an online Professional English language course in the university LMS Blackboard. The student's achievements were tracked for two semesters in the academic year 2016/17. The research was completed by a questionnaire survey, created by the course instructors, which deplored how students evaluated this learning and teaching approach.

Closed format Likert questions were distributed online in the e-course of professional English language. The students (86%) appreciated mostly the system of regular course tests. This formative assessment was used to conduct in-process evaluations of students' comprehension, learning needs, and academic progress during lessons. Based on the individual students' results teacher or instructor identified concepts that students were struggling to understand, skills they were having difficulties acquiring, or learning standards they have not yet achieved so that adjustments could be made, as well as relevant academic support. The students (65%) apparently valued that regular testing led to a reduction in stress. The fact that they (58%) were able to collaborate, to a certain extent, on the testing format, e.g. multiple questions, gapped text, was very motivating. The possibility to communicate with an instructor through an online course was appreciated least (47%), as our students still prefer direct (face to face) communication with the teacher, see Fig. 4.

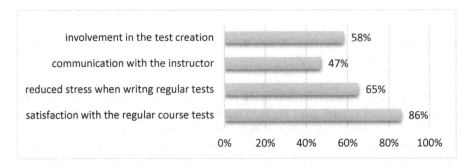

Fig. 4. Students' view on the environment, evaluation in AfL learning %. (Source: author)

The results were statistically processed and they clearly showed that there was no statistically significant improvement in students' performance in the Professional English language course. We also did not find a statistically significant difference among the students from the point of view of gender, see Figs. 5 and 6.

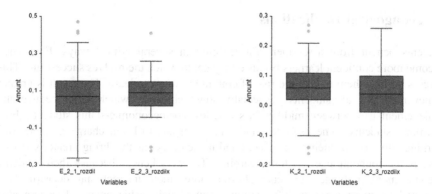

Fig. 5. Correlation between pre-tests and post-tests in winter and summer semesters in academic year 2016/17. (Source: author)

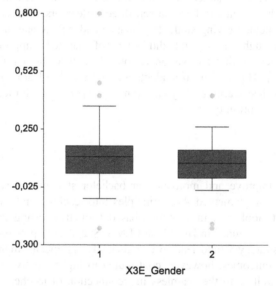

Fig. 6. Academic performance and correlation from the point of view of gender in the monitored group of students. (Source: author)

While we cannot confirm the improvement in academic performance in this group of students, it is clear from the results of the questionnaire survey that Afl strategy is appreciated by the students as a motivating element in the learning process. Variability and individualized approach gives students more confidence and reduces the stress level.

4 Pedagogical Implications

Students benefit from assessment for learning in several critical ways. First, they become more confident learners because they get to watch themselves succeeding. This success permits them to take the risk of continuing to try to learn. The result is greater achievement for all students—especially low achievers, which helps reduce the achievement gap between middle-class and low-socioeconomic-status students. Furthermore, students come to understand what it means to be in charge of their own learning—to monitor their own success and make decisions that bring greater success. This is the foundation of lifelong learning. Teachers benefit because their students become more motivated to learn. Furthermore, their instructional decisions are informed by more accurate information about student achievement. Teachers also benefit from the savings in time that result from their ability to develop and use classroom assessments more efficiently.

Godwin-Jones [13] remarked that the biggest current challenge for teachers nowadays is to help students to become self-directed learners. That is why important roles for teachers include giving students guidance and AfL is one of the appropriate environments. Although our research did not proof that AfL supports the students' performance, we believe that motivation is core element to the learning process. As Mawer and Stenly [14] point out, if students are motivated to learn and know how to direct and monitor their learning, they can turn any experience with technology into a language-learning opportunity.

5 Conclusion

In the attempt to improve and motivate our bachelor students of Management and Economy, we have implemented AfL principles into teaching and learning environment. Our students took part in computer-based formative testing in the course of professional English language in Blackboard LMS. Statistically-processed data did not confirm that this strategy would lead to a statistically significant improvement in the student's learning outcomes, however, contributed to higher motivation to study the online course, as well as to the seamless interconnection of teacher and student and students with each other.

Acknowledgement. The paper was written with the support of the specific project 6/2018 grant "Determinants of Cognitive Processes Impacting the Work Performance" granted by the University of Hradec Králové, Czech Republic and thanks to help of student Tomáš Valenta.

References

1. Black, P., Wiliam, D.: Assessment and classroom learning. Assess. Educ.: Principles Policy Practice **5**(1), 7–73 (1998)
2. Ausubel, D.P.: Educational Psychology: A Cognitive View. Holt, Rinehart & Winston, New York (1968)

3. Bloom, B.S.: The search for methods of instruction as effective as one-to-one tutoring. Educ. Leadership **41**(8), 4–17 (1984)
4. Guskey, T.R.: Formative assessment: the contributions of Benjamin S. Bloom. In: Andrade, H.L., Cizek, G.J. (eds.) Handbook of Formative Assessment, pp. 106–124. Taylor & Francis, New York (2010)
5. Black, P.J., Wiliam, D.: The formative purpose: assessment must first promote learning. In: Wilson, M. (ed.). Towards Coherence Between Classroom Assessment and Accountability: 103rd Yearbook of the National Society for the Study of Education (Part 2), vol. Part II, pp. 20–50. University of Chicago Press, Chicago (2004)
6. Harlen, W., Deakin-Crick, R.: A systematic review of the impact of summative assessment and tests on students' motivation for learning. In: EPPI-Centre (ed.), Research Evidence in Education Library, 1.1 ed., p. 153. University of London Institute of Education Social Science Research Unit, London (2002)
7. Perry, W.G.: Cognitive and ethical growth: the making of meaning. In: Chickering, A.W., Associates (eds.) The Modern American College, pp. 76–116. Jossey-Bass, San Francisco (1981)
8. Kohlberg, L.: Development of moral character and moral ideology. In: Hoffman, M.L., Hoffman, L.W. (eds.) Review of Child Development Research, vol. I, pp. 381–431. Russel Sage Foundation, New York (1964)
9. Sadler, R.: Formative assessment and the design of instructional systems. Instr. Sci. **18**, 119–144 (1989)
10. Atkin, J.M., Black, P., Coffey, J.: Classroom Assessment and the National Science Education Standards. National Academy Press, Washington, DC (2001)
11. Shepard, L.A.: Using assessment to help students think about learning. In: Keynote address at the Assessment Training Institute Summer Conference, Portland, OR, July 2001
12. Black, P., Wiliam, D.: Inside the black box: raising standards through classroom assessment. Phi Delta Kappan **80**(2), 139–148 (1998)
13. Godwin-Jones, R.: Emerging technologies: mobile apps for language learning. Lang. Learn. Technol. **15**(2), 2–11 (2011)
14. Mawer, K., Stanley, G.: Digital Play. Computer Games and Language Aims. Delta Publishing, Peaslake (2011)
15. Sadler, D.R.: Formative assessment and the design of instructional systems. Instr. Sci. **18**(2), 119 (1989)

A Service-Oriented Architecture for Student Modeling in Peer Assessment Environments

Gabriel Badea[1], Elvira Popescu[1], Andrea Sterbini[2],
and Marco Temperini[2(✉)]

[1] Computers and Information Technology Department, University of Craiova,
Craiova, Romania
[2] Sapienza University, Rome, Italy
marte@diag.uniroma1.it

Abstract. Peer assessment functionalities are provided in several Learning Management Systems; data coming from the peer evaluation sessions could be used for automated or semi-automated grading, for the management of student modeling, and for providing the teacher with feedback about the learners. Various models for the representation of peer assessment data have been proposed in the literature. In this paper we build on the availability of such a model based on Bayesian Networks, and introduce: (1) a web service capable of representing data coming from peer evaluation sessions, in which student modeling is based on learners' *Competence* and *Assessment capability* features; (2) a protocol of communication, and the design of a related API, making the service available, i.e., allowing the exchange of data between the web service and the LMS supporting the peer assessment sessions; (3) a working example of using this API in the Moodle LMS, by means of enhancing the existing *Workshop* plugin.

Keywords: Peer evaluation · Bayesian Network Model · Student model
Web service

1 Introduction

Analysis and evaluation are high level metacognitive skills, entailing knowledge well beyond the result granted by passive acquisition of notions [1]. While learning, a student can train such abilities through the participation in sessions of peer assessment [2], in addition to verifying and improving her own comprehension of a topic [3].

Moreover, peer assessment provides support for a wide range of assignments, including open-ended questions. Free text answers, short essays, programming code, discussion and motivation of the chosen solution to a problem, are examples of activities that can be proposed to students through open-ended questions, resulting as much more challenging and informative than multiple choice tests [4]. The feedback produced by a peer evaluation system can be useful in several ways: it can be directed to the teacher, in order to support monitoring the student's progress, or it can be aimed at the student, to provide assessment and suggestions for improvement. In such a system, student modeling can provide a powerful tool, supporting the production of meaningful feedback.

© Springer Nature Switzerland AG 2018
T. Hao et al. (Eds.): SETE 2018, LNCS 11284, pp. 32–37, 2018.
https://doi.org/10.1007/978-3-030-03580-8_4

In particular, the use of Bayesian Network models to represent significant student traits has been investigated with success [5], also in the context of peer assessment systems [6]. In this paper we build on the availability of one of such models, and present: (1) a web service capable of representing data coming from peer evaluation sessions (described in Sect. 2); (2) a protocol of communication, and the design of a related API, making the service available, i.e., allowing the exchange of data between the web service and the LMS supporting the peer assessment sessions (described in Sect. 3); (3) a working example of using this API in Moodle LMS [7], by means of enhancing the dedicated *Workshop* plugin [8] (described in Sect. 4). Our plans for future development are summarized in Sect. 5.

2 Student Modeling Service Concept and Architecture

First we describe the model of Bayesian Network (BN) data representation, for a peer assessment session, as proposed in [9]. A student is rendered in the network as a set of discrete variables (probability distributions), representing: (1) his knowledge level on the question's topic (variable K); (2) his ability to evaluate (variable J); (3) his answer correctness/grade (variable C). In addition, a variable G is associated to the student's answer, for each grade given to it by peers. K, J and C are computed by evidence propagation, based on the peer assessments (G values), and possibly on the grades added in the network by the teacher, in relation to some of the answers. The final value of C is the estimated answer's grade. Dependencies are assumed among the above variables and are given by conditional probability tables: C and J depend probabilistically on K; G depends on J and C.

If the model is applied in a framework calling for teacher's grading work, then also the teacher's grades can be used as evidence (fixing the value of a C variable) and determine the network update by propagation, which has positive effects on the overall correctness of the grades inferred by the system [9]. On the other hand, also the bare use of the model, to just represent the data and make inferences on the final grades of the answers, with no grading work done by the teacher, has been shown effective [9].

Hence, the application of the model described above can enhance the management of data coming from a session of peer assessment, or from a sequence of sessions. We therefore believe it is worthwhile to implement the model in a web service, and make its functionalities available to teachers using peer evaluation on a web-based platform. In what follows, we describe the steps of use of such a service, in a realistic situation. The next section shows a more detailed description of the web service, and of its API.

Let us consider a typical peer assessment session, taking place in a web-based learning environment, which requires from each student the answer to an open-ended question and the evaluation (and grading) of a number of her peers' answers. After the session, the teacher can visualize the answers and the peer evaluations; this data can be analyzed in order to recognize the proficiency and difficulties of each student. In this context, the Bayesian Network modeling service can provide additional useful information regarding students' competence and assessment capability. In order to do that, the learning environment needs to provide an implementation of the API exposing the service. A schematic representation of the proposed architecture is included in Fig. 1.

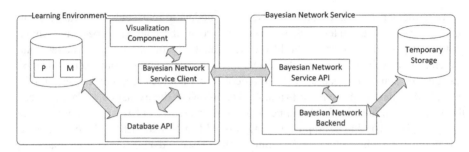

Fig. 1. Schematic system architecture (P represents the peer assessment data related to a given session, and M represents the student models, as computed by the BN service)

Based on the peer evaluation dataset sent by the educational platform, the service computes and returns the following data: (1) the students' models (in terms of the K and J variables of each student); (2) the answers' grades, as inferred by the service according to the available data; (3) a ranking of the answers, suggesting what is the most convenient answer to be graded by the teacher, in order to add the highest amount of information in the network and make the inferred grades more precise. At the first interaction, only the peer evaluation data would be sent to the service. In the following interactions, however, the current models can be sent as well, in order to allow the service to further enhance the modeling process.

3 Bayesian Network Service and Corresponding API

We designed and implemented a Bayesian Network Service (BNS), as a Python-based library applied for modeling *Competence* and *Assessment capability* features of the learner, as mentioned in the previous section: K, the level of knowledge; J, the ability to assess peers' work; and C, the correctness of the answer provided by the student. The BNS accepts as input the peer assessment session data, i.e.: (1) the peer evaluations, (2) those teacher's grades that are available, and, optionally (3) the previous K values of the students. Then, it returns as output the computed student models and inferred grades.

In addition, we implemented a Python-based BNS API, which can be used to extend the functionality of any peer assessment platform. The main method provided by the API is *getStudentModels*, which accepts as input the peer evaluation session data, processes it and returns the corresponding student models. The exchanged data is represented in JSON format. In what follows we present some examples of input data:

(1) *The list of grades assigned by each student to her peers*

```
"peer-assessments": {
    "S1" : { "S2": 0.83, "S3": 0.56 },        # grades given by student S1 to S2 and S3
    "S2" : { "S1": 0.70, "S3": 0.62 },
    ...    }        # grades given by all other students participating in the peer assessment
```

Here the student with identifier S1 assigned a grade of 83 to student S2 and a grade of 56 to student S3 (on a 1 to 100 scale). Notice that all grades are normalized in the range 0-1 (e.g.: 83 → 0.83, 56 → 0.56).

(2) *The list of grades assigned by the teacher to each student*

```
"teacher-grades": {
    "S1": 0.6,                  # grade given by the teacher to student S1
    "S2": 0.72,
    ...    }                    # grades given by the teacher to all other students
```

Notice that the teacher can assess the entire class of learners or only a subset of them.

(3) *The current student models, in terms of the K variables*

```
"student-models" : {
    "S1" : { "K": [ 0.32, 0.31, 0.20, 0.10, 0.05, 0.02 ] },
    "S2" : { "K": [ 0.15, 0.20, 0.35, 0.17, 0.08, 0.05 ] },
    ...    }                    # all other students' models
```

The students' knowledge level (K) is represented as a distribution of probabilities over the grades A-F; e.g., in case of student S1: $p(A) = 0.32$, $p(B) = 0.31$, $p(C) = 0.20$, $p(D) = 0.10$, $p(E) = 0.05$, $p(F) = 0.02$.

Starting from this input data, the BNS API computes the student models (K and J), and the answers' inferred grade (C). An example output, for the student S1, is as follows:

```
"S1" : {
    "C" : {
        "value" : 0.77,                                 # inferred grade (answer's Correctness)
        "probs" : [ 0.11, 0.15, 0.34, 0.21, 0.16, 0.03 ]  # inferred probability distribution for C
    },
    "J" : {
        "value" : 0.82,                                 # inferred ability to Judge
        "probs" : [ 0.14, 0.35, 0.24, 0.21, 0.05, 0.01 ]  # inferred probability distribution for J
    },
    "K" : {
        "value" : 0.85,                                 # inferred Knowledge about the topic
        "probs" : [ 0.25, 0.36, 0.21, 0.12, 0.05, 0.01 ]  # inferred probability distribution for K
    }, ...
}
```

Moreover, the service orders the answers not yet graded by the teacher, to suggest which one should be given precedence, in case of further grading on teacher's part.

4 Proof of Concept - Integrating BNS in Moodle

We put our Bayesian Network Service to trial, by using it in Moodle LMS; more specifically, we extended the Moodle Workshop plugin with student modeling functionality. The *Workshop plugin* [8] is an effective peer assessment module based on sessions in which learners submit their own work and assess the work of peers according to the teacher's specifications. A session consists of several phases: (1) *setup phase* where the teacher sets the session description, provides instructions for the submission and assessment forms; (2) *submission phase* where the learners submit their work; (3) *assessment phase* where learners evaluate other peers' work; (4) *grading evaluation phase* where students are graded based on their competences; and (5) *closed phase* where the session ends and the teacher and learners can view the outcomes in a grades report.

A PHP-based client using BNS API was developed and integrated into the Workshop plugin. When an evaluation session moves to closed phase, the session data is encoded in JSON format and sent to the BNS. The service is responsible for creating the student models and sending them back to the client. The Workshop plugin decodes the response and stores the models in the database using the Moodle Database API; the Moodle database was also extended in order to accommodate the new functionality.

Furthermore, in order to provide better insights into the student *Competence* and *Assessment capability*, the Workshop plugin was modified to support the computation of two additional *inter-session* grades: *overall submission grade* and *overall assessment grade*. The *overall submission grade* reflects the student's abilities of solving tasks; it is computed as the average of the grades obtained for all his submitted answers, throughout the sessions. The *overall assessment grade* reflects the student's abilities of assessing other peers' work; it is computed as the average of the grades obtained for all the assessments provided by the student, throughout the sessions.

We are currently using Moodle Workshop in a class of around 60 students enrolled in a course on Programming Techniques (first year Bachelor course in Computer Engineering, at Sapienza University, Rome). Each peer assessment session consists of one programming task, whose solution entails the definition of an algorithm and its implementation in the C programming language. Three criteria are associated to each task, to provide the students with some guidelines regarding the evaluation process. In each session, a student is requested to solve her own task, and to evaluate three of her peers' solutions (randomly assigned). Each answer is assessed also by the teacher, in order to provide the students with expert evaluation, and to have a complete dataset that we plan to use in order to analyze the behavior of the BNS. We also aim to investigate the effectiveness and reliability of the enhanced Workshop plugin, compared to the base version. The results of our experimental study will be reported in a future paper.

5   Conclusion

This paper proposed a service-oriented approach for student modeling in peer assessment platforms. More specifically, we designed and implemented a web service based on a Bayesian Network model, which computes learners' *Competence* and *Assessment capability*, basing on data coming from peer assessment sessions, and on teacher's assessment of a subset of the answers. A corresponding Python-based API was also proposed for the Bayesian Network Service. As proof of concept, we used this API in Moodle, by enhancing the Workshop plugin with student modeling functionality.

As future work, we plan to further extend the Workshop module, by integrating open learner model visualization features (including ranking, comparison with peers, evolution over time). These could be used both by the teacher, for providing feedback and remedial interventions, and by the student, for spurring metacognitive awareness. We also plan to provide various metrics regarding students' activity (level of involvement, consistency etc.), as well as regarding the reliability of the computed student model.

Furthermore, our BNS API was conceived to be used by any platform offering peer assessment functionalities; we would therefore like to integrate it also with another system, in order to prove its flexibility and broad applicability. Finally, experimental studies need to be performed, in order to provide real world validation of our approach.

References

1. Bloom, B.S., Engelhart, M.D., Furst, E.J., Hill, W.H., Krathwohl, D.R.: Taxonomy of Educational Objectives: The Classification of Educational Goals. Handbook I: Cognitive Domain. McKay, New York (1956)
2. Sadler, P.M., Good, E.: The impact of self- and peer-grading on student learning. Educ. Assess. 11(1), 1–31 (2006)
3. Li, L., Liu, X., Steckelberg, A.L.: Assessor or assessee: how student learning improves by giving and receiving peer feedback. Br. J. Educ. Technol. 41(3), 525–536 (2010)
4. Palmer, K., Richardson, P.: On-line assessment and free-response input - a pedagogic and technical model for squaring the circle. In: Proceedings of 7th Computer Assisted Assessment Conference (CAA), pp. 289–300 (2003)
5. Conati, C., Gertner, A., VanLehn, K.: Using Bayesian networks to manage uncertainty in student modeling. User Model. User-Adapt. Interact. 12(4), 371–417 (2002)
6. Sterbini, A., Temperini, M.: Analysis of open answers via mediated peer-assessment. In: Proceedings of 17th International Conference on System Theory, Control and Computing (ICSTCC) (2013)
7. Moodle learning management system. https://moodle.org/. Accessed 28 May 2018
8. Workshop plugin. https://docs.moodle.org/35/en/Using_Workshop. Accessed 28 May 2018
9. De Marsico, M., Sciarrone, F., Sterbini, A., Temperini, M.: Supporting mediated peer-evaluation to grade answers to open-ended questions. EURASIA J. Math. Sci. Technol. Educ. 13(4), 1085–1106 (2017)

Emerging Technologies Support for Intelligent Tutoring

Technology Enhanced Learning Experience in Intercultural Business Communication Course: A Case Study

Marcel Pikhart[✉]

Faculty of Informatics and Management, University of Hradec Kralove,
Hradec Kralove, Czech Republic
marcel.pikhart@uhk.cz

Abstract. Intercultural business communication courses have become a must in today's world and they have already been implemented into university curricula. However, due to their novelty, they still lack detailed methodology how to introduce them to the students using modern communication technologies. The presented paper focuses on hands-on experience of web-based learning in an intercultural business communication course at the Faculty of Information Technology and Management, University of Hradec Kralove, Czech Republic. The course itself was introduced in 2014, as an academic effort to improve intercultural competence of the students of business and IT. However, after a few years, the tutor realised that the standard ways of transferring information were not sufficient and tried to create a supporting online (web-based) course for the participants to help them develop intercultural awareness in a modern interactive way. The students follow classic educational patterns of university curriculum and also they have an opportunity to use the online course with additional materials to enhance their learning experience. The conducted comparative research clearly proved that the students benefited from the introduction of technology enhanced learning experience significantly. The results of the research will thus be very important for curricula makers and for the tutors themselves as well.

Keywords: Business communication · Intercultural communication
Managerial communication · E-learning · Online learning
Technology enhanced learning · University curricula

1 Introduction

There is enough research into the use of mobile technologies in various aspects of educational process [2, 6, 9, 10], academic education [3], learning aspects for seniors [4, 5, 7], or even the use of technological devices in business [1, 8]. However, we still lack research into technology enhanced learning of the currently modern courses of intercultural business communication. The author of the paper introduced the course in the academic year 2014/2015 at the Faculty of Informatics and Management at the University of Hradec Kralove, Czech Republic. The course still runs regularly with dozens of participants from all over the world. Each year there are more than 50

© Springer Nature Switzerland AG 2018
T. Hao et al. (Eds.): SETE 2018, LNCS 11284, pp. 41–45, 2018.
https://doi.org/10.1007/978-3-030-03580-8_5

participants of the course, mostly from China, Taiwan, Hong Kong but also from many European universities and also a few students from Latin America.

The author attempts to compare research from 2016 when the students did not have any technology enhanced learning experience with recent research from the winter semester of 2017 when the technology enhanced learning was introduced. The participants were asked about their satisfaction with the course and also about their recommendation about the course. The possibility to compare the results (before the technology enhanced learning and after it was implemented) provide us with a very important insight into the efficiency and attractiveness of this kind of teaching techniques at our universities.

During the academic year of 2016/2017 the tutor of the course used standard frontal education methods without any use of technology enhanced learning. The technology enhanced learning was introduced into the course in the academic year of 2017/2018 and was facilitated by these tools and environments:

- The use of cloud as a store for texts to study - mostly Google Docs,
- Use of YouTube videos - e.g. Hofstede and Lewis interviews,
- Blackboard - used to communicate with the students, share information and links to the given texts to study,
- Communication with the students via email and blog portal (blogspot.com)
- Online testing through Blackboard platform during the semester and the final test at the end of the semester.

2   Research Questions

These were the research question we wanted to focus on during the research:

1. How much are the participants of the course satisfied **without** the use of technology enhanced learning? (participants of the course 2016/2017)
2. How much are the participants of the course satisfied **with** the use of technology enhanced learning? (participants of the course 2017/2018)
3. What are their recommendations regarding practical use of technology enhanced learning tools in the classes of intercultural business communication? (participants of the 2017/2018 course only)

3   Purpose of the Study

The purpose of the study was to obtain systematic data about the satisfaction of the students without and with the use of technology enhanced learning which could lead to implementation of new methods and thus enhance the learning experience of them as the participants of the course.

4   Research Methodology

4.1   Research 1

After the winter semester 2016/2017, quantitative research was conducted in the group of the participants of the course of intercultural business communication at the Faculty of Informatics and Management of the University of Hradec Kralove. The data were collected by using a questionnaire distributed during the last seminar of the semester. The research sample comprised of 48 participants. They were the foreign students of our university from Taiwan, Hong Kong, China, Greece, the Netherlands, Italy, Spain, Bulgaria, Nigeria and Turkey. Their age was between 19 and 23 years.

4.2   Research 2

After the winter semester 2017/2018, quantitative research was conducted in the group of the participants of the course of intercultural business communication at the Faculty of Informatics and Management of the University of Hradec Kralove. The data were collected by using an online questionnaire during the last seminar of the semester. The research sample comprised of 54 participants. They were the foreign students of our university from Taiwan, Hong Kong, China, Mexico, Italy, Spain, Bulgaria and Turkey. Their age was between 19 and 23 years.

5   Results of the Research and Their Discussion

5.1   Research 1

The research proved that the students were quite satisfied with the contents of the course; however, many of them expressed their dissatisfaction with its monotonous nature. Some of them also expressed their idea about using some modern technological tools to communicate the information from the course with them. These ideas were not very specific but motivated the effort of the tutor to implement these technological achievements into the class the following academic year.

The results of the research clearly showed that the students naturally need technological devices and technology enhanced learning methods to reach the information better, study on the go, reach the data online, etc.

5.2   Research 2

The research proved that the vast majority of the participants are totally satisfied with extra materials and sources provided through the web-based platform because they supply them with new information and stimuli they cannot get from standard lectures and textbooks. This form of blended learning proves to be very useful and improves both learning curve and experience for the participants.

The participants equally confirmed that the used tools are adequate and that there is no need to introduce any more, i.e. the cloud usage, YouTube videos, Blackboard, email communication, blog communication and online testing were sufficient and they did not express any need to introduce anything else.

5.3   Comparative Results

The research proved that the vast majority of the participants are totally satisfied with extra materials and sources provided through the web-based platform because they supply them with new information and stimuli they cannot get from standard lectures and textbooks. These findings are supported by already a classic theory of Generation Z, who desperately needs electronic means of communication not only for pleasure and social encounters but also for work, education and professional life. This supports the idea of the necessary implementation of blended learning into intercultural business communication courses, and therefore proves to be useful for academics that need some guidance when creating identical or similar courses as this one.

The urgent need for us as creators of curricula described by the research must be taken into account as we still lack this approach in many academic areas still untouched by technology enhanced learning. The research only supports the idea that modern technological tools have a great opportunity to enhance the learning process which can become more efficient.

When the two tested groups are compared, we can clearly see the difference in their satisfaction and also their feeling that they have obtained and learned new information in an easy and modern way. The aspects of modernity and trendy technological features are very important for the current generation much more than ever before. The unprecedented changes in the way new technologies are used but also viewed are clearly seen in the research results – the modern generation not only needs the technologically enhanced learning, but it needs it to make the learning process more efficient.

6   Conclusion

The comparative research which was conducted clearly showed that the difference of the level of satisfaction before and after introducing technology enhanced learning is dramatic. The participants clearly showed their dissatisfaction with the monotonous classes before the introduction of the technology enhanced learning, and on the contrary, the second group of participants who took the class after the introduction the technology enhanced learning clearly showed their interest and enthusiasm.

Curriculum creators and tutors of similar courses must take into account the differences in generation, i.e. the current generation of university students desperately needs modern communication tools implemented even into the teaching process; otherwise we as educators can never succeed. The information obtained from the research leads us to a challenge of implementing technology enhanced learning into all aspects of educational process because the participants of this process will benefit from it much more than from traditional approaches.

Acknowledgement. This paper is supported by the SPEV 2018 project at the Faculty of Informatics and Management, University of Hradec Kralove, Czech Republic.

References

1. Cerna, M., Svobodova, L.: Internet and social networks as a support for communication in the business environment - pilot study. In: Hradec Economic Days 2017, vol. 7, no. 1, pp. 120–126 (2017)
2. Cheung, S.K.S.: A case study on the students' attitude and acceptance of mobile learning. In: Li, K.C., Wong, T.L., Cheung, S.K.S., Lam, J., Ng, K.K. (eds.) Technology in Education. Transforming Educational Practices with Technology. CCIS, vol. 494, pp. 45–54. Springer, Berlin (2015). https://doi.org/10.1007/978-3-662-46158-7_5
3. Klimova, B.: Assessment in the eLearning course on academic writing – a case study. In: Wu, T.-T., Gennari, R., Huang, Y.-M., Xie, H., Cao, Y. (eds.) SETE 2016. LNCS, vol. 10108, pp. 733–738. Springer, Cham (2017). https://doi.org/10.1007/978-3-319-52836-6_79
4. Klimova B.: Senior tourism and information and communication technologies. In: Park J., Chen S.C., Raymond Choo, K.K. (eds) Advanced Multimedia and Ubiquitous Engineering. FutureTech 2017, MUE 2017. LNEE, vol. 448, pp. 440–445. Springer, Singapore (2017a). https://doi.org/10.1007/978-981-10-5041-1_71
5. Klimova B.: Smart teacher. In: Uskov V., Howlett R., Jain L. (eds) Smart Education and e-Learning 2017. SEEL 2017. SIST, vol. 75, pp. 321–328. Springer, Heidelberg (2018). https://doi.org/10.1007/978-3-319-59451-4_32
6. Oz, H.: Prospective English teachers ownership and usage of mobile devices as M-learning tools. Procedia - Soc. Behav. Sci. **141**, 1031–1041 (2013)
7. Poulova, P., Klimova, B.: Mobile learning and its potential for engineering education. In: Proceedings of 2015 IEEE Global Engineering Education Conference (EDUCON 2015), pp. 47–51. University of Technology, Talinn (2015)
8. Teodorescu, A.: Mobile learning and its impact on business English learning. Procedia - Soc. Behav. Sci. **180**, 1534–1540 (2015)
9. Wu, Q.: Pulling mobile assisted language learning (MALL) into the mainstream: MALL in broad practice. PLoS ONE **10**(5), e0128762 (2015)
10. Yang, J.: Mobile assisted language learning: review of the recent applications of emerging mobile technologies. Engl. Lang. Teach. **6**(7), 19–25 (2013)

Using the iPeer LMS Feature to Evaluate Peer Participation in Teamwork for Assessment "as learning": Lessons Learned

Adriana Botha[1](✉) , Riana Steyn[1] , Lizette Weilbach[1] ,
and Erika Muller[2]

[1] Department of Informatics, University of Pretoria, Pretoria, South Africa
adriana.botha@up.ac.za
[2] Department of ENGAGE, University of Pretoria, Pretoria, South Africa

Abstract. The competency gap between the teamwork skills of undergraduate students and that, which is required by employers, has caused many undergraduate programmes within a faculty at an urban University in South Africa to introduce learning outcomes, which focus specifically on teamwork skills and student participation within teams. Despite the provision of well-designed rubrics, module lecturers and support staff reported to still have limited control over team dynamics and outcomes of peer assessments. The educational consultant at this University identified the iPeer tool for formative assessment of teamwork participation within the official LMS of the institution. The paper illustrates that iPeer provides module lecturers with the opportunity to utilise technology for assessment 'as learning'. An iPeer research collaborative team was established and some module lecturers opted to pilot the tool as part of their large group projects.

The purpose of this paper is to share with other academics the lessons learned from implementing the iPeer tool to create an awareness of the online technology available to assist with peer participation evaluation challenges. This is done by reporting on the insights gained from the pilot projects, with the aim of sharing assessment possibilities that could influence individual behaviour in teams and as a result contribute to improved teamwork skills such as communication, collaboration and the ability to meet team deadlines. The learning is based on peer feedback which is readily available to all team members.

Keywords: Peer participation evaluation (PPE) · Teamwork skills
Assessment as learning · LMS feature · iPeer tool

1 Introduction and Background

Several authors emphasise the importance of teaching effective communication and teamwork skills to engineering students (Lingard [1], Martinez, Romero, Marquez and Perez [2], Kashefi, Ismail and Yusof [3], Isaac, Kolawole, Funsho and Adesiji [4] and Ercan and Khan [5]), while the ten top soft skills needed in today's workplace as reported by Robles [6] include, integrity, communication, courtesy, responsibility, social skills, positive attitude, professionalism, teamwork, and work ethic. In line with

© Springer Nature Switzerland AG 2018
T. Hao et al. (Eds.): SETE 2018, LNCS 11284, pp. 46–55, 2018.
https://doi.org/10.1007/978-3-030-03580-8_6

this, education authorities incorporate exit level programme learning outcomes that focus specifically on teamwork and students' participation within a team to prepare them for the world of work. In this regard the Engineering Council of South Africa (ECSA) [7] and the Accreditation Board for Engineering and Technology (ABET) [8] has placed an emphasis on teamwork skills in its criteria for the accreditation of engineering and computing programs. The ECSA exit level outcome 8 states that "Individual, team and multidisciplinary working requires that a student is able to demonstrate knowledge and understanding of engineering management principles and apply these to one's own work as a member or leader in a diverse team and to manage projects [7]". In the same way, the ABET computing student outcome criteria (d), requires students to have "an ability to function effectively on teams to accomplish a common goal." [8].

The emerging hybrid drive within a seamless learning environment forced lecturers at our University to revisit the constructive alignment of their curricula to the outcomes set by these and other South African Educational authorities (Fig. 1).

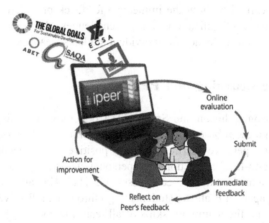

Fig. 1. The process and alignment of technology driven team participation evaluation to the outcomes set by the South African Educational Authorities and External Accreditation Bodies.

Although teamwork forms an integral part of the Engineering and Computing programs at our University, the question of the validity and reliability of the marks awarded for teamwork are often questioned. To assess teamwork effectively, both the team's final product (task) and the process by which they arrived at that product (group processes such as participation, collaboration and contribution) need to be evaluated [9]. In an online document of the Columbia Center for Teaching and Learning for graduate students [10], the author confirms that it is hard to determine a sense of understanding of an individual student's group participation and contribution. This can become even more complex, despite the provision of well-designed rubrics, when group work takes place outside the scheduled lecture time where lecturers are unable to observe the way in which the team members collaborate and contribute. When group conflict arises, lecturers are often challenged to give advice on team dynamics without objective hard evidence of group processes.

In this paper we argue that technology supported peer participation evaluation (PPE) seems to provide the solution to these group work assessment challenges, and that care should be taken to use it as formative assessment 'as learning' and not only in a summative way 'for learning'.

In the next section, we elaborate on PPE as a construct of collaborative learning and the opportunities it poses to enhance the formative assessment of teamwork skills, after which we reflect on the challenges experienced with the implementation of PPE practices in the Faculty of Engineering, Built Environment and IT (EBIT) at our University, in Sect. 3. PPE as a form of 'assessment as learning' and the value it can add to individual students' learning curves for self-regulated learning and metacognition is discussed in Sect. 4. In Sect. 5 we report on how technology was utilised for assessment 'as learning', by implementing the iPeer tool within the LMS of our institution as a pilot and discuss the feedback received from the module lecturers involved. In Sect. 6 we discuss the findings of our research and in the last section we share our lessons learned on how the immediate feedback provided by the iPeer tool assisted with the early identification of team challenges, the improvement of team dynamics, as well as the influence on individual students' team behavior.

2 Cooperative Learning and PPE

According to Johnson, Johnson and Smith [11] Cooperative Learning (CL) provides the foundation for problem-based; team-based; collaborative and peer-assisted learning. The elements of cooperative learning include positive interdependence; individual accountability; face-to-face interaction; interpersonal and small group skills and group processing. PPE is a method to be used to assess CL [12]. The latter forms the point of departure for this paper. PPE allows students to go through a reflective process of their group's dynamics and the teamwork skills of all team members.

The skills obtained through these reflections are used to ensure effective future work relationships. It is also the element which allows students to adjust their future behaviour based on their own reflection and on the qualitative feedback obtained from their peers [13]. A broad understanding of the underlying theories informing PPE can assist lecturers in the design of rubrics for evaluating some of the hidden curriculum aspects of PPE, namely team dynamics, power play, the management of conflict and being cooperative, commitment, performance and motivation, self-regulation and communication. Providing feedback on teamwork leads to the development of skills such as critical reflection, and sensitively providing feedback on the work done by others. Apart from learning from the feedback itself, students also attain lifelong skills through meta-processes such as reflecting on and justifying what they've done [14].

Another advantage of peer evaluation is the fact that students receive more feedback from peers much quicker than that which can be offered by their lecturer. It therefore offers a valuable solution in cases of constrained resources and minimal academic capacity [14, 15].

3   Current Challenges with PPE Practices

The implementation of PPE is often accompanied by remarks and attitudes such as: "Group work and projects aren't fair if we do not get a mark for it"; "If not well structured, peer evaluation marks are not a true reflection of individual participation"; "The mark allocation for group work is not fair" and "I do all the work myself but everyone in the team gets the distinction". The focus of involving students in teamwork needs to move towards the aim of facilitating peer learning and through this process cultivating collaboration and graduate attributes. As learning is strongly influenced by assessment, lecturers are faced with the notion that in order to improve peer learning the assessment practices they use need to support it.

Finding innovative solutions for PPE in our University was born from the challenges lecturers experienced with teamwork assessment and the drive of the institution towards offering 25–30% of its programmes as hybrid programmes. This in effect forced lecturers to seek alternative ways of assessment, such as PPE as formative assessment.

The following section will point out some of the challenges experienced by lecturers with regards to the implementation of PPE in their modules.

3.1   Second Year Engineering Module in Manufacturing and Design (MOW217) - 497 Students

It is challenging to evaluate a student's ability to participate in teamwork, as it is not possible to rely purely on the group's feedback to rate the students' participation. When students have the choice of team formation, it leads to friends working together and this raises the question of whether their loyalty towards each other weighs more than their honest feedback, even if it is anonymous. The administration involved in arranging and rearranging self-enrolled groups is very significant. Students sometimes do not integrate with different ethnic groups when they self-enroll in groups and this is not at all representative of what will happen in the work environment. The students work in teams throughout the module and PPE takes place on two occasions.

Due to the large number of students the lecturer searched for a new way to improve PEE without overloading the current administration burden. He also wanted to change the quality of the PPE feedback. As the module is seen as a potential high-risk module, the aim was to improve throughput, but more importantly, to improve students' competency levels in the subject. The iPeer tool was implemented to comply with the expected ECSA outcomes, and to investigate if one could change students' attitude towards PPE and at the same time enculturate individual team participation and contributing behaviour. Additionally, two Qualtrics surveys, which address aspects of transformation and access within teamwork, were also introduced.

Previously a manual system was used where group members rated their team members and included their ratings in their report. This yielded very unsatisfactory results with students rating each other equally high. An anonymous online quiz was also done, which yielded similar results as described above.

3.2 Third Year Engineering Management Module (BSS310) - 982 Students of Nine Different Engineering Programmes

Due to the number of enrolled students, the groups were too large (10 students per group) and all team members were not equally contributing. Students exhibited an inability to (independently) apply their knowledge or seek knowledge without exact instructions which manifested in a 'babysitting' or 'spoon feeding' phenomena. Proactivity was in general lacking, with issues and problems visible at the onset of team formation. As always, the student syndrome of leaving everything for the very last-minute surfaced once again. Students fail to read instructions and show little under-standing of such. Furthermore, they tend not to ask questions when they do not understand. The self-reflection evaluation and immediate peer feedback could, together with a well-structured rubric indicating competency levels, support students to develop and grow self-regulating and metacognitive skills. A major challenge in this module is the inability of students to seek information independently, e.g. using a simple Google search.

To date PPE practices were executed through team diaries and meeting memos - in some cases there were none of these.

3.3 Third Year Systems Development Project Module for Information System Students (INF370) - 122 Students

History shows that when INF370 students are able to freely form their own teams well in advance, they tend to find a way to work well together. In cases where teams have to be put together with the "remaining" students or "students without groups" due to late registration, the tendency is that these groups experience a lot of conflict throughout the year due to: free riders; unequal goals set by the individual members; poor commu-nication and misunderstandings. Although a few methods are in place to inter alia handle free riders and team conflict, the need for early identification of group problems is essential. Students tend to carry free riders for the first few deliverables without reporting them. This is a problem as these issues need to be visible early on so that one could rectify them immediately before all the trust between the members is completely lost.

Teams have a project management file in which they plan ahead and report on team meetings held and team member participation. This file is handed in with every deliverable and signed off by all group members. Team participation is though not evaluated per se. Each deliverable (there are 11) is a group deliverable and teams get scored on their final product only. This poses a problem, as the curriculum requires students to demonstrate PPE skills, which is not currently measured. Team problems are reported to the course coordinator after which a meeting is called to raise and discuss issues. The process is very time consuming and involves manual peer evalu-ation to determine the non-contributing culprits. Peer evaluation therefore only took place manually when group issues arose. As this was not sufficient, the iPeer tool was introduced in May 2018, allowing team members to assess their peers' team skills such as communication, conflict handling and the ability to meet team deadlines.

3.4 Engineering Augmented Degree Programme (ENGAGE) - 156 Students

Students are introduced to teamwork through a 'Go Green project' in the skills and practice-based Professional Orientation module. The project serves as an initial introduction to the importance of teamwork in an engineering context. Various challenges were faced. Hard copy rubrics were used during face-to-face presentation sessions.

During 2015 and 2016, challenges were faced to get all students on campus during the student unrests. The Qualtrics online survey tool was used as alternative to the hard copies. In 2017 students only did one peer evaluation at the end of the total project which was not seen to be so effective. There was a need for an online tool to be used at three different instances during the project in order to provide immediate feedback and evaluation regarding: participation in the initial idea for a project; research and literature review; participation in the practical execution of the planned project and a final report; and the team's presentation of the project once it was completed.

The general challenges experienced in the project are: (1) Students do not appreciate working in teams, despite allowing them to choose their own teammates. The selection of own teammates is motivated by practical considerations such as proximity in living quarters and timetable issues; (2) Sticking to a pre-planned time schedule during the course of the semester; (3) Monitoring the quality of work submitted by each team member; (4) Heavy admin load of the lecturers who coordinate the project to make sure that all teams consist of only 4 members and that submissions are done timeously, during the different phases of the project.

This section provided a snapshot of some of the challenges lecturers in the EBIT Faculty face concerning the manual implementation of PPE. All the above lecturers showed a willingness to enhance their assessment practices, applying technology in the form of the iPeer tool to ensure that PPE becomes more than just a formative scoring process.

4 PPE for Assessment "as learning"

Quality feedback as part of PPE has the potential to enhance and promote student learning [14]. Peer feedback 'as' learning is a process during which the rich and detailed comments of peers on their fellow learners' performance and the standard of their work, lead to an improved understanding and consequently to enhanced learning. To appreciate PPE's pedagogical value and the influence it has on improved learning and student success, reference is given to what PPE is not in the context of this paper. PPE is not primarily for summative assessment, which is about assessment 'of' learning and for marks only. In summative assessment there is no opportunity for qualitative feedback and the mark or grade indicates the level of achievement. This type of assessment is usually done at the end of a semester or during an end of year examination when students will not necessary see their feedback to learn from it.

Although PPE is a type of formative assessment, it can still be distinguished from assessment 'for' learning in the sense that 'for' provides student feedback that contributes a great deal to encourage learning. Important to note is that feedback needs to be well-justified to have a positive effect on learning. Assessment 'for' learning is also ongoing and provides opportunities for early intervention support. However, according to Gupta [16], PPE is considered to be assessment 'as' learning as it provides students with the opportunity to monitor their own learning (it is self-regulated) with self-correction (which leads to metacognition). It therefore allows students to reflect on their work and as such learn about themselves as learners, as well as about their role within a team. In this process, they also become aware of the way in which they learn, and they consequently similarly discover what they don't know.

5 Creating an Awareness of Online Technology for Peer Participation Evaluation

Various online peer evaluation tools are available. Examples include Turnitin, CATME, PEAR, SPARK, Teammate and Blackboard's Peer Assessment Tool. New features that form part of an LMS are often not visible to lecturers or tend not to be used due to: a lack of understanding of its educational value; the absence of training in its use; or the absence of an existing framework to be used for its implementation. Lecturers also seem to be reluctant to use technology if its future is not secure, as time spent on the development of such content and assessment would be valuable time wasted. After being introduced to the iPeer tool, the educational consultant (EC) of the EBIT Faculty identified the value it could add to lecturing practices where new innovative ways to implement PPE were already tried out, or where formative 'assessment as learning', using the old fashioned good old paper-based approach, was still utilised.

To introduce the iPeer tool, the EC demonstrated the tool during a lunch hour workshop to lecturers who had the opportunity to experience the tool 'as students' and were able to follow the creation of an assessment event. Prior to the workshop, some module lecturers who were experiencing challenges with assessing teamwork for large classes were also invited to pilot the iPeer tool. An iPeer Research Collaborative Team was established to further support the investigation and implementation of the tool.

The four types of evaluation events available within the iPeer tool include: simple evaluations, rubrics, mixed evaluations and surveys. The tool allows a lecturer to implement PPE in 5 easy steps: (1) Set up student groups; (2) Create an evaluation event; (3) Launch the event; (4) Students assess their peers using grades and comments according to the selected type of evaluation. Note that if these comments are enforced, it provides their peers with valuable information on why they received a specific score - providing for assessment 'as learning'. Students/groups who did not submit their assessments are also clearly indicated for follow up. During step (5) details on peer grades and comments can be released to students (see Fig. 2).

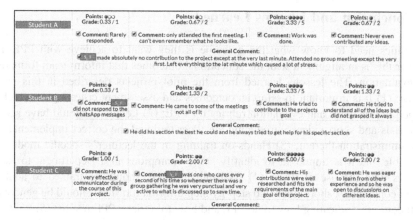

Fig. 2. Example feedback using a teamwork assessment rubric with enforced peer comments

6 Findings and Discussion Across the Pilot Projects

In all the pilot projects mentioned in the previous section of the paper, the lecturers observed significant buy-in from the majority of students, with no negative feedback or highlighted concerns. The students embraced and accepted iPeer as a PPE tool. The quality of the marks allocated to team members by their peers, were significantly more valuable and distributed. Constructive qualitative feedback was obtained via a compulsory comment entry for each evaluation criteria (see Fig. 2 for examples of these comments), providing team members with the opportunity to use it as part of their assessment 'as learning' process.

With regards to group randomisation, the tool proved to be invaluable. Previously students were allowed to select their own group members, which typically resulted in them selecting their friends and subjectively scoring all group members to have contributed equally towards the teamwork processes. The use of the random group allocation functionality offered by the iPeer tool resulted in varied group member ratings, which presented a much more realistic picture of the groups' skills and processes.

Due to the transparency of the qualitative data obtained through the compulsory feedback comments, lecturers were able to gain a deeper insight and understanding of the teams' dynamics and the way in which the students participated within their groups. Non-contributors were also exposed. Lecturers were able to identify the problem teams early on and could start with rectifying actions in these teams as soon as the evidence were provided, especially in the modules where a number of evaluation events were used for milestone assessment. The enforcement of required comments allowed students the opportunity to gain more insight in their skills and to improve their behavior, team participation and contribution before moving on to a next team or to a next deliverable within the same team project. Students are also able to see their average marks and the anonymous feedback they got from their peers in the LMS Grade Centre. More benefits from the lecturers' perspective include the effortless administrative task required to create the evaluation event and the different types of evaluation events available that could be adapted in line with the required outcomes of the evaluation.

7 Conclusion and Lessons Learned

Academics need to know what the outcome is they want to achieve with PPE and whether this is in alignment with the educational outcomes that inform team formation and evaluation. The lessons learned from the pilot projects described in this paper include: (1) It is important to setup an outcomes and assessment criteria plan which is mapped to due dates and evaluation rubrics for PPE; (2) Lecturers should have access to tutorials and short videos introducing the iPeer tool and the correct implementation and administration thereof; (3) Hands-on training in the lecturer's specific module is invaluable and it is important to identify some champions in a Department to assist lecturers with the use of iPeer; (4) Assistant lecturers should be trained to address student concerns. A short video and step-by-step information sheet should be generated for student use, indicating how to do PPE and how to retrieve PPE results; (5) Students should be informed of the value of the iPeer tool and be motivated to use the feedback they receive from their peers 'as learning'; (6) A survey should be distributed to find out what students' perception of the iPeer tool is with regards to its ease of use, fairness of mark allocation, anonymity, value of immediate feedback and influence on behavioural change; (7) Administration with groups can be done through self-enrolment or random enrollment. If there is no motivation for self-enrollment, randomised groups created by the LMS or iPeer is recommended; (8) The pushing of class lists and groups from the LMS needs to be updated in iPeer if there are any changes to teams or team members. The tool provides a wraparound using Excel to update the data from LMS to iPeer; (9) If your username/user ID is not pushed with the student list you will find it challenging to get access to the iPeer course. The LMS administrator can assist with this; (10) Structure due dates/result dates well, so that this process is automated. Marks and feedback can be released manually, as you would, especially with large classes, need to have consistency and fairness in mind when you handle these; (11) There is a maximum of 25 marks that can be allocated per criteria. Keep this in mind when the marks get pushed back to the LMS Grade Centre; (12) Make participation and comments when scoring compulsory, this forces the students to explain the mark they give and provides valuable information for learning and self-growth to take place. Also include a penalty for late submission and non-completion to force students to do the assessment timely.

The iPeer Research Collaboration Team aim to achieve with PPE through the utilisation of iPeer, more responsible students who take accountability for their own learning; who are able to understand the shortcomings (if any) in their team skills; and who can grow and adjust their skills and behavior accordingly. Lecturers should be in a position where they can promptly identify the challenges and problems of both the individual team members, as well as that of the team as a whole. For purposes of reporting, the information and anonymous feedback to peers could be used to plan workshops and interventions to develop and improve team skills and dynamics. Ultimately, the vision for implementing iPeer for PPE for assessment 'as' learning is to foster changed behaviour, self-regulated learning, and metacognition, in alignment with the concept map for aligning PPE outcomes to cooperative learning and technology implementation.

Acknowledgements. A big thank you to Lisa Ransom from the Centre for Learning and Teaching at the Auckland University of Technology, who shared her insights and students' feedback with us.

A special thank you to Lucas du Plessis and Saija Bezuidenhout from our University for their invaluable support for and feedback on this project.

References

1. Lingard, R.W.: Teaching and assessing teamwork skills in engineering and computer science. Syst. Cybern. Inform. **8**, 34–37 (2010)
2. Martinez, M.L., Romero, G., Marquez, J.J., Perez, J.M.: Integrating teams in multidisciplinary project based learning in mechanical engineering. In: Proceedings of the IEEE EDUCON 2010 Conference, pp. 709–715 (2010)
3. Kashefi, H.K., Ismail, Z., Yusof, Y.M.: The impact of blended learning on communication skills and teamwork of engineering students in multivariable calculus. Procedia – Soc. Behav. Sci. **56**, 342–347 (2012)
4. Isaac, T.S., Kolawole, O.J., Funsho, A.A.G., Adesiji, O.J.: Reviewing engineering curricula to meet industrial and societal needs. In: Proceedings of the IEEE International Conference on Interactive Collaborative Learning (ICL), pp. 55–59 (2014)
5. Ercan, M.F., Khan, R.: Teamwork as a fundamental skill for engineering graduates. In: 2017 IEEE International Conference on Teaching, Assessment, and Learning for Engineering (TALE) (2017)
6. Robles, M.M.: Executive perceptions of the top 10 soft skills needed in today's work-place. Bus. Commun. Q. **75**, 453–465 (2012)
7. ECSA: Engineering Council of South Africa: Standards and Procedures System (ECSA), South Africa (2018)
8. ABET: Criteria for Accrediting Engineering Programs. Online (2018). http://www.abet.org/wp-content/uploads/2017/12/C001-18-19-CAC-Criteria-Version-1.0-12-21-17-FINAL.pdf, http://www.abet.org/wp-content/uploads/2018/02/E001-18-19-EAC-Criteria-11-29-17.pdf
9. Kollar, I., Fischer, F.: Peer assessment as collaborative learning a cognitive perspective. Learn. Instr. **20**, 344–348 (2012)
10. Bauer, M., Brooks, S.B., Dandrock, C.: 19th World Congress the International Federation of Automatic Control Cape Town (2014)
11. Johnson, D.W., Johnson, R.T., Smith, K.: Cooperative learning: improving university instruction by basing practice on validated theory. J. Excellence Univ. Teach. 1–26 (2013)
12. Gueldenzoph, L.E., May, G.L.: Collaborative peer evaluation: best practises for group member assessment. Bus. Commun. Q. **65**, 9–20 (2002)
13. Johnson, D.W., Johnson, R.T., Smith, K.A.: Cooperative learning returns to college: what evidence is there that it works? Change **30**(4), 27–35 (1998)
14. Liu, N., Carless, D.: Peer feedback: the learning element of peer assessment. Teach. High. Educ. **11**, 270–290 (2006)
15. Cho, K., MacArthur, C.: Student revision with peer and expert reviewing. Learn. Instr. **2**, 328–338 (2010)
16. Gupta, K.: Assessment as learning. Sci. Teach. **83**, 43–47 (2016)

Applying Diffusion of Innovation Theory to Learning Management System Feature Implementation in Higher Education: Lessons Learned

Adriana Botha[✉] , Hanlie Smuts , and Carina de Villiers

Department of Informatics, University of Pretoria, Pretoria, South Africa
adriana.botha@up.ac.za

Abstract. In today's rapidly changing world, information technology is transforming the higher education (HE) domain through an increase in accessibility of fast, multimedia-capable computers and broadband access. HE institutions are adopting new ways of enhancing their traditional ways of teaching, resulting in the emergence of seamless learning scenarios with a consequential need for flexible tools able to support experiences across various dimensions in such seamless learning environments. Learning Management Systems (LMS) in turn have fulfilled this requirement for enablement, however, technology alone is not sufficient as the potential it offers in order to be able to use it effectively in redesigning their educational scenarios, are often not understood or implemented. In order to achieve seamless learning while optimizing capital investment in learning management systems, this paper focuses on LMS feature implementation by applying the diffusion of innovations theory as a guideline. This paper presents two real-world examples that illustrate the proposed steps taken for LMS feature implementation and presents a number of lessons learned in doing so. It was established that there was synergy between the lessons learned for HE and industry and that HE could draw on the findings from industry.

Keywords: Learning management system · Diffusion of innovation
Higher education

1 Introduction

The workplace of today is dramatically different from the workplace of the past and what people produce together is what counts [1, 2]. The most common capabilities demanded of graduate job entrants include communication, team work, integrity, intellectual ability, and confidence [3]. The employability of graduates is an increasingly important topic within HE and it is important for universities to better understand employer capability and skills requirements, so that their graduates can better meet those requirements as well as the wider educational objectives of an HE qualification [3]. In this regard, the HE authorities require of institutions to conduct an annual programme review of programmes offered at the institution to improve learning for

© Springer Nature Switzerland AG 2018
T. Hao et al. (Eds.): SETE 2018, LNCS 11284, pp. 56–65, 2018.
https://doi.org/10.1007/978-3-030-03580-8_7

student success. External professional boards also require proof of evidence that students achieved the desired learning outcomes before they can enter the work place. The Engineering Council of South Africa (ECSA) for example expect proof of evidence that all engineering programmes adheres to eleven exit level outcomes with respect to where these outcomes were implemented, practiced and integrated assessed. This is also the case with programmes in the Informatics and Information Technology disciplines which need to comply to the Accreditation Board for Engineering and Technology (ABET) [7].

Update and optimization of HE qualification programmes involve a continued emphasis on the role of HE in preparing students both for highly skilled work and for whatever unknowns the future will bring. While in many cases it will be impossible to predict what this specific practice will be, it is anticipated that students will go out to practice in even more complex social, ethical and economic worlds [1]. Making graduates aware of the concept and importance of skill transfer is the responsibility of HE. Helping students understand and appreciate those factors which influence skill transfer is critical and will assist their career progression, lifelong learning and productivity [4].

An outside observer might conclude that HE possesses all there is to know about learning, and that with a few digital enhancements, its knowledge was complete [1]. However, persistent industry criticism of HE efforts in producing work-ready graduates and evidence of poor performance in certain employability skills are still evident [4, 6]. There has been far less attention to the transition of graduate skills and knowledge from university to the workplace [4]. The use of LMS features not only supports reporting on assurance of learning and graduate readiness over the past few years, but also enabled institutions to use data analytics to inform the actions for improvement of programmes to be in alignment with inter alia industry expectations [5].

Therefore, the purpose of this paper is to share lessons learned from the implementation of LMS features in HE through the application of the diffusion of innovation theory as a guideline. This is achieved through considering two real-world examples – one related to HE and the other to industry.

The next section presents the background to the study, where after technology adoption based on the diffusion of innovation theory will be explored in Sect. 3. Section 4 concludes the paper.

2 Background

In the next sections a brief overview of the expectation of industry with respect to providing evidence that institutions are complying with HE standards and industry requirements are presented. The affordances of LMS features in HE to address the current student in order to meet industry expectations are highlighted. In the final section, reference will be provided on how the diffusion of innovation theory can inform the decision to adapt technology and more specifically, the implementation of LMS features successfully.

2.1   Learning Management Systems in Higher Education

An LMS is a software application for the administration and reporting through analytics of educational programmes and modules. It affords the creation and uploading of various forms of content, provides assessment opportunities online and a platform for collaboration. Various types of LMS's are available such as Blackboard Learn, which is a licensed enterprise package. Other open source LMS's are for example Canvas and Moodle. Various tools within the LMS are available for early identification of challenged students and means to monitor and track these students' performance. Some LMS's have features to align outcomes with content and assessment through reports, for example the Goals Tool in Blackboard.

Dahlstrom et al. [8] reported on an information technology practices survey with nearly 800 institutions and explored the perspectives of faculty and students on the LMS in the context of institutional investments. It was found that "faculty and students value the use of the LMS as an enhancement to their teaching and learning experiences, but relatively few use the advanced features and even fewer use these systems to their fullest capacity" [8]. The faculty and students also indicated that they wanted to use analytics to enhance learning outcomes.

Although academics and learning developers highly value the learning and teaching features within the LMS [9], one often hear that the decision for academics to adopt and accept the use and implementation of the LMS into educational practice still remains a challenge and they often are sceptical of the successful implementation of underutilized features in the LMS. The next generation LMS should have specific attributes to meet user needs and expectations: for seamless learning it should be mobile friendly; to enculturate self-regulated learning it should allow personalization and be customizable; for successful implementation as part of a move to hybrid learning the LMS should be adaptive, intuitive and integrated; the design should enhance student learning and be able to easily report on the assurance of learning.

However, it was questioned if a lecturer's intention level for using an LMS are influenced by the combination of the LMS in use, the specific instructional task that needs to be performed and the specific user interface [10]. Dahlstrom et al. [8] found that lecturers are more willing to receive training to make better use of the LMS if they have evidence that it will improve student outcomes. Furthermore, a clear vision towards next generation learning environments was depicted, and summarize the use of an LMS and underutilization thereof as follows [8]: "Faculty and students perceive today's LMS as augmenting their teaching and learning experiences. However, relatively few students or faculty uses the more advanced features, and even fewer use these systems to their fullest capacity. Tomorrow's digital learning environment will find ways to bridge these gaps, through making users aware of system features, providing integrated training and support, setting expectations or standards for use, and/or prioritizing the user-friendliness of system interfaces. These systems (or ecosystems) will be optimized to enhance the teaching and learning experience."

2.2   The Profile of the "Current" Student

Students are increasingly crossing back and forth between higher education and the working world. It is common for undergraduates to have significant work experience prior to enrolment, with many also maintaining concurrent part time work alongside full time study [1]. Self-management encompasses the ability to multi-task, work autonomously, achieve work-life balance, self-regulate emotions and tolerate stress; all vital to employability [4]. The general consensus amongst employers is that graduates that make themselves as 'work ready' as possible are in a much stronger position [3].

HE institutions are faced with a new generation of students, often referred to as the millennials and more recently, generation Z [11]. These students are characterized as determined, driven achievers, express a need for immediate feedback, and have a sense of entitlement and are often experienced as a generation with unrealistic expectations. They expect a "how to" guide to succeed in the lecture environment and depend on technology for achieving their educational goals, as expected by HE and industry. Howe and Strauss [12] further characterize millennials as: "special, sheltered, team orientated, confident, pressured, achieving and conventional."

The Millennials want to spend less time on tasks and reach success with little effort [13]. To ensure that students can experience the connection between what they learn and the real-world application thereof, change on the lecturer side is inevitable. This changing educational environment calls for lecturers to reflect and revisit their teaching practices. It also asks of lecturers to 're-purpose' and change their adaption behavior to their use of technology to support this new generation who are also in some instance working full- and part-time jobs while taking lectures.

2.3   Diffusion of Innovation Theory (DIT)

The DIT by Rogers [14] is a well-known framework and still relevant in HE where new technology are being investigated for adoption [15]. The framework consists of 4 main elements in the diffusion of a new idea: (1) The innovation itself, (2) Communication channels, (3) Time and (4) Social system or the context. For purpose of this paper underutilized or unknown LMS features can also be referred to as an innovation if perceived by an individual as 'new'. Diffusion, as referred to in the DIT, is the process where an innovation is communicated over a period. People first have knowledge about the innovation, then forms an attitude towards the innovation after which they decide if they want to adopt or reject the implementation of the innovation. The final stage of communication is the confirmation stage where the individual evaluates the results of the innovation-decision that has been made. The communication takes place within a social system through certain channels and with specific people who create and share the information with each other to reach a mutual understanding of the adoption of the innovation. The stages through which people move to decide on the acceptance or rejection of an innovation is called the adoption process.

The adoption rate of an idea, object or practice is determined by five characteristics, namely: (1) Relative advantage of the innovation to the ones it supersedes; (2) Compatibility to existing needs and past experiences, (3) Complexity in relation to the difficulty and use; (4) Trialability with respect to the limited experimentation and the

(5) Observability of results of the innovation to the people within the social system. There are five categories of adoption and range from innovators, early adopters and majority, late majority and laggards.

3 Exploration of Technology Adoption Based on Diffusion of Innovation Theory

In this section, two real-world examples illustrate how the application of the DIT enabled the technology feature implementation. The first example is shared from HE, while the second example is drawn from industry.

3.1 Example 1 – Higher Education

The first example is related to an ABET accredited BCom Informatics programme offered at an emerging hybrid higher education institution in South Africa (SA) [15]. This programme needs to provide proof of evidence of assurance of learning compliance.

Head of departments, programme coordinators and module lecturers often fail to provide hard coherent evidence to report on assurance of learning. According to the Sydney Business School [16] assurance of learning (AoL) refers to: "The systematic process of collecting data about student learning outcomes, reviewing and using it to continuously develop and improve the School's degree programs. AoL ensures our graduates achieve the goals and outcomes we say they will achieve when we advertise our degree programs. It is a means of holding ourselves accountable to delivering what we say we will deliver to students and other stakeholders, as well as a way of supporting the continuous improvement of our degree programs."

Management and lecturers are not always aware of technology already available to them to assist with the collection of data for AoL and the reporting opportunities already available within these licensed enterprise packages. There can be a few reasons for this such as that not all features of the LMS are visible or advertised for use, unknown educational value of these features, or no policies for ensuring a quality assured process in place for the potential roll-out of these features.

The head of department (HOD) and education consultant investigated alternative methods of collecting data and reporting on AoL utilizing the institutions official LMS Blackboard Learn (Bb). They discovered that the Goals Tool feature and Goals Performance Dashboard feature within Bb could address the need for reporting to ABET as well as their annual programme review. The automated reports generated by Bb can inform the direction for programme and module improvement as well as actions to be taken for effective student learning. Another affordance discovered was the Goals Performance dashboard feature that informs students how they are progressing with their outcomes covered and achieved. Through this automated function, students can on a daily basis, monitor their performance against the aligned graduate attributes and industry expectation, enhancing their self-regulated and metacognition skills.

Another key objective was to introduce the Goals Tool to lecturers and at the same time motivate the lecturers to use the feature. In order for lecturers to adopt the Goals Tool successfully as part of their education practice, the DIT (Sect. 2.3) directed the design of the framework with reference to the innovation element and the persuasion communication resource (channel). The education consultant conducted a workshop, attended by all lecturers in the department, to introduce the perceived characteristics of the Goals Tool where after they completed an online proof of concept survey. The questions designed were informed by the five characteristics for the decision to adopt an innovation. Although the overall feedback was positive in the potential use of the feature, there remain resistance and concern with the additional administration load this feature could hold.

Lessons Learned
The diffusion of innovation decision process enabled the HOD and the education consultant to introduce the Goals Tool feature of the official LMS of the institution to lecturers. Reflection on the lessons learned provided the opportunity for a follow-up workshop with the aim to fully implement Goals Tool as a feature for reporting on AoL to ABET and programme improvement. The following highlights some of the key lessons learned during the feature implementation process:

Get to know your LMS and all the possible features included in the licensed enterprise package. Do not hesitate to take the risk to experiment with unknown and undiscovered features within your LMS, especially if continuation of the feature is a threat. These challenges can be addressed once the actual discontinuation eventually happens – lessons would have been learned and productive and proven recommendations can be offered at that stage to the institution to motivate for the continuation or alternative to the LMS feature.

Communicate through 'show and tell' the educational value of the LMS features and potential advantages it holds for lecturers and students. Engage with lecturers to experience the features in a 'sandpit' environment where it is save for them to make mistakes. See this as opportunities for learning and getting 'buy-in'.

Do not ignore the 'receiver variable' component of Rogers' [14] DIT. Know your audience especially regarding to their attitude toward change and their perceived need for the innovation (Fig. 1 grey boxes). The knowledge phase of the diffusion process, where a lecturer becomes aware of an innovation and how it functions, cannot be underestimated. The lecturer is part of a social system which Rogers [14] defines as: "a set of interrelated units that are engaged in joint problem-solving to accomplish a common goal." The social system institutes borders within which an innovation such as the Goals Tool feature diffuses. Norms manifest in the behavior patterns of the social system, the department in this instance, which influence the diffusion process. Recognize the role of change agents and influence of opinion leadership (who are usually the early adopters) within this social system to ensure a positive direction towards successful adoption of an innovation (Fig. 1 grey boxes).

For successful implementation of an innovation such as the Goals Tool feature on institutional level, an established partnership is indispensable. The following stakeholders should be part of this partnership: the institutions quality assurance office, institutional planning office, offices of the vice-chancellors for academic matters, offices

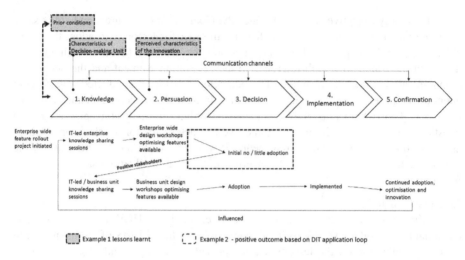

Fig. 1. Example 1 and 2 feature implementation lessons learned

of the deputy deans for teaching and learning, the departments and finally the support departments who is responsible for the institutional LMS and the learning developers and teaching and learning advisors.

3.2   Example 2 - Industry

As industry places significant emphasis on industry-ready graduates, our second example and lessons learned are drawn from this domain. This example stems from one of the telecommunication companies in South Africa that operates in a competitive market and in an advanced technology environment. Product and services are key differentiators and technology enablement plays a significant and key role within this company in order to achieve strategic objectives and customer experience imperatives. The processes utilized for system development and implementation of technology solutions follow standard system development lifecycle steps, traditionally initiated by a business owner. Business owners utilize their – in many instances – limited knowledge of the enablement technologies to design, develop and innovate new products and services. During a business owner/technology optimization and collaboration drive, one of the enterprise architects highlighted additional technology features of purchased software that were not utilized at all, either because business owners were not aware of it or that the business owners did not realize what value a particular system feature would add. This realization triggered an assessment process where technology capability was mapped to technology usage with the aim to identify a gap i.e. what system features are available, but not utilized.

From the gap analysis concluded, it was clear that the capital investment into multiple platforms and systems at an enterprise level, was not utilized fully as all available features were not exploited and in some instances, sub-optimal product design was considered as minor tweaks using the system features might have resulted in a much better, innovative outcome. A management decision was then taken to, under the leadership of the Head of Information Technology (IT), kick off a programme in order to address the implementation and roll out of the already present technology features. The reason this initiative was IT lead was that the knowledge of the technology features, were held in IT. The programme was defined according to the organisation's project methodology with particular pillars such as stakeholder identification and communication, scope definition, risk and issue management, and behavioural change management. Specific scope steps were defined guided by the innovation-decision process consisting of knowledge, persuasion, decision, implementation and confirmation.

The programme team initiated an enterprise wide multiple-step process in order to achieve the objective of enabling under-utilized or not used system features. Firstly, multiple sessions were scheduled for IT to share knowledge with business stakeholders and owner about the multiple system features available. Secondly, workshops were then scheduled in order to consider product design using the prior knowledge of the entire feature set that is available. As most of these workshops were led by IT, business owners started to share their discomfort, and in some instances, business stakeholders stopped to attend the workshops. A robust debate followed about whether the company is product-led, customer-led or technology-led. The final outcome based on lack of consensus, was to place the programme on hold – irrespective of pockets of business support for the initiative.

The programme team assessed the project and it was agreed that the approach and process followed to achieve the programme outcomes, were revised. Instead of fol-lowing a "big bang" approach, the steps were updated to continue with the programme, but with the stakeholders willing to follow the process as defined and by executing pilot projects. This revised approach resulted in a positive outcome and in the end created a critical mass that "naturally" placed pressure on the rest of the enterprise to follow suit.

Lessons Learned
The innovation-decision process followed enabled the definition of an agile and innovative process through identifying the components that should be addressed first. The following highlights some of the lessons learned during the innovation-decision process and is summarized in Fig. 1:

Diffusion is a social process that involves interpersonal communication relation-ships. In this instance it was found that the interpersonal channels were powerful to change strong attitudes held by individuals, which became pertinent at the decision stage (1). By looping back and by changing this element, the second decision stage was navigated successfully.

The initial focus was on sharing how-to knowledge, while the success of deciding to adopt was based on focusing on awareness-knowledge. The focus on awareness-knowledge ensured that individuals in departments learned more about the features and, eventually, adopted it.

The degree of uncertainty about the feature's functioning and "peer" pressure from colleagues, etc. must not be underestimated as it affects opinions and beliefs. The focus on pilots addressed this concern as it enabled the feature experience so decisions, and in particular adoption decisions, could be taken knowingly. In addition, by linking the feature (innovation) outcome to the department's key performance indicators and ensuring that the link was understood, took uncertainty out of the discussion and ensured a better holistic understanding.

Do not assume that rejection is only present in the *decision* step. Rejection is possible in every stage of the innovation-decision process. By pro-actively monitoring this may be addressed at core in order to enable progression to the next step. The innovation diffusion steps could not merely be applied in a linear fashion as the initial decision pointed to "no adoption" and the project would end if the steps were not considered again and updates made by looping back.

4 Conclusion

The strain between industry requirements of graduates and HE's delivery of work-ready graduates, are acknowledged. In order to enable HE to deliver on its mandate, technology enablement such as LMS features are utilized. However, not all LMS features are implemented or used, often because there is no awareness of the presences of these features. Therefore, the purpose of this paper was to consider two real-world examples where the diffusion of innovation theory was applied in order to establish lessons learned in feature implementation. This paper presented two examples from two very different enterprise domains: to guide the implementation of additional features in an LMS in a HE institution and the technology feature implementation process prevalent in a telecommunication company in South Africa. The lessons learned during the two initiatives are complementary, but in both cases highlighted that the social system and change agents (opinion leaders) as depicted in diffusion of innovation theory, play a key role for successful implementation of technology features. In addition, both examples used a workshop approach, show-and tell and a pilot to inform and train potential users on the technology features.

Underutilization of technology features is not unique to higher education and in this instance higher education can learn from the approach and steps followed by industry as indicated in Fig. 1. Valuable contribution from industry which can seamlessly be integrated into higher education include the consultation with major stakeholders and owners of the technology, as well as conducting workshops to determine entire feature sets e.g. the institutions LMS.

Lastly, one of the key realizations of the paper pointed to the fact that value was extant in not following the diffusion of innovation steps in a linear fashion, but that holistic consideration in each step as well as looping back where necessary, added value towards successful adoption of features.

It was established that there were synergies between the lessons learned for HE and industry and that HE could draw on the findings from industry for the successful implementation of technology features, in this instance specifically pertaining to LMS features.

References

1. Boud, D., Rooney, D.: What can higher education learn from the workplace? In: Dailey-Hebert, A., Dennis, K.S. (eds.) Transformative Perspectives and Processes in Higher Education. ABET, vol. 6, pp. 195–209. Springer, Cham (2015). https://doi.org/10.1007/978-3-319-09247-8_11
2. Kennan, M.A., Willard, P., et al.: What do they want?: a study of changing employer expectations of information professionals. Aust. Acad. Res. Libr. **37**, 17–37 (2016)
3. McMurray, S., Dutton, M., McQuaid, R., Richard, A.: Employer demands from business graduates. Educ. Train. **15**, 1–32 (2016)
4. Jackson, D.: Modelling graduate skill transfer from university to the workplace. J. Educ. Work **29**, 199–231 (2016)
5. Muller, E., Botha, A.: Moving towards hybrid teaching in alignment with accreditation requirements: curriculum review of professional orientation in the ENGAGE programme. In: CSET ODL Conference (2017)
6. Bauer, M., Brooks, K.S., Sandrock, C.: Industry expectations and academic practice in control engineering education: a South African survey. In: 19th World Congress the International Federation of Automatic Control, Cape Town (2014)
7. Shuman, L.J., Besterfield-Sacre, M., McGourty, J.: The ABET 'professional skills' - can they be taught? Can they be assessed? J. Eng. Educ. **94**, 41–55 (2015)
8. Dahlstrom, E., Brooks, D.C., Bichsel, J.: the current ecosystem of learning management systems in higher education: student, faculty, and IT perspectives. Research report. ECAR, Louisville, September 2014
9. Lonn, S., Teasley, S.: Saving time or innovating practice: investigating perceptions and uses of Learning Management Systems. Comput. Educ. **53**, 686–694 (2009)
10. Schoonenboom, J.: Using an adapted, task-level technology acceptance model to explain why instructors in higher education intend to use some learning management system tools more that others. Comput. Educ. **71**, 247–256 (2014)
11. Werth, E.P., Werth, L.: Effective training for millennial students. Adult Learn. **22**, 12–19 (2011)
12. Howe, N., Strauss, W.: Millennials Rising: The Next Greatest Generation. Vintage Books, New York (1993)
13. Monaco, M., Martin, M.: The millennial student: a new generation of learners. Athl. Train. Educ. J. **2**, 42–46 (2007)
14. Rogers, E.M.: Diffusion of Innovations. The Free Press, New York (2003)
15. Botha, A., De Villiers, C.: From accreditation compliance to improving reporting on learning outcomes: the use of an LMS. In: International Conference for Research and Innovation (ICERI) (2017)
16. University of Sydney Business School. http://sydney.edu.au/business/about/accreditations/AoL

Emerging Technologies Support for Game-Based and Joyful Learning

Is a Picture Truly Worth a Thousand Words? Infographics for Undergraduate Teaching

Riana Steyn[(⊠)] ⓘ, Adriana Botha, and Nita Mennega

Department of Informatics, University of Pretoria, Pretoria, South Africa
Riana.steyn@up.ac.za

Abstract. Infographics, have emerged as an appealing academic tool. Supplementing traditional learning material such as textbooks, or PowerPoint slides, infographics allow for summarised versions of the same material.

Millennials want access to relevant information literally at the click of a button. As educators, we have to find a way of engaging these students with new teaching practices and new learning styles. The researchers commenced on a quest to see how they could engage these students, not only by teaching them the relevant knowledge, but also by allowing these students to use a simple infographic, which covers an entire study theme, and testing the students' perception of the use of infographics as a substitute for or even to replace "traditional" PowerPoint slides. The infographic was guided based on the 5 principles of the Gestalt theory.

The study was conducted on 210 student participants, with limited prior experience of infographics.

The infographic was perceived as a great tool and of good quality, which they would prefer to use as a study method over PowerPoint slides.

As educators, we need to find ways in which to incorporate infographics as a learning approach, to enhance the learning experience of students.

It is recommended that educators explore visual tools to enhance the learning experience and to retain the knowledge to which our students have been exposed. It is further recommended that infographics should be evaluated based on the five principles of Gestalt to not only improve designs, but also student experience.

Keywords: Infographic · Visual communication tool · Learning tool
Hybrid learning · Traditional learning approaches

1 Introduction

Teaching has long surpassed the handing out of a textbook, which includes all the content required for the term, semester or even year, or giving students a set of PowerPoint slides that they are expected to use, and add additional notes or summaries. Students are engaged with technology everywhere one looks. As educators, we need to find the means to embrace these technologies to engage more effectively with the students. As Puttnam [1] rightfully states: "If we want to win back the trust of young people, we need to engage far more effectively with their world – learn to view technology, and the way in which they relate to it – through their eyes." The reality of

© Springer Nature Switzerland AG 2018
T. Hao et al. (Eds.): SETE 2018, LNCS 11284, pp. 69–78, 2018.
https://doi.org/10.1007/978-3-030-03580-8_8

the students with whom we work is "always on/never off", as coined by Ashraf [2] and Pullan [3]. Turpie [4] said that "new technology and digital media engage young people from the day they enter the world". The students referred to here are millennials, who are "the first generation growing up with the internet" or even further Generation Z [5], which are students born after 1995. Kalantzis [6] says that, with this ever-changing world, perhaps we – as educators – should lead the change. Bradshaw and Porter [7] note that most people are visual learners. Therefore, using visual aids as a teaching mechanism is inevitable.

Many universities are forced to engage in a blended learning environment where technology-mediated learning and face-to-face sessions have to merge [8]. Kirkwood and Prince [9] also noted that technology is no longer a field only for enthusiasts or novel users. All lecturers should engage with technology [10, 11]. This new context of technology needs to be understood [10], and as educators, we should find the means to embed our understanding of technology within the existing classroom. Davidson, Major and Michaelsen [12] talk of the notion of getting students to become "*active participants in the learning process*", and not just having them sit in a classroom, listening to a lecturer and then repeating the theory back to the lecturer.

Vanichvasin [13] confirms three aspects of infographics in the learning process: appeal (as a communication tool to engage students), comprehension (to connect subject matter and conceptualise it) and retention (to make knowledge more memorable).

This paper explores this notion by allowing students to give their viewpoint on the use of an infographic as an additional learning tool to assist them by supporting the traditional PowerPoint slides that educators love to use.

2 Literature Review

Yildirim [14] notes that many teaching approaches have adopted a hybrid approach. Bonk and Graham [15] define blended learning as the combination of "face-to-face instructions with computer-mediated instruction". Bender [16] talks about hybrid learning, where a course that has face-to-face classes on campus has an additional web component that is linked to the course. Woods, Baker and Hopper [17] confirm this when they talk about the web-based augmentation of the traditional classroom setting. Bender [16], Rosenberg [18] and Wilson [19] talk of the best of both worlds: this phenomenon of combining physical classroom interactions with some sort of web component.

Yildirim [14] states that one of the most crucial forms of presenting information is through the use of visual aids. Visuals evoke emotions and create experiences [7], which is one of the reasons for the effective use of visual aids in a classroom environment. However, Yildirim [14] also says that no matter what visual aid, tool or technology one uses, each aid has its own properties of information, intended use and learner preferences.

Yildirim [14] continues to note that graphics allow for the visual presentation of information and that, in today's teaching environment, infographics are seen as a new type of material that provides information to fit within a certain scope or flow. "Too much information can be presented with very little explanation," [14]. He further defines an infographic as "presenting information within a certain flow with the help of various visuals and texts in a visual form," [14] which is similarly defined by Sudakov et al. [20], who use words such as "images combined with knowledge". It is important to note that the information should be presented in a logical sequence, this is where the Gestalt theory plays a crucial role. Gestalt says that one should not only focus on the individual parts, but that the whole effect of the picture should also create a "whole effect" [21] or "gestalt" and that one experience perceptual wholes, and not necessarily isolated parts. Wertheimer and Riezler [22] defines gestalt as "what happens to a part of the whole is, in clear-cut cases, determined by the laws of the inner structure of its whole", thus the individual pieces are driven or determined by the structure of the entire whole, also mentioned as the context.

Infographics stimulate a human's visual system in order to recognise certain patterns and trends [20], and effective infographics present the data in pleasing and simplistic ways. Williams [23] defines infographics as "the statistics, patterns and trends in information; the characteristics of the information landscape" However the "trick" is to see how the whole picture says something relevant and once one starts looking at the individual parts, these also convey their own message [21]. Wang [24] confirms the use of Gestalt as "there are many ways Gestalt principles can help us organize and present visual information better in an infographic, especially if you are dealing with complex information" and this paper uses complex information in an academic setting.

Infographics are increasing in popularity in the education environment [7, 14, 20, 25]. Yildirim [14] notes that the strongest aspects of infographics are their flexible structure, the fact that they allow information to be visual, and that they can be prepared in alternative forms, which means that each infographic can look different.

For the purpose of this research, an infographic was designed based on the first study unit of a first-year undergraduate course in business analysis and design. The infographic is a one-page view (see Annexure A), which is broken down into the four study units, from a broader viewpoint, but once you start reading the context, you will note each section relates to a theme within the broader study unit, thus gestalt.

2.1 Quality of Infographics

Gestalt theory has five principles which should be followed during design. These principles [24, 26] will now briefly be discussed.

- Similarity: Relationships are created by sharing visual characteristics. Colour was used extensively in the infographic to create relationships amongst objects, as well as borders around the various sub-themes within the study unit. See Annexure A, Section A for an example.
- Continuation: an object will allow the eye to follow in a specific direction once the eye is fixed on the object, until another object interrupts the flow. An example of how it is applied can be seen in Annexure A, Section B. The bold green lines show that three topics exist, but the bold green arrow indicates the flow and thus ensures continuation is achieved.

- Closure: this principle is applied which allows the eye to close the loop, or the gap, it is also mostly recommended in art work, mosaics or sculptures. This infographic did not include this principle due to the nature of the work. As this infographic already summarises almost 69 academic slides and content in total, we did not want to create confusion amongst the students to allow them to try and close the loop or fill the gaps.
- Proximity: Placing objects together makes them seem like a group, this can be applied in various ways. This was applied by breaking down the infographic into the various study themes within the entire study unit and placing borders around these themes.
- Figure/ground: This is the relationship between objects and its surroundings. The layout was based around a clock, where one moves clockwise around the various study units.

In addition to Gestalt's theory which purely focuses on design, various other authors have also listed certain points or aspects which they consider to be relevant for creating infographics specifically. The infographic used for this study was designed to ensure a positive learning experience for the students. To determine if the infographic designed for this paper was considered good, the researchers addressed the characteristics of a good infographic according to various authors as follows (Table 1):

Table 1 Infographic characteristics

Characteristics	Applied for this study
Purpose of the infographic [14]	The infographic was designed to determine if one can replace the traditional PowerPoint slides with one view. Thus, 90 slides were consolidated into one view
Quality of the visuals and design [7, 14, 21, 22, 24, 25] Level of visualising the information [14, 25] Information and visualisation of the information should be top quality (no errors, no unnecessary information should be displayed) [14]. Every element should do something [25].	The students were asked to evaluate the infographic, in two ways. First, they had to answer a question in an Answer Garden: "Type one word that you think describes the infographic." Secondly, they had to complete a questionnaire based on the quality by answering the following question: "Rate the quality of the infographic based on the following": Content/Layout/Visuals/Consistency between information and visuals/No errors/No unnecessary information/Colour appropriate/Preferred layout

2.2 Further Background to the Study

This infographic was designed by the researchers with the help of an instructional designer, as Yildirim [14] highlighted that instructional design is a crucial element to creating infographics.

The content of the specific study unit, Systems Theory, was analysed to determine the most important concept of the study unit. Thus, the main information required on the infographic was determined and extracted from the PowerPoint slides as a consolidation of the main concepts, normally presented in 90 slides, into one view. This information was handed to the graphic designer with a brief plan or layout of what the researchers had in mind. The infographic evolved through various iterations. The final version can be viewed in Annexure A.

3 Method

As part of a first-year course called Systems Analysis and Design, which was presented at an urban university, the students had to grasp key concepts of the Systems Theory study unit. This research was conducted on completion of the first study unit, four weeks into the students' first semester of studies. Although it was assumed that the students had little experience of infographics as a learning tool, this was one of the questions asked during the data gathering. The classes were split up into three groups, with their first contact session of the week either a Monday or a Tuesday. This is relevant since the infographic was distributed in colour, printed in an A4 format, to all the students who attended the classes during their first contact session of the week, thus either on a Monday or a Tuesday.

The teaching of this study unit was traditionally through additional reading material in a portable document format (PDF) and PowerPoint slides that were created and made available to students through the learning management system (LMS) Blackboard. In total, there were 91 slides for the entire Study Unit 1, of which 22 were seen as being "empty" thus no new content. They were the introduction slides, the exercise slides or a few recap slides. Thus, 69 slides contained the content for Study Unit 1.

At the end of each study unit, the students have to write a quiz based on all the work covered in the slides. The quiz is online and they write it in their own time, this was written on the Friday before the infographic was distributed in class. They could use their learning material if they wanted to. During the following class (the Monday or Tuesday class), the students all received a hard copy of the infographic in colour, which was the first time they had seen the infographic. They also had to complete an Answer Garden stating what they love or hate about the infographic in one word. Of the 352 students enrolled for this subject, 209 completed the questionnaire, implying a 59.4% response rate. The Answer Garden received 290 responses. The assumption the researchers made due to the difference in responses was that a student could have provided more than one word in the Answer Garden. They were given 10 min to read it, and were then given a quiz consisting of 10 questions, randomly selected from the same question bank as their first quiz on the Friday. They then had to complete the quiz using the infographic to answer the questions. After the quiz, they were asked to navigate to the Answer Garden and type one word they thought best described the infographic. The students then had to complete an online questionnaire on Google Forms, consisting of 16 questions, on their experience and perception of the infographic, as well as the quality of the infographic. The feedback from the questionnaire was then analysed.

4 Findings

An Answer Garden is a free tool available on https://answergarden.ch/ [27] that allows one to generate responses based on a specific question. As the respondents give their answers, a word cloud instantly grows, with repeating words growing bigger. The responses from the students can be seen in Fig. 1.

Fig. 1. Answer Garden word cloud

It is evident from the word cloud that the word "helpful" was the most repetitive word, by accumulating 51 responses. This was followed by: Informative – 21 responses; Useful – 19 responses; Convenient – 18 responses.

Thus, overall, there was a positive response from the students' side towards the infographic. The students were asked to be brutally honest and, if they hated it, they could also state that. There were a few negative responses, such as "useless" (1 response), "boring" (1 response) and "busy" (2 responses). This was expected as people do not agree on everything. However, the low negative response showed that, overall, the majority of the students could see the value of infographics.

The students then had to complete the questionnaire on Google Forms. This was completed during class time. Of the 209 respondents, the majority were male students (69.4%), followed by female students (58.7%) and those who preferred not to say (1.9%). Looking at their ages, 97.1% of the students belonged to Generation Z, thus were born after 1995.

Asking them if they had ever used or seen an infographic as a study tool before, 56.5% said "No". The rest said "Yes".

Printed textbooks, infographics and PowerPoint slides were the most preferred study methods. Interestingly, videos were only selected by 42% of the respondents, which is in contrast with the findings of Steyn et al. [11] and Yildirim [14]. By Selecting other one respondent said: "By making personal notes from information collected during class and out of a textbook".

The next section of questionnaire related to the actual focus of this paper, which was the link back to a good-quality infographic. These questions were asked in the form of a Likert scale, with 1 being poor and 5 being excellent.

The main question asked was: "Rate the quality of the infographic based on the following": (1.) Content; (2.) Layout; (3.) Visuals; (4.) Consistency between information and visuals; (5.) No errors; (6.) No unnecessary information; (7.) Colour appropriate; (8.) Preferred layout. It is evident from Fig. 2 that most of the students thought the infographic was excellent to above average for all the categories. Thus, did the infographic meet the characteristics as set out by the literature? The answer is: "Yes, most definitely".

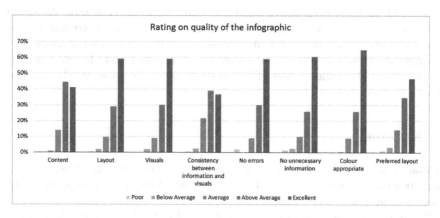

Fig. 2. Quality rating

Their opinion on whether they thought the infographic was an effective tool from which to study for Study Unit 1. Some 94% of the students said "Yes".

Students were asked their perception or opinion on the successful use of Infographic in the following contexts: (1.) In Presenting lectures; (2.) In explaining study material; (3.) Used in learning activities; (4.) Showing examples; (5.) In summarizing content. Figure 3 clearly show various areas where student felt infographics could successfully be applied during their studies.

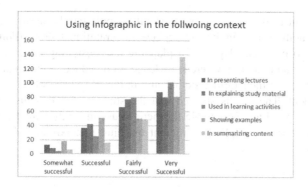

Fig. 3. Using infographic in the following context

Additional comments about the infographic were: "Brilliant thank you!"; "It is a really good tool and I'm glad you did it for us."; "It is a good summarisation of the work but it is a bit too clustered."; "Loved it."; "Really enjoyed it. Glad it was made."; "Supercalifragilisticexpialidocious."; "This infographic is extremely helpful. I hope this form of study is implemented in all modules."; "Why have we not done this before? This is a great way of learning…"

Some of the more constructive comments were: "Examples and short definitions, would not recommend for studying but as a nice summary of the content I would recommend every student to have an infographic."; "The infographic is an excellent assisting tool. However, it does not contain all the required detail for someone who knows nothing about the content of the work. Brilliant for someone who has been through the work before."

5 Discussion

As educators, we have to engage students in "their" world, and one of the ways this paper focused on was designing an infographic to assist the students in grasping large amounts of information at a glance.

The infographic that was produced clearly ticked all the boxes when it came to the design and characteristics of a good infographic as a teaching tool as identified [7, 14, 22]. It also followed the Gestalt theory's principles for design [22, 24] to ensure that it is not just pictures and words placed onto a page to try something, but with careful planning and design, the end result can ensure that knowledge is not only transferred, but also laid down in the foundation of the students.

The next part of this research will focus on the true impact of the infographic on the knowledge retention of students.

6 Conclusion

This paper set out to determine whether an infographic can be used to enhance students' learning abilities and, in the end, replace the "traditional" PowerPoint slides that educators love to hand out. By careful planning and designing these types of interventions, one can get to a place where knowledge is embedded in these student's minds which they can use in their further studies and in the end apply when they enter their work environment. The results showed that the students felt that the quality of the infographics was good and acceptable for them to use in Study Unit 1 and they were excited that lecturers are exploring different teaching methods to truly engage with them.

Annexure A

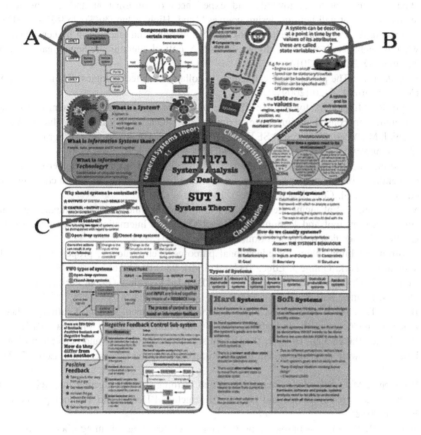

References

1. Puttnam, L.: Creative learning through technology. In: Wright, S., Kieffer, J., Holden, J., Newbigin, J. (Eds.) CreativityMoneyLove: Learning for the 21st Century (2012)
2. Ashraf, B.: Teaching the Google-eyed YouTube generation. Educ. Train. 51(5/6), 343–352 (2009)
3. Pullan, M.C.: Student support services for millennial undergraduates. J. Educ. Technol. Syst. 38(2), 235–253 (2009)
4. Turpie, J.: Creative engineers. In: Wright, S., Kieffer, J., Holden, J., Newbigin, J. (Eds.) CreativityMoneyLove: Learning for the 21st Century (2012)
5. Wikipedia: Generation Z (2017). https://en.m.wikipedia.org/wiki/generation_Z. Accessed 9 Feb 2017
6. Kalantzis, M.: Changing subjectivities, new learning. Pedag.: Int. J. 1(1), 7–12 (2006)

7. Bradshaw, M.J., Porter, S.: Infographics: a new tool for the nursing classroom. Nurse Educ.: Technol. Corner **42**(2), 57–59 (2017)

8. Kirkwood, A., Price, L.: Learners and learning in the twenty-first century: what do we know about students' attitudes towards and experiences of information and communication technologies that will help us design courses? Stud. High. Educ. **30**(3), 257–274 (2005)

9. Kirkwood, A., Prince, L.: Technology-enhanced learning and teaching in higher education: what is 'enhanced' and how do we know? A critical literature review. Learn., Media Technol. **39**(2), 6–36 (2014)

10. Laurillard, D.: The pedagogical challenges to collaborative technologies. Comput.-Support. Collab. Learn. **4**, 5–20 (2009)

11. Steyn, R., Millard, S., Jordaan, J.: The use of a learning management system to facilitate student-driven content design: an experiment. In: Huang, T.-C., Lau, R., Huang, Y.-M., Spaniol, M., Yuen, C.-H. (eds.) SETE 2017. LNCS, vol. 10676, pp. 75–94. Springer, Cham (2017). https://doi.org/10.1007/978-3-319-71084-6_10

12. Davidson, N., Major, C.H., Michaelsen, L.K.: Small-group learning in higher education - cooperative, collaborative, problem-based and team-based learning: an introduction by guest editors. J. Excell. Coll. Teach. **25**(3&4), 1–6 (2014)

13. Vanichvasin, P.: Enhancing the quality of learning through the use of infographics as visual communication tool and learning tool. In: ICQA 2013 International Conference on QA Culture: Cooperation or Competition, Bangkok (2013)

14. Yildirim, S.: Infographics for educational purposes: their structure, properties and reader approaches. Turk. Online J. Educ. Technol. **15**(3), 98–110 (2016)

15. Bonk, C.J., Graham, C.R.: The Handbook of Blended Learning: Global Perspectives, Local Designs. Pfeiffer, San Francisco (2006)

16. Bender, T.: Discussion-Based Online Teaching to Enhance Student Learning: Theory, Practice, and Assessment, 2nd edn, p. 256. Stylus Publishing, LLC, Virginia (2012)

17. Woods, R., Baker, J.D., Hopper, D.: Hybrid structures: faculty use and perception of web-based courseware as a supplement to face-to-face instruction. Internet High. Educ. **7**, 281–297 (2004)

18. Rosenberg, M.J.: Knowledge management and learning: perfect together. In: Reiser, R.A., Dempsey, J.V. (eds.) Trends and Issues in Instructional Design and Technology. Pearson, Boston (2012)

19. Wilson, R.W.: In-class-online hybrid methods of teaching planning theory: assessing impacts on discussion and learning. J. Plan. Educ. Res. **28**, 237–246 (2008)

20. Sudakov, I., Bellsky, T., Usenyuk, S., Polyakova, V.V.: Infographics and mathematics: a mechanism for effective learning in the classroom. Probl., Resour., Issues Math. Undergrad. Stud. **26**(2), 158–167 (2016)

21. Behrens, R.R.: Art, design and gestalt theory. Leonardo **31**(4), 299–303 (1998)

22. Wertheimer, M., Riezler, K.: Gestalt theory. Soc. Res. **11**(1), 78–99 (1944)

23. Williams, F.M.: Diversity, thinking styles, and infographics. In: 12th International Conference of Women Engineers and Scientists (2002)

24. Wang, L.: Gestalt principles for information design. In: HOW Magazine (2017)

25. Saunders, D.H., Horrel, A., Murray, A.: Infographics for students assessment: more than meets the eye. BJSM (2017)

26. Staff: Gestalt theory in typography & design principles. In: HOW Magazine (2015)

27. AnswerGarden: Answer Garden (2018). https://answergarden.ch/. Accessed 20 Feb 2018

Collaborative Style of Teaching and Learning with Information and Communication Technology (ICT) from University Teachers and Student's Perspectives

Hana Mohelska[(⊠)] and Marcela Sokolova

Faculty of Informatics and Management, The University of Hradec Kralove,
Hradec Kralove, Czech Republic
hana.mohelska@uhk.cz

Abstract. The collaborative form of education places on students the following requirements in particular: distribution of social roles, planning of their own activities, division of partial tasks, learning to consult and help, controlling each other, solving partial conflicts, combining partial results into a whole, evaluating the contribution of individual members. Many models of collaborative learning such as The Structural Approach to Cooperative Learning (Spencer Kagan), have been tested at universities. Collaborative learning (CL) is directly linked to information and communication technologies (ICT) that seem to be the best environment for this form of learning. This review article seeks to define the structures of the CL model in the higher education environment, the basic elements of it and the strengths and weaknesses and to give examples of good practice.

Keywords: Collaborative learning · Definition · Concept · Elements

1 Introduction

The definition of Collaborative learning (CL) is as a set of teaching and learning strategies promoting student collaboration in small groups (two to five students) so they would optimise their own as well as each other's learning during collaborative learning [3]. There are three broad categories into which collaborative working can fall:

Collaborative learning could be also defined as an individual progress made by students in tandem with others working to achieve a common goal. Students are held responsible to one another and will manage it themselves with appropriate direction. Students learn to understand and anticipate difference in a better way and to recognise this in themselves as well as others, and they use this understanding to their advantage.

Co-operative learning is a co-operation that involves inherent interdependence – For example in a theatre, the cast and crew of a production. Roles and responsibilities are defined in a clear way; however they are open for negotiation. This particular method of collaboration brings a strong sense of accountability with it.

Competition is an effective means of developing students' collaborative skills if used properly. It can especially be effective while working with teams (particularly

© Springer Nature Switzerland AG 2018
T. Hao et al. (Eds.): SETE 2018, LNCS 11284, pp. 79–86, 2018.
https://doi.org/10.1007/978-3-030-03580-8_9

when students are incentivised with rewards), and could be helpful to develop entrepreneurship and leadership skills. It is important to mention that students' learning to collaborate in this way need to be monitored closely, in order to ensure they are developing the correct skills in the correct way.

CL is being used in many different fields and disciplines and in many different variations, the definition remains unagreed on [2]. Even when there's no clear definition of CL, there are some features we can use to identify it.

Collaboration is a trend that became very popular in 21st century. The demand on society to work together on important issues as increased [1]. The importance has been shifted from individualism and independence to group efforts and community [6].

To solve a task or create a product, the CL uses an educational approach to teaching and learning, involving groups of people working together.

With the CL method the learners are required to listen to ideas of others, while they have to defend their own, which can be emotionally and socially challenging. While doing so, the group forms its own unique opinions which isn't based just on experts or textbooks.

In the CL environment the learners have the possibility of discussing with others, presenting and defending their own ideas, questioning the ideas of others and questing the opinions of others while being actively engaged [3, 5].

In the CL we can see a great shift from the classical teacher-centred classes in college environment. In the classes, where the collaborative learning is implied, the classical process of giving the lecture, listening to it and taking notes doesn't vanish entirely, but it works alongside the processes that emerge from the work of groups formed by students.

Teachers using the CL method do think about themselves more as coaches or designers of intellectual experiences for students, rather than being just transmitters of the information [12].

Collaborative learning can be used in traditional classrooms as well, combining the intellectual efforts by students or joint efforts of teachers and students. The students are mainly working in groups of two or more, trying to understand the tasks together, solving problems, finding solutions to different issues or co-creating a product. There is a big diversity in the CL activities, but the most important is the fact, that all students are involved in researching or using the course material, rather than just focusing on their presentations or expositions [13]. CL tries to shift the responsibility of information pursuit on students. CL forces the students to engage in dialogue between themselves, taking charge of their own learning process. The students have a common goal set and are forced to exchange their ideas and thoughts actively while completing the group activities. There is a great resemblance between collaborative activities and social activities. In addition, the process of CL helps the students to become more self-sufficient because it brings various experience to all the group members. That's why the CL leads students to obtaining and perfecting their social skills and helps them to develop a positive attitude towards learning.

1.1 Methods

The concept of CL was defined by the method of literature research of domestic and foreign academic papers from the Web of Knowledge and Scopus databases. The information necessary to formulate the requirements on students and teachers were obtained by methods of analysis and synthesis. The structure of the CL model in higher education environment and its fundamental elements are schematically visualized. The strong and weak sides, the ICT support included, are identified by the literature research of academic papers as well.

2 Requirements on Students and Teachers

2.1 Definition of the Requirements on Students

CL as a form of education requires:

- Dividing of the social roles – allocation of hierarchy inside the group in which the students of all performance levels are represented – advanced, average and below average, regardless of race, gender, etc. The ideal amount of people inside group are 3–5.
- Planning their activities – analysis of the problem and brief insight into possibilities of its evaluation and separation to smaller segments.
- Dividing the tasks – assigning the activities, the segments of task separated in previous step to individual members of the group.
- Learn to advise and help each other and to coordinate efforts – not all students can complete the assigned task. The one-sided view might be misleading, individually completed parts blend into one another and the group can't have contradictory opinions on the subject.
- Controlling one another – observing the activity of others which is related with obtaining the responsibility not only for themselves but for the whole group as well.
- Solving the arguments – being able to express themselves, motivate the others to work, agreeing on collective approach, being able to step down from their opinions.
- Combining partial results into a whole.
- Rating the contribution of individual members of the group – and justly rating those who didn't make appropriate effort, but only inside the group.

2.2 Definition of the Requirements on Teachers

CL is defined by very important factor – the individual isn't rated; the whole group is. The objective of the rating is the task itself, not one's share in it. Rating of one's share is inner concern of the group, because its members know the best how each of them worked on given task. The group work cannot lead to group members competing, their individualism won't lead to anything, because the group is rated as whole [7].

CL accents the cognitive aspects and the individual social dimension is combined in tasks and goals of the group work as suggested by following scheme:

This approach to education recorded promising advance in social relations between the students during experiments; the others were accepted better, the racism and segregation appeared in less circumstances, better self-awareness appeared and the ability to cooperate with others grew. Positive results have emerged in greater numbers with elementary types of teaching and with younger students. With more difficult tasks and higher education students the results seemed to be unconvincing and CL less effective [6].

Many different approaches of cooperative and collaborative learning were tried in universities. Kagan and Kagan [4] provide that the structural approach to cooperative learning is based on the creation, analysis, and systematic application of content-free ways to organize classroom interactions. Structures (outlined in a Fig. 1) have differing uses in the academic, cognitive, and social domains, such as team building, communication building, mastery, and concept development [4].

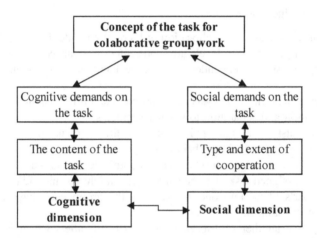

Fig. 1. Combination of cognitive aspects and the individual social dimension in tasks of the group work [3], own elaboration

Johnson and Johnson [3] state that for collaboration to be efficient, it must involve considerable conflicts between the members of the group. If the conflicts aren't solved constructively, the efforts in cooperative learning will fail. Students must become involved in academic controversy and be able to solve their conflicts constructively (integrative negotiations and peer mediation) [3]. When the conflicts are resolved a constructive manner, the cooperative hard work lead to learning of the civic values that are essential to the establishment of a successful learning community, while competitive and individualistic efforts could teach students values that are opposite to those of healthy community [6].

ICT Support. Computer-Supported Collaborative Learning (CSCL) is a fast-growing branch of pedagogical science which concerns itself with a question how people can learn with the use of computers. The education process happens mainly through the interactions between students. Students learn how to formulate their questions, follow the lines of the teaching process together, teach themselves and watch how others learn. This branch studies how ICT facilitates the sharing and distribution of the knowledge and reports between members of the collaborating community which can be physically separated.

The CSCL process can however be perceived as process of convergence during which people convince one another about their opinions which leads to achieving of collective representations [12]. CSCL doesn't necessarily have to be represented only by online communication platform. The group of students can also use a computer to search information online and gather, discuss and present those facts they found together. CSCL then doesn't have to be in the distant form (the above-mentioned physical separation) but can happen face-to-face as well [10, 13].

The CL learning model creates different structures than those usual in current school systems and the computer provided environment is the ideal for CL. The computers arrange communication and cooperation of students during the CL [6].

2.3   Multi-user Virtual Environment, MUVE

The environment that was created by connecting the possibilities of today's internet and gaming world. At the beginning there was a RPG game Dungeons and Dragons which inspired the developers to create Multi-User Dragon (MUD), which were online games in which the players were in same space and were in contact with each other [11]. In MUD the actions were described by text only. Later however the graphic interface was implemented, and one path of development has led to creation of Multi-User Virtual Environment (MUVE). In this environment allows its users to enter a virtual world, where they use their "avatars" to communicate with other users and allows them to realize the activities of collaborative learning [12]. The virtual environment can be used as constructive style education. Many universities have already realized this fact and use the virtual environment as a background for a scientific works, or in public relations (with their applicants) [9, 14]. There are many alternative terms used to describe MUVE: Collaborative Hypermedia Environment (CHE), Avatar Cyberspace, Desktop Virtual Reality, Avatar Virtual Environment, Virtual Worlds, Social Virtual Worlds, or Moving Worlds [8].

The expansion and further development of ICT have brought a third dimension and with it new opportunities:

- 3D Virtual Learning Environment, 3D VLE;
    - An educational environment created based on above-defined MUVE technology. It's different from the classic VLE, as suggested by its name, by being in third dimension as well as higher interactivity and its own space-time.
- 3D Collaborative Hypermedia Environment, CHE;
    - Synonym of above-defined 3D VLE.
- Massively Multi-Learner Online Learning Environment, MMOLE.

3 Results and Discuss

Many benefits of the CL were discovered during the research. Recommended way of sorting the CL's benefits is dividing them into categories as explained for example by [4, 6].

For the use of this article the above-mentioned way of sorting has been used.

It's composed of these benefit's categories:

1. Social benefits
   - CL helps to develop a social support system for learners;
   - CL leads to build diversity understanding among students and staff;
   - CL establishes a positive atmosphere for modelling and practicing cooperation, and;
   - CL develops learning communities.
2. Psychological benefits
   - Student-centred instruction increases students' self-esteem;
   - Cooperation reduces anxiety, and;
   - CL develops positive attitudes towards teachers.
3. Academic benefits
   - CL Promotes critical thinking skills;
   - Involves students actively in the learning process;
   - Classroom results are improved;
   - Models appropriate student problem solving techniques;
   - Large lectures can be personalized;
   - CL is especially helpful in motivating students in specific curriculum.
4. Alternate student and teacher assessment techniques
   - Collaborative teaching techniques utilize a variety of assessments.

4 Conclusion

The systems described in Sect. 2 have these characteristic strong features;

- space and time are shared by all users (the user, or his avatar, moves around the environment, which is a 3D landscape, freely);
- the user interface is graphic and intuitive (no special training is necessary);
- the environment itself can be changed and expended by users;
- the time goes by independently on user's presence (fully-fledged reality is created);
- the users, or their avatars, form groups (formal and informal);
- communication can be in a form of text (chat), voice chat or as a communication between avatars in the 3D landscape reminding of a conversation in the real world, greatly expanding the possibilities of a traditional LMS environments.

MUVE allows the realization of so called situational and constructive education in which the student (or his avatar) is in the centre of attention which in the theme of the lecture – for example he can be part of building of the pyramids in ancient Egypt or walk through circulatory system of a human. Presence in such environment and contact with the avatars of other students makes this experience unique and easily remembered.

Among the weak sides we can find higher demands on teachers, selection of suitable tasks, technical facilities of the universities. Also, the fact, that MUVE allows the realization of situational a constructive education when student (or his avatar) finds himself in the centre of attention, that is the subject of a lecture, can also be a weak side. Student can be brought into the game to the point, where he misses the main point of lecture.

The results of the paper appear to require special attention by educators in order to balance the cognitive and collaborative aspects of CL. Integration of the before mentioned aspects could be helpful in ensuring the social interaction, which is prominent to the efficacy of CL. In order to back up this argument, Law et al. [6] stated: 'to understand the nature of productive collaboration, we need to articulate how social goals and discourse practices interact with knowledge-building processes that lead to co-construction of understanding' [6].

Acknowledgement. The paper was written with the support of the specific project 6/2018 grant "Determinants of Cognitive Processes Impacting the Work Performance" granted by the University of Hradec Králové, Czech Republic and thanks to help of student Tomáš Valenta.

References

1. Austin, J.E.: Strategic collaboration between nonprofits and businesses. Nonprofit Volunt. Sect. Q. **29**, 69–97 (2000). https://doi.org/10.1177/0899764000291S004
2. Jenni, R.W., Mauriel, J.: Cooperation and collaboration: reality or rhetoric? Int. J. Leadersh. Educ. **7**, 181–195 (2004). https://doi.org/10.1080/1360312042000211446
3. Johnson, D.W., Johnson, R.T.: Learning together and alone: overview and meta analysis. Asia Pac. J. Educ. **22**, 95–105 (2002). https://doi.org/10.1080/0218879020220110
4. Kagan, S., Kagan, M.: The structural approach: six keys to cooperative learning. In: Sharan, S. (ed.) Handbook of Cooperative Learning Methods. Greenwood Press, Westport (1994)
5. Laal, M., Laal, M.: Collaborative learning: what is it? Procedia - Soc. Behav. Sci. **31**, 491–495 (2012). https://doi.org/10.1016/j.sbspro.2011.12.092
6. Law, Q.P.S., So, H.C.F., Chung, J.W.Y.: Effect of collaborative learning on enhancement of students' self-efficacy, social skills and knowledge towards mobile apps development. Am. J. Educ. Res. **5**(1), 25–29 (2017). https://doi.org/10.12691/education-5-1-4
7. Leonard, P.E., Leonard, L.J.: The collaborative prescription: remedy or reverie? Int. J. Leadersh. Educ. **4**, 383–399 (2001). https://doi.org/10.1080/13603120110078016
8. Mohelska, H., Sokolova, M.: The creation of the qualitative scenarios in the virtual three-dimensional environment second life. Procedia Comput. Sci. **3**, 312–315 (2011). https://doi.org/10.1016/j.procs.2010.12.053
9. Mohelska, H., Sokolova, M.: Effectiveness of using e-learning for business disciplines: the case of introductory management course. EM Ekon. Manag. **17**, 82–92 (2014). https://doi.org/10.15240/tul/001/2014-1-007

10. Pikhart, M.: Managerial communication and its changes in the global intercultural business world. In: SHS Web of Conferences (2017). https://doi.org/10.1051/shsconf/20173701013. ISSN 2261-2424
11. Říha, D.: Avatar Cyberspace - Matrix v embryonálním Stadiu? (2011). http://www1.cuni.cz/~rihad/med/AVATARCB.htm. Accessed 13 May 2018
12. Sawyer, R.K.: The Cambridge Handbook of the Learning Sciences. Cambridge University Press, Cambridge (2005)
13. Smith, B.L., MacGregor, J.T.: What is collaborative learning? In: Collaborative Learning: A Sourcebook for Higher Education, pp. 10–30. National Center on Postsecondary Teaching, Learning, and Assessment (NCTLA), University Park (1992)
14. Welch, M.: Collaboration: staying on the bandwagon. J. Teach. Educ. **49**, 26–37 (1998). https://doi.org/10.1177/0022487198049001004

Geocaching as Unconventional Method
for Foreign Language Teaching

Sarka Hubackova[✉]

Department of Applied Linguistics, Faculty of Informatics and Management,
University of Hradec Kralove, Hradec Kralove, Czech Republic
sarka.hubackova@uhk.cz

Abstract. Geocaching is being used as a medium for identification of new places and for dwelling in nature, which might influence even the proper selection of a target destination. Its feature is not only regional. The basic principle is to seek and look for and eventually find that secret hiding device called cache. There stands an individual or a group of people on one side, who made the box. They had hidden it at an interesting place and had registered it on the internet with accurate coordinates. We have tried to retell the state among Czech cachers. We wanted to know how they can cope with foreign language listing. As a very suitable it seem to appear students' presentations in foreign language on interesting finds both home and abroad. Students love to show those findings, which achievement was not so simple. Students may also create their own Geocaching dictionaries; seek for new expressions and their translations into mother tongue. Finally they can try to translate listings both to mother tongue and foreign language. Students understand that they need good knowledge of foreign language for their future job: for contacts with foreign travel agencies, tour operators, business partners, visitors, tourists etc.

Keywords: Geocaching · Education · Teaching methods · Foreign languages
Unconventional method

1 Introduction

Geocaching came into being in May 2000. Then the American president Bill Clinton had decided that the so called selective accessibility in the army GPS should be deactivated. (The selective accessibility is an artificial error of measurement conducted by an ordinary user. The error runs between 50–100 m). In that way the accuracy of GPS heightened to some meters. New opportunities for GPS owners had been opened worldwide. Geocaching owes its spread into other states to the fact that very significant part of that activity happened by means of the internet whose number of users had increased just about 2000. Even the internet had likely been the main medium; by means of it some knowledge of geocaching had spread. In most cases it had most likely happened by means of social nets and discussion for a through involvement and recommendation of personal experience to its users. Another fact contributing to the spread of geocaching is that you need – except the GPS apparatus – no specific and expensive equipment to its operating and performing [1, 2].

© Springer Nature Switzerland AG 2018
T. Hao et al. (Eds.): SETE 2018, LNCS 11284, pp. 87–94, 2018.
https://doi.org/10.1007/978-3-030-03580-8_10

That activity was growing in popularity and it only was the question of time when it would come even into the Czech Republic. The first cache Tex-Czech had been founded in June 2001, one year and one month from the depositing of a small box in Beaver Creek in the USA. The cache was initially only a plastic bag. Later it was substituted by a solid box. It can be found at a conservation area by Stramberk and it has got 3,689 finds now (by October 5th 2015). The mostly visited traditional cache in the Czech Republic is now in Prague and is called Prague bridges 1 – Charles Bridge, which has got 23,614 finds (by October 5th 2015). The second one is Terezka which used to be at the first position with 20,250 findings. Geocaching is being used as a medium for identification of new places and for dwelling in nature, which might influence even the proper selection of a target destination. Its feature is not only regional. Its participants use it abroad as well [5]. Thanks to the fact that it can be combined with other activities, it may be conducted practically anywhere. Its social significance is first of all in its feature of a collective activity. Its main part happens in real space; but the major part of participants' communication happens via internet.

When speaking about main motivating factor towards Geocaching, we often mention the possibility to learn new places, to spend free time in an interesting way, to meet new friends and to learn a foreign language or to get better in it. Most of geocachers visit thanks to the game such places, they would never learn otherwise. No matter if it was the main course of their trip, but also places they visit incidentally by adjusting the route to finding a cache.

The basic principle is to seek and look for and eventually find that secret hiding device called cache. There stands an individual or a group of people on one side, who made the box. They had hidden it at an interesting place and had registered it on the internet with accurate coordinates. On the other side, there stands an individual or a group of people, who had found that cache on internet or by means of a smartphone or of GPS and now they embark to look for it. Such people are called geocachers. Looking for a cache they should be quite common and ordinary and try not to catch attention of disinterested persons - muggles.

Caches are deposited worldwide, usually at such places that are exceptional in a way: nearby a historic building, in a landscape with a beautiful view. We might find them also in tree tops or under a bridge. In such cases you must have special equipment. As for the box under discussion, there is some information on the official web concerning the size, difficulty, terrain of finding place. Further, there is a description of the cache proper, but also of the environment of the finding place. A clue plays an important part of the information. The box itself is hidden in such a way that it possibly cannot be seen or stolen. Sometimes it is hidden in tree caves, under stones, under trees cut etc. It is more difficult to fancy a suitable hiding place, because some disinterested people can be found everywhere. Some gaps, parapets, travel signs may occur as useful. Most of boxes contain magnets. Everyone looking for a cache has to avoid damages of environment or private property.

If the box is found, the registration of the name and the date into a logbook follows. In some cases the registration of time as well. After that the finder has to return at the same place and to cover the box in the way that it should prevent a random find. As necessary it is considered to log the find by means of a smartphone or official web.

Sometimes a so called Geotour is made. Basically, some caches are located not far from each other. The aim of such a proceeding is to make the game participants familiar with the area, with its development and current state, to point out some places of interest and to give some information about them. In the Czech Republic, there exists one at the Václav Havel Airport. It came into being in 2014 in collaboration with experienced players of the Czech Geocaching Association. Thanks to them a highly appreciated series of caches of caches has been made. When looking for boxes, the participants learn a lot of interesting pieces of information. The whole Geotour is guided by an explorer. He explains the history of airport and sightseeing of its neighborhood. At the same time he mentions the security rules of luggage transport. He also may give a piece of advice how to use a free time at the airport. The players of Geotour can gain a small remembrance of their visit to the airport. It is a wooden coin designed for collectors.

2   Methods

Firstly, a method of literature review of available sources exploring the issue of modern teaching methods was used. A search was performed in the databases Web of Science, Scopus, Springer and Science Direct. Secondly, on the basis of evaluation of these literature sources, the researched issue was explored.

3   Geocaching Used in Foreign Language Teaching and Learning

3.1   Work with the Foreign Language Listing

In the last years geocaching became an interesting tool for promotion in tourism. This game is played by about six million of registered players all over the world and it represents big segment of tourism market. These people are mostly interested not only in travelling and visiting new and interesting places, but they are very often connecting and planning their tours with geocaching, too [3]. It is a big opportunity for tourism industry to cooperate with municipalities and regions in preparing their inviting campaigns in paper materials or on web pages. Also geocaching tours or only visiting interesting places that are not often mentioned in tourist guides are connected with finding caches. Density of interesting caches in certain location is very often main parameter in choosing final destination while planning holidays or trips for geocaching players [4].

To make the caches deposited and located in our territory available to foreigners it is necessary to translate the listing into a foreign language, most often into English, less often into German. So it is in other European countries as well. It is suitable to make such a translation while it is a chance that at least some foreign players will try and find the cache.

Zábranská [6] explores the occurrence of a foreign language listing in the Czech Republic in her degree thesis. Some of her figures – even only as general numbers – are given here. Her overview cannot be complete for many reasons. She gives the most listings in German around Karlovy Vary – 30%. The second position holds Prague with 18%. It is quite clear that most listings written in German occur further in border areas neighboring with German speaking countries. The English listings are mostly common in Prague – 40%, followed by some tourist regions with over 20%. With decreasing attractiveness of a region, the number English listings is lower (Fig. 1).

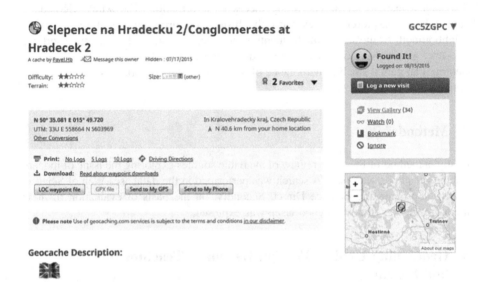

Fig. 1. Listing in english

4   Findings

When looking for a cache abroad, you are supposed to have at least a partial knowledge of a foreign language. Of course, in some cases you may collaborate with a translator. A large number of caches abroad are written in the relevant native language, or in English.

We have tried to retell the state among Czech cachers. We wanted to know how they can cope with foreign language listing. The following graphs show some results:

My usage of a foreign language in Geocaching

- While caching in a foreign country I read the listing
- in native language – 12%
- in native language using translator – 24%
- in English without trouble – 19%
- in English using translator – 38%
- I work only by means of coordinates – 6% (Fig. 2).

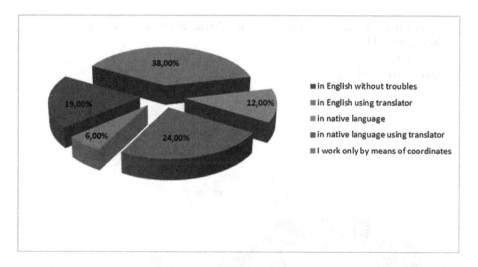

Fig. 2. Chart 1

The foreign language I use most often
English – 53%
German – 32%
Spanish – 9%
Other – 7% (Fig. 3).

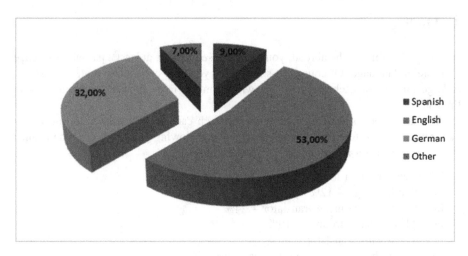

Fig. 3. Chart 2

My coming into play in foreign language discussion on Geocaching web:
Ordinarily – 11%
Exceptionally – 22%
Never – 67% (Fig. 4).

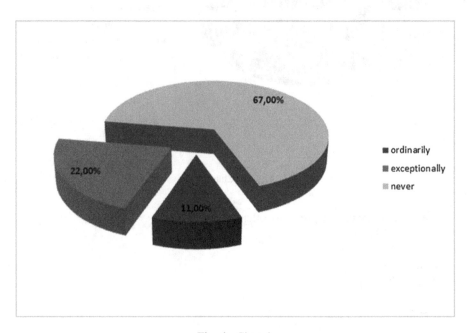

Fig. 4. Chart 3

5 Discussion

5.1 Geocaching Used in Foreign Language Learning

Concerning the facts given and for reason of Geocaching spreading the same become a good helper in a foreign language learning.

Reading through and working on a foreign language listing you broaden your vocabulary, you learn new expressions, you practice some grammar rules. You often meet foreigners, you have to speak with them in their native languages, you ask for advice. At the same time you get familiar with many interesting places. You get familiar with other countries and their people.

5.2 Geocaching Used in Foreign Language Teaching

As a very suitable it seem to appear students' presentations in foreign language on interesting finds both home and abroad. Students love to show those findings, which achievement was not so simple. Sometimes they can also bring along their special skills, for example as regards finding caches placed e.g. in tree top, on a cliff above the river, underground or other hard to reach location.

Another possibility is to promote conversational skills on topics that are bound with Geocaching and are often very close to the students, e.g. on suitability of some placements, on number of caches in different countries, on suitability and means of giving hints. Very interesting proved discussions on some troublemaking caches, their location, terrain, placement an so on.

Students may also create their own Geocaching dictionaries; seek for new expressions and their translations into mother tongue. Finally they can try to translate listings both to mother tongue and foreign language.

6 Conclusion

Students understand that they need good knowledge of foreign language for their future job: for contacts with foreign travel agencies, tour operators, business partners, visitors, tourists etc. Use of Geocaching in foreign language teaching involves plenty of areas. The significance of Geocaching for foreign language teaching is already considerable. Given that Geocaching is constantly developing, its further extended usage for teaching can be assumed.

References

1. Geocaching.com (2015). https://www.geocaching.com/. Accessed 12 Sept 2015
2. Geocaching (2015). https://en.wikipedia.org/wiki/Geocaching Accessed 29 Sept 2015
3. Hubackova, S.: Foreign language teaching with WebCT support. Procedia Soc. Behav. Sci. **3** (2010), 112–115 (2010)
4. Pikhart, M.: New horizons of intercultural communication: applied linguistics approach. Procedia Soc. Behav. Sci. **152**, 954–957 (2014)

5. Rylich, J.: Geocaching: turistika, hra a dobrodružství s GPS. Ikaros: Elektronický časopis o informační společnosti. 2012, roč. 16, č. 8 (2015). http://ikaros.cz/node/7608. Accessed 10 Sept 2015
6. Zábranská, V.: Vliv geocachingu na cestovní ruch. Diplomová práce (2015). https://www.vse.cz/vskp/30702_vliv_geocachingu_na_cestovni_ruch. Accessed 21 Sept 2015

Emerging Technologies of Pedagogical Issues

A Corpus-Based Study on the Distribution of Business Terms in Business English Writing

Shili Ge[1] and Xiaoxiao Chen[2(✉)]

[1] National Experimental Teaching Center of Simultaneous Interpreting,
Guangdong University of Foreign Studies (GDUFS), Guangzhou 510420, China
geshili@gdufs.edu.cn
[2] School of English for International Business, GDUFS,
Guangzhou 510420, China
gracekot@qq.com

Abstract. In order to explore the integration of business knowledge and English language in Business English teaching, all the writing samples from three Business English writing textbooks were collected to construct a corpus; a Business English terminology database was constructed; and a computer program was coded to automatically annotate and analyze business terms in the corpus. The results show that the corpus covers all ten disciplines of business terms under study but the distribution is obviously different. Therefore, Business English teaching text does reflect the integration of business knowledge and English language to some extent, but it mainly relates to the simple business knowledge and needs to expand substantially for Business English writing teaching.

Keywords: Business English writing · Business term · Business knowledge
Writing course book · Corpus

1 Introduction

The features and advantages of Business English (BE) lie in its interdisciplinarity integrating language skills and business knowledge [1]. BE implies "emphasis on particular kinds of communication in a specific context" [2]. BE shares general Englsih (GE) features and contains a wealth of business knowledge. "Business terminology is a salient linguistic feature of business knowledge" [3]. BE teaching has to pay attention to business knowledge, e.g., business terms. However, there are still few studies on this topic so far. This study aims to investigate the infiltration of business knowledge in course books of BE writing so as to facilitate its teaching in China.

2 Literature Review

2.1 Business English Writing and Its Teaching

National teaching guidance to BE in China indicates that "BE BA program has interdisciplinary features" [4], aiming to cultivate applied and interdisciplinary talents

© Springer Nature Switzerland AG 2018
T. Hao et al. (Eds.): SETE 2018, LNCS 11284, pp. 97–106, 2018.
https://doi.org/10.1007/978-3-030-03580-8_11

being able to handle international business. They would master the basic theory and knowledge of linguistics, economics, management and law (international business law), familiarize with common rules and convention of international business, embrace the ability of English application, business practice, cross-cultural communication, critical thinking, innovation and independent study and be equipped with international vision and humanistic literacy [5]. BE writing is "one of the most principal communication form in the internal and external of an organization" [6], which is also one of the core courses required in the National Curriculum for BA Program in Business English of China [7], aiming to cultivate students' writing ability for their future business communication.

BE writing, as an interdisciplinary writing, involves language skills as well as business knowledge. Zhang [8] investigates the opinions of international business professionals on the writing of BE major undergraduate students. Among the formal, process, rhetorical, and subject-matter dimensions of genre knowledge, subject-matter is listed as the second important category right behind formal category. This research indicates that business writing "need to be taught in a holistic way", and it "should be treated from the outset as performing a business activity where the four dimensions of genre knowledge are equally relevant and important" [8]. BE, as an interdisciplinary subject, mainly reflects in the compound of language and business knowledge. "The cultivation of compound talents is a systematic project and it cannot be achieved with the addition of one or two courses" [9].

2.2 Business Knowledge and Business Terms in BE Writing

The teaching of BE major needs the combination of business knowledge and language skills. Zhong et al. [5] compare the national curricula for BA programs in English, Translation and BE and find out that Management, Economics, Law, and business knowledge related to business discourse are the core knowledge requirements of BE distinguishable from traditional English and translation BA programs.

Term is the node of a concept network and concept comes from subject-field knowledge [10]. Therefore, term is a textual reflection of filed knowledge and business term is a significant linguistic reflection of business knowledge. One of the most important aspect in BE writing is the application of business terms.

Yan [11] indicates that BE BA program aims at the cultivation of applicable compound English talents who can communicate between cultures effectively according to the conventions of common professional discourse community. Discourse community refers to a community with common goals, mutual communication mechanism, and application of specific genres and specialized vocabulary [12]. "Specialized vocabulary" includes business terms naturally. Therefore, business term is the linguistic reflection that BE major students have mastered the relevant business knowledge and BE writing is one channel of this reflection.

To cultivate compound BE talents for business discourse community, business term, as a joint of English language and business knowledge, has to be emphasized. Business communication stresses clarity and accuracy, and the reflection of the two features is impossible without the application of business terms. Ellis and Johnson [2] indicate that "there is a preference for clear, logical, thought" in business communication and "certain terms have evolved to save time in referring to concepts which people in business are familiar with". Guffey & Loewy [13] emphasize that in business writing, especially in the revision stage, clear and precise words should be adopted. From their illustration, it can be seen that business terms are used to replace GE expression for each and every example. There is similar conclusion in BE study in China. In the long history of BE communication, a series of business terms are created for clear and concise expression and frequent business term application is typical stylistic and linguistic features for BE [14].

Russian terminologist B. Golovin points out that term is a tool for professional thinking and a core part in professional communication language [15]. Therefore, as a part of international business communication, the unification and wide application of business term will become the lubrication of international business communication and significantly promote international business. This is the reason that the teaching of BE writing has to pay attention to the application of business terms.

In the teaching of BE writing, "there is no doubt that course books of BE writing, as the carrier of teaching, are very important in BE talent cultivation" [16]. Business terms in course books, in fact, reflect clearly the combination situation of English language and business knowledge in present BE teaching.

2.3   Terminology, Corpus and Term Recognition

"It is a well-known fact that terminology has attracted the interest of researchers with very different backgrounds and motivations" [17]. Terms are defined as "the words that are assigned to concepts used in the special languages that occur in subject-field or domain-related texts" [18]. Similar idea occurs in BE study, too. "In the late 1960s and early 1970s, specialist vocabulary was seen to be what distinguished Business English from General English, and there was preoccupation with business-related words and terminology" [2].

The descriptive terminology research method based on communicative theory of terminology [19] and sociocognitive approach of terminology description [20] is different from traditional prescriptive method. The descriptive method focuses not on the standardization of terms, but on the organization and description of terms based on semantic relationship, so as to analyze the distribution of terms in authentic texts with the help of specialized corpus or other authentic language materials.

Automatic recognition and extraction is the first step in terminology resource construction and it is the most important step. Automatic extraction "methods include statistically based procedures, linguistically-based procedures and hybrid procedures" [21]. Dictionary-based procedure is a linguistic rule-based approach and it is the simplest approach. By comparing the candidate term with entries in term dictionary one by one, the candidate term can be determined that it is a term if it is found in the dictionary and not if it is not in the dictionary. This approach is effective and efficient, only that an electronic term dictionary is required and complex term recognition needs supplementary of statistical procedures.

3 Research Design

3.1 Research Questions

The rational and precise application of business terms in BE writing is a reflection of high writing quality. The model essays in writing course books are an exemplar of learning and training for BE writing learners. Terms in the model essays have a direct influence on learners and therefore, their distribution is worthy of detailed investigation. Research questions from the perspectives of business discipline and course book type are as following:

(1) What business disciplines do the terms in BE writing course books fall in? What is the distribution feature of terms in these disciplines?
(2) What is the feature of term distribution among different kinds of BE writing course books? How is business knowledge reflected in different kinds of BE writing course books?

3.2 Corpus Construction of BE Writing Model Essays

With a brief survey of BE writing course books adopted for BA program of BE majors in China, three course books of different types from different years were selected: Practical Business Writing (PBW), Business English Writing (BEW), and Up-To-Date Correspondence for Import & Export (UCIE). Among them, the former two books are comprehensive BE writing course books and the last one is a traditional correspondence writing course book. There are 203 model essays in all three book and they were collected to form the model essay corpus for this study. The detailed data are shown in Table 1.

Table 1. Information of BE writing course books model essay corpus.

Course books	PBW	BEW	UCIE	Total
Essay number	52	59	92	203
Word number	11320	12157	15010	38420
Chapter number	18	16	11	32

As shown in Table 1, the numbers of chapter are different in three course books, but some chapters share the same themes such as Letter of Invitation, Letter of Thanks, Inquiry and Quotation, etc. The total number of themes without repetition is 32.

3.3 Term Bank Construction of Business Terms

Term matching procedure is adopted in this study to recognize and annotate terms in BE writing corpus, which requires the digitalization of a BE term dictionary to construct a BE term bank. The detail of BE Term Bank (BETB) is reported in [3].

3.4   Term Recognition, Annotation and Statistical Analysis

Among three approaches of term recognition, the simplest and most efficient one is maximum matching algorithm based on dictionary. Certainly, there are some short-comings in this approach, such as ignorance of new terms and low recall rate of terms, etc. However, this is not a big problem for term recognition in BE writing. The total amount of terms required in BE writing curriculum for foreign language learners is not very large.

To identify and annotate terms in model essays, a maximum matching algorithm is designed and coded in Python. The algorithm is rather simple:

```
Read in all term entries and categories from BETB
for each composition in the corpus:
  for each sentence in a composition:
    Lemmatize all words
    Match the longest term from the first word with the
original word or lemmatized word
      if matched:
        Annotate the first category of the term
        Move on to the next word after the term
      if not matched:
        Move on to the next word
Output the annotated result
```

To illustrate the identification and annotation procedure, an annotated sample is given as following:
Tina Mao
Great Wall <Import> [IB] & <Export> [IB] Co. <Ltd.> [LAW]
[…]
Dear Mr. Smith,
We would like to extend to you an invitation for your visit to the 106th Chinese <Export> [IB] <Commodities> [ECO] <Fair> [MAR] in Guangzhou, which is to be held from Sept. 6 to Sept. 16. All of our new items will be on display in the <Fair> [MAR]. Our <manager> [HR] and <sales representatives> [MAR] will be there to meet you and conduct <negotiations> [MAN] with you.
We sincerely hope you could come for a visit in the <Fair> [MAR]. We are confident that our meeting at the <Fair> [MAR] will be fruitful and <lead> [MAR] to the advance of our <Business> [ECO] <relations> [IT].
Please confirm your visit at your earliest convenience so that we could make the necessary arrangements.
Sincerely yours,
Tina Mao

There are 15 terms in the 147 words model essay (punctuations excluded), among which 14 are single-word terms and 1 is a two-word term. Terms are annotated in the essay with angle brackets, <>, and their categories are annotated with square brackets,

[]. Most terms are matched with their original forms, such as <import> and <export>; some are matched with lemmatized forms, such as <negotiations> with <negotiation> and <sales representatives> with <sales representative>.

There are also some problems in the recognition and annotation of terms. First, some term candidates should be annotated as business terms only when their semantic meanings match the definitions given in the dictionary. For example, the word "lead" should be annotated as a term in marketing category [MAR] when it means "A person or organization that might possibly have a need for the company's product or service" in the context. Otherwise, it should be considered as a common word. Yet, in the above model essay, it is labeled as a term though it is in fact only a common word. In present, this type of words is just annotated as terms due to their small fraction and the explorative nature of this study.

Another problem is the multiple-category that a term belongs to. In this case, the category label should be annotated according to its context. For example, if the term "relation" means "A two-dimensional table in the relational database model", it should be classified in information technology category, [IT]. And if it means "A principle whereby effect is given to an act done at one time as if it had been done at a previous time", it should be put into law category, [LAW]. The solution of this problem for present study is to annotate the first label since the first is the most frequent used one.

At last, only matched original or lemmatized words are identified as terms. Some other words, in fact, are terms, too. For example, "Co." is the abbreviation of term "corporation" of economics category [ECO] in BETB, but it is not annotated.

To partially solve the three problems of term recognition and annotation, part of annotated texts are manually checked and term bank is supplemented and revised by adding in some abbreviated terms, adjusted the category order of some terms according to the themes in model essay corpus, so as to decrease the recognition and annotation error in corpus as much as possible.

4   Results and Discussion

Based on the revised and expanded BETB, business terms in BE writing model essay corpus were recognized and annotated with Python program. The distributions of business terms and their categories in the corpus are listed in Tables 2 and 3 according to their type and token.

From the type analysis of business terms, i.e. the terms without repetition, the answer to the first research question can be found: the distributions in categories and disciplines of business terms in BE writing model essay corpus.

The model essays in the three course books contain 401, 262 and 248 terms, respectively, and the total amount of term type without repetition is 564, covering all 10 management disciplines under study and covering also the business knowledge that is required to master by BE undergraduate students according to the National Curriculum. From the perspective of BE writing course book design, the combination of BE language skills and business knowledge is adequately reflected.

From the percentage of terms in different disciplines in Table 2, it can be seen that the distribution of terms in disciplines is not proportionate, mainly concentrating upon

Table 2. Distribution of term type from BE writing model essay corpus.

	PBW	Percent (%)	BEW	Percent (%)	UCIE	Percent (%)
ACC	31	7.73	32	12.21	28	11.29
MAN	68	16.96	45	17.18	21	8.47
MAR	61	15.21	35	13.36	35	14.11
LAW	26	6.48	20	7.63	18	7.26
OPE	43	10.72	18	6.87	22	8.87
HR	41	10.22	29	11.07	13	5.24
IB	50	12.47	24	9.16	48	19.35
ECO	48	11.97	33	12.60	39	15.73
FIN	27	6.73	22	8.40	20	8.06
IT	6	1.50	4	1.53	4	1.61
Total	401	100.00	262	100.00	248	100.00

the fields of accounting, management, marketing, human resources, international business and economics, and especially marketing and economics. This is in concordance with the discipline position of BE study. Marketing occupies a key position in business knowledge system in BE teaching. Cao [1] indicates that in the practice of BE teaching, every university can determine their own research direction and fields based on the position and resource they possess in the discipline, such as international business or finance, but "the core theory is international marketing because marketing is indispensable no matter how you treat the discipline of BE". The emergence of large amount of economics and management terms in the result also shows the close relationship between BE and the two disciplines of economics and management. Lin [22] believes that business linguistics is "the collection of theory and research methodology from the three disciplines of linguistics, economics and management". The terms of accounting, human resources and international business occupy a relatively large proportion. However, from the requirement of National Curriculum of BE, terms of international business law, international finance and information technology are deficient, and especially information technology terms are scarce.

As we all know, laws and regulations play an important role in international trade and other business activities. In the course of business cooperation and trade, all countries must abide by the laws of various places; at the same time, relevant knowledge of international business law and economic law also helps international business practitioners seek appropriate ways to avoid risks and losses. Therefore, in BE writing teaching, the integration and penetration of business law knowledge need to be strengthened. The inadequate use of international financial terms reflects the rare involvement of relevant knowledge in BE writing.

Survey by Zhu [23] indicates that many BE majors feel that they fail to master the knowledge of the core courses of economics and management well enough, and the "professional knowledge they learnt in class is superficial or too simple". The less use of financial terms in writing course books also reflects this problem. The lack or even absence of information technology terminology is particularly urgent in the context of today's business computerization. The possible reasons include at least two aspects.

One is that the era of textbook compilation has not been able to keep up with the trend of e-commerce; the other is that BE writing teachers and researchers are not involved in advanced information technology such as the management information system. Whatever the reason, the supplement of information technology knowledge in BE writing is a top priority.

Table 3. Distribution of term token from BE writing model essay corpus.

	PBW	Percent (%)	BEW	Percent (%)	UCIE	Percent (%)
ACC	59	5.49	154	15.34	92	6.55
MAN	126	11.72	143	14.24	172	12.25
MAR	139	12.93	98	9.76	188	13.39
LAW	156	14.51	74	7.37	105	7.48
OPE	148	13.77	77	7.67	214	15.24
HR	91	8.47	118	11.75	114	8.12
IB	91	8.47	52	5.18	201	14.32
ECO	206	19.16	239	23.81	286	20.37
FIN	50	4.65	43	4.28	26	1.85
IT	9	0.84	6	0.60	6	0.43
Total	1075	100	1004	100	1404	100

From Tables 2 and 3, the answer to the second research question can be found out, namely, the distribution of business terms and the similarities and differences of business knowledge coverage in different types of course books can be analyzed.

In terms of marketing and economics terms, both the comprehensive BE writing course books and the English correspondence writing course book, whether it is in terms of terminology type, the number of terms in a particular category, or terminology token, that is, the absolute frequency of terms, presents similar characteristics: the term resource is rich, and the average term frequency is high.

In terms of the distribution of other disciplines, there are some differences between the two kinds of course books, especially between the two disciplines of management and human resources. From the perspective of term type, the two comprehensive BE writing course books are obviously rich in terms of these two disciplines, while the two kinds of term numbers in correspondence course book are relatively low. However, from the perspective of term token, the numbers of these two kinds of terms in correspondence course book are also very high. This shows that in correspondence writing, a small number of terms of management and human resources are heavily reused. Through browsing the course book, it can be seen that these large number of reused terms belong to commonly used business terms, and most learners will soon master them. From the use of these two kinds of terms, the correspondence writing course books have some defects in the coverage of business knowledge, which should also be one of the reasons why the teaching materials are more inclined to use comprehensive writing course books in recent years.

Another obvious difference between the two kinds of course books is the use of international business [IB] terms. No matter measured by token or type, comprehensive writing course books are obviously lower than correspondence course book. Therefore, the application of international business knowledge should be a significant feature of the writing of foreign trade correspondence, and the distribution of [IB] term is relatively small in comprehensive business writing course books. Therefore, if comprehensive course books are adopted in teaching, appropriate ways should be taken to enhance the teaching and application of international business knowledge.

The terms of other disciplines, such as finance [FIN] terminology, are less frequent in both kinds of course books. The numbers are especially lower in correspondence course book. This shows that all kinds of BE writing course books need to enhance the coverage and depth of business knowledge.

5 Conclusion

A large number of business terms are included in the model essays of BE writing, which is an undoubted empirical proof of the interdisciplinary properties of BE, and it is also the distinguishing feature of BE major, which shows the significance of the major. In the research data, the large numbers of management, marketing, and economics terms prove the hypothesis that one of the three sub-systems of BE study is international business, that is, "the basic support theory of the international business subsystem is economics, management and law" [1]. But at the same time, research data show that the frequency of legal terms is not high, indicating that legal knowledge in BE writing teaching still needs to be strengthened. In the process of comparison between the comprehensive BE writing course books and the traditional correspondence writing course books, it is found that the comprehensive course books have more advantages in the coverage of business knowledge than the traditional correspondence ones, which has a certain guiding significance for the selection of the teaching materials.

Acknowledgements. This work is financially supported by the National Social Science Fund (No. 13BYY097).

References

1. Cao, D.: A theoretical framework for China's business English based on international business communication. Foreign Lang. China **9**(3), 10–15 (2012)
2. Ellis, M., Johnson, C.: Teaching Business English. Oxford University Press, Oxford (2014)
3. Ge, S., Zhang, J., Chen, X.: Corpus-based correlational study of terms and quality in business english writing. In: Wu, T.-T., Gennari, R., Huang, Y.-M., Xie, H., Cao, Y. (eds.) SETE 2016. LNCS, vol. 10108, pp. 349–358. Springer, Cham (2017). https://doi.org/10.1007/978-3-319-52836-6_37
4. Wang, L., Ye, X., Yan, M., Peng, Q., Xu, D.: Interpretation of the National Standard of BA program teaching quality for business English majors. Foreign Lang. Teach. Res. **47**(2), 297–302 (2015)

5. Zhong, W., Zhang, W., He, J.: On positioning BA in business English program in higher education. Foreign Lang. China **12**(1), 4–10 (2015)
6. Chen, X., Ge, S.: An exploration of procedural business english writing ability from the perspective of business communication. Foreign Lang. Res. **2**, 58–62 (2016)
7. Chen, H., Wang, L.: Developing national curriculum for BA program in business English of China. Foreign Lang. China **6**(4), 4–11 (2009)
8. Zhang, Z.: Business English students learning to write for international business: what do international business practitioners have to say about their texts? Engl. Specif. Purp. **32**(3), 144–156 (2013)
9. Qin, X., Wu, G.: Give full play to the advantages of science and technology universities and strive to cultivate compound English Majors: a review of the running mode of English Majors in science and technology universities. Foreign Lang. World **4**, 10–14 (1999)
10. Riggs, F., Matti, M., Gerhard, B.: Descriptive terminology in the social sciences. In: Sue, E., Gerhard, B. (eds.) Handbook of Terminology Management, vol. 1. Basic Aspects of Terminology Management, pp. 184–195. John Benjamins Publishing Company, Amsterdam/Philadelphia (1997)
11. Yan, M.: The construction of "curriculum-instruction-assessment" model for undergraduate business English major. Foreign Lang. Res. **5**, 95–98 (2015)
12. Yan, M.: The theoretical construction of discourse community. Foreign Lang. Res. **6**, 85–88 (2010)
13. Guffey, M., Loewy, D.: Essentials of Business Communication. Cengage Learning, South-Western (2010)
14. Liao, Y., Mo, Z.: Researches for Language and Translation on International Business English, 2nd edn. University of International Business and Economics Press, Beijing (2007)
15. Liu, Q.: The Research and Exploration of Terminology in China. The Commercial Press, Beijing (2009)
16. Mo, Z., Sun, W.: The present development of business English writing course books. Foreign Lang. Educ. **31**(5), 81–85 (2010)
17. Bourigault, D., Jacquemin, C., L'Homme, M.: Introduction of Recent Advances in Computational Terminology. John Benjamins Publishing Company, Amsterdam/Philadelphia (2001)
18. Wright, S.: Term selection: the initial phase of terminology management. In: Wright, S., Budin, G. (eds.) Handbook of Terminology Management, vol. 1, Basic Aspects of Terminology Management, pp. 13–23. John Benjamins Publishing Company, Amsterdam/Philadelphia (1997)
19. Cabré, M.: Theories of terminology: Their description, prescription and explanation. Terminology **9**(9), 163–199 (2003)
20. Temmerman, R.: Towards New Ways of Terminology Description: The Sociocognitive-Approach, vol. 3. John Benjamins Publishing, Philadelphia (2000)
21. Ahmad, K., Rogers, M.: Corpus-related applications. In: Wright, S., Budin, G (eds.) Handbook of Terminology Management. Application-Oriented Terminology Management, vol. 2, pp. 725–760. John Benjamins Publishing Company, Amsterdam/Philadelphia (2001)
22. Lin, T.: The establishment of business linguistics. Foreign Lang. World **2**, 2–9 (2014)
23. Zhu, W.: Investigation and analysis of the English immersion education. Int. Econ. Trade Res. **21**(9), 50–53 (2005)

Dimension of a Learning Organisation in the IT Sector in the Czech Republic – Case Study

Vaclav Zubr$^{(\boxtimes)}$ (iD)

Faculty of Informatics and Management, The University of Hradec Kralove,
Hradec Kralove, Czech Republic
vaclav.zubr@uhk.cz

Abstract. Implementing a learning organisation model enables organisations to obtain a strategic advantage. This paper deals with implementing an organisational learning model in organisations in the IT sector in the Czech Republic. The Czech version of the questionnaire "Dimension of a Learning Organisation" is used to evaluate the organisations. The rating of most dimensions is balanced (3.527–4.454). From the seven dimensions of the learning organisation, Dimension 4 – Create systems to capture and share learning is the lowest score while Dimension 1 – Create continuous learning opportunities has the highest score. The assessment of dimensions reflects the respondent's position. The difference between senior and line staff assessment is statistically significant (p = 0.002). In the future, it would be appropriate to conduct this research on a larger number of respondents and interdisciplinary compare the obtained results.

Keywords: Learning organisation · DLOQ · Learning, IT sector

1 Introduction

In many organisations, we can see human resources development models that consider education to be a separate function [17]. In the case of a learning organisation, the whole organisation is considered to be a system in which individual learning is supported and the organisation learns from their synergies [3].

The learning organisation supports individual learning as well as the whole organisation's learning; it's based on discovering and correcting shortcomings within its activities. Interaction between individuals is then a key aspect of organisational learning. This way, the organisation seeks to detect and remove hidden causes in both the internal and external environment [15, 20].

The introduction of the learning organisation concept, among other things, allows organisations greater flexibility, competitiveness, improved performance, achieving goals and long-term prosperity in comparison with their competitors [14].

On the basis of a literature search of domestic and foreign sources it was discovered that the introduction of the learning organisation concept in Czech companies hasn't been dealt with to a large extent and only basic references, assumptions and assertions

© Springer Nature Switzerland AG 2018
T. Hao et al. (Eds.): SETE 2018, LNCS 11284, pp. 107–116, 2018.
https://doi.org/10.1007/978-3-030-03580-8_12

can be found in the literature. This finding opened up space for carrying out a study that, using the "Dimension of a Learning Organisation" questionnaire, evaluated the rate of introduction of the learning organisation concept in the surveyed companies.

2   Research Background

The importance of small and medium-sized enterprises in the Czech Republic is relatively high given the high percentage of people they employ (more than 70% of employees in the private sector) [6].

Small and medium-sized enterprises are defined by the Czech Statistical Office as enterprises that employ up to 250 people. In detail, small and medium-sized enterprises can be divided into small enterprises (also micro-companies) with 1 to 9 employees, small enterprises with 10 to 49 employees and medium enterprises employ between 50 and 250 people. We can also see a more detailed division of small enterprises into groups from 10 to 19 and from 20 to 49 employees and a more detailed division of medium-sized enterprises into groups ranging from 50 to 99 employees and from 100 to 249 employees. Enterprises with more than 250 people are called large enterprises [5, 6].

Workers in a learning organisation strive to achieve their potential, share the targeted vision within a team of colleagues and their personal goals are in-line with the organisation's mission [20]. People's sub-system in a learning organisation includes managers, employees as well as customers, business partners and alliances, suppliers and retailers, as well as surrounding communities [10].

Leaders must fully understand the knowledge process to be able to influence it properly. Therefore, they should understand how information and knowledge resources (databases, web resources, resources available through the library system) are created, organised, made accessible and how they can use all information (internally and externally). Leaders focus directly on the employees' internal motivation and their higher needs, trying to create a working environment that encourages employees to test new approaches (without fears of punishment for negative results) [16].

For companies wishing to learn as part of an organisational strategy, a number of features play a key role: learning as part of strategy, participatory approach, IT, formative accounting, internal exchange, flexible remuneration system, supporting structures, gathering information on the external environment, inter-organisational learning, a learning-friendly atmosphere and a personal development opportunity for everyone. For all these characteristics, correct functioning should be ensured [1, 18].

According to more studies, several factors, which are illustrated in Fig. 1, are involved in the good functioning of the learning organisation concept.

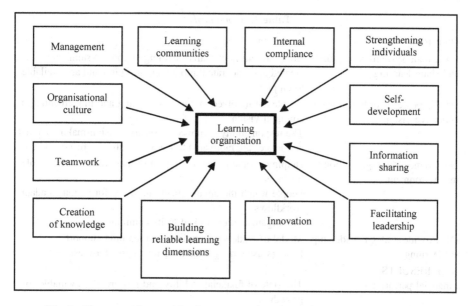

Fig. 1. Factors with a positive impact on a learning organisation (Source: [21])

There are many tools to measure and diagnose learning organisations. This number is directly dependent on the number of learning organisation definitions. The definition of learning organisation by Marsick and Watkins [19] is also one of these tools.

According to Marsick and Watkins, there are seven dimensions that characterise a learning organisation culture (Table 1).

Table 1. Seven dimensions of a learning organisation

Dimension	Definition
D1: Create continuous learning opportunities	Learning is designed so that people can learn by working; opportunities for continuing education and growth are provided
D2: Promote inquiry and dialogue	People have the ability to think reasonably so that they can express their opinions; people have the ability to listen and examine the opinions of others; Organisation culture supports polling, feedback and experimentation
D3: Encourage collaboration and team learning	The work is designed to use a group approach to different ways of thinking; groups are expected to learn and work together; co-operation is appreciated by the organisation culture and is rewarded

(*continued*)

Table 1. (continued)

Dimension	Definition
D4: Create systems to capture and share learning	Both old and new shared learning support systems are created and integrated into the organisation and are available to employees
D5: Empower people toward a collective vision	People are involved in creating, owning and implementing a common vision The responsibility is moved closer to decision-making so that employees are motivated to learn what they're responsible for
D6: Connect the organisation to its environment	Helping people to see the impact of their work on the whole business People watch the environment and use information to adapt workflows The organisation is linked to its communities
D7: Provide strategic leadership for learning	Model of leaders, champions and learning support Leaders use strategic learning to support business results
KEY RESULTS Financial performance	The state of financial stability and resources is available for growth
Knowledge performance	Improving learning and knowledge products and services (core indicators of intellectual capital)

Source: own processing with the use of [9, 11]

3   Methods

Between December 2017 and February 2018, a cross-section questionnaire survey was carried out, the survey focused on small and medium-sized businesses in the IT sector in the Czech Republic. The focus of the study on small and medium-sized enterprises is largely due to their significant position in the employment of people in recent years [6]. Contacts for small and medium-sized businesses that were contacted to participate in the study, were obtained from the Albertina for Business and Marketing Database [2]. The size of the enterprise and the sector of activity were selected as a business selection criterion. The business sectors were entered by the CZ-NACE code, the predominant activity, specifically: [12].

J – Information and communication activities – 62.0 – Activities in the Information Technology field – 62.01 – Programming – 62.02 – Information Technology Consultancy – 62.03 – Computer Equipment Management – 62.09 – Other IT activities.

For the purpose of this study, a shorter version Dimensions of the Learning Organisation questionnaire [11] was used with 21 questions focused on 7 dimensions of the learning organisation. To maintain the validity of the questionnaire, the questionnaire was translated by two independent translators from English into Czech and then back to English. At the same time, retaining the meaning of the questionnaire was considered. For each dimension, Cronbach confidence coefficient was calculated using IBM SPSS Statistics Version 24. The Alpha coefficient ranged from 0.683 to 0.860 for each dimension. Overall, the value of the coefficient was 0.933. The calculated values of the Cronbach coefficient appear to be satisfactory (the coefficient higher than 0.7 is "satisfactory") [4, 8]. Individual dimensions were assessed by the respondents on the 6-point Likert scale.

A pilot study was carried out in the introduction to verify the questionnaire's clarity. This study was attended by a total of 20 students (11 male, 9 female) from the combined form of follow-up Master's degree in Information Management. It was concluded from follow-up interviews to the questionnaire's completion, that there is a good understanding of individual questions and that the questionnaire is easily understood.

After the pilot study, a final version of the questionnaire was created using "docs.google.com". The link to the questionnaire was then sent to the respondents' email addresses which were obtained from the Albertina database. The survey included companies from all over the Czech Republic. In total, 2,884 respondents were addressed. Approximately 250 submitted e-mails returned as a non-deliverable message due to non-existence of the e-mail addresses, 25 respondents responded to the e-mail with the response that they don't currently operate a business.

The obtained data was analysed using Microsoft Excel 2016 and IBM SPSS Statistics version 24 using descriptive statistics, parametric and non-parametric tests at confidence levels $\alpha = 0.01$ and $\alpha = 0.05$.

4   Results

For the study, a shortened 21 questionnaire version of the "Dimension of a learning organisation" questionnaire was used, which included the seven dimensions. A pilot study was first conducted to verify the understanding of the questionnaire.

Respondents' responses were ranked according to the seven dimensions of the learning organisation. None of these dimensions were rated with less than 3 points, the fourth dimension's (average score 3.70) and the sixth dimension's (average score 3.90) were scored worst. The highest rating was achieved by dimension 2 (average score 4.67).

Following the pilot survey's evaluation, several questions were modified in the questionnaire. Information regarding the size of the organisation and the position in the organisation were added to the questionnaire.

To verify the questionnaire's validity, reliability was measured for each dimension using the Cronbach alpha reliability indicator. The reliability value should be higher than 0.7 [4]. All dimensions except dimension 4 met the required reliability value. Although dimension 4 didn't reach 0.7 value, it's significantly close to this value (0.017 difference), so this value can also be considered satisfactory. The reason for the lower Cronbach alpha value is probably different respondents' answers within dimension 4.

A total of 2,884 respondents from small and medium-sized companies from the Czech Republic with a focus on information technology activities were addressed. A total of 201 respondents (137 male, 64 female) answered the questionnaire (Table 2).

Table 2. The respondents' demographic profile

	Number of respondents (n = 201)	% (n = 201)
Organisation size		
Up to 10 employees	65	32.3%
Up to 50 employees	91	45.3%
Up to 250 employees	45	22.4%
Age		
21–30 years	30	14.9%
31–40 years	76	37.8%
41–50 years	57	28.4%
51–60 years	32	15.9%
61 years and over	6	3.0%
Position in employment		
Staff member	72	35.8%
Executive member	129	64.2%
Learning time (monthly)		
0 h	9	4.5%
1–10 h	109	54.2%
11–20 h	48	23.9%
21–35 h	15	7.5%
36 h and over	20	10.0%

Source: own processing

4.1   Evaluation of All Dimensions

In the overall evaluation of all dimensions, respondents' no. 31 and 87 seem to be the key respondents with the most remote values. Apart from the position in the workplace (staff worker), there is no connection between the two respondents. For more dimensions, we can see the remote values of other respondents - for example respondents' numbers 61, 103 and 161. These three respondents combine characteristics such as university degree, work as a staff worker, and relatively short employment in a given company (3 and 6 years). Given that all respondents with remote values work in the staff workers ranks, the question is whether their assessment of individual dimensions merely reflects the ignorance of the company's operation and their own lack of interest in engaging in joint organisational activities.

According to the table of average ratings by to the position of the worker (Table 3), it is clear that average workers score lower in all dimensions compared with management. On average, the management ranks the individual dimensions better by 0.677 points than standard staff members. There is a statistically significant difference in the t-test ($p = 0.002$, $\alpha = 0.01$) (Fig. 2).

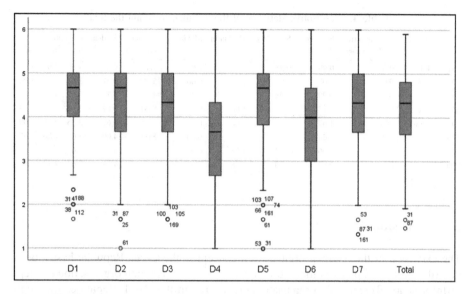

Fig. 2. Boxplot 7 dimensions and the whole study (Source: own processing)

The assessment of most dimensions is fairly balanced, (Table 4) it can't be claimed that organisations in the Czech Republic don't have the features of a learning organisation (values close to four can be compared to agreeing with assertions in individual dimensions). Since all dimensions are mutually related, we do not determine the most important dimension.

Table 3. Comparison of respondents' answers with different rankings

	D1	D2	D3	D4	D5	D6	D7
Staff members	4.123	4.012	3.752	3.227	3.819	3.433	3.745
Executive members	4.638	4.593	4.435	3.695	4.612	4.230	4.649

Source: own processing

If we compare the average assessment of the dimensions by the respondents from different sized organisations by means of t-test, there is no statistically significant difference between respondents from small enterprises (1–9 employees) and enterprises employing up to 50 employees ($p = 0.843$, $\alpha = 0.05$). At the same time there is no statistically significant difference between small enterprises and enterprises employing up to 250 employees ($p = 0.102$, $\alpha = 0.05$). When comparing organisations employing up to 50 employees and up to 250 employees, there is also no statistically significant difference ($p = 0.061$, $\alpha = 0.05$).

Table 4. Descriptive statistics of the 7 dimensions and the total

	Average	Medium error of the average	Standard deviation	Scattering	Minimum	Maximum	Median variation	Median	Percentile		
									25	50	75
D1	4.45	0.07	0.99	0.98	1.67	6.00	4.33	4.67	4.00	4.67	5.00
D2	4.39	0.07	1.03	1.06	1.00	6.00	5.00	4.67	3.67	4.67	5.00
D3	4.19	0.07	0.99	0.98	1.67	6.00	4.33	4.33	3.67	4.33	5.00
D4	3.53	0.08	1.17	1.36	1.00	6.00	5.00	3.67	2.67	3.67	4.33
D5	4.33	0.08	1.07	1.15	1.00	6.00	5.00	4.67	3.75	4.67	5.00
D6	3.94	0.07	1.04	1.08	1.00	6.00	5.00	4.00	3.00	4.00	4.67
D7	4.33	0.08	1.06	1.13	1.33	6.00	4.67	4.33	3.67	4.33	5.00
Total	4.19	0.06	0.84	0.70	1.48	5.91	4.43	4.33	3.62	4.33	4.83

Source: own processing

5 Discussion

The extension of the learning organisation concept in the Czech Republic hasn't been described yet. This paper is focused on evaluation of the learning organisation concept in Information Technology organisations registered in the Czech Republic. Although data was collected for three months, the correlations within the group are high, which contributes to the credibility of the detected data.

21-question questionnaire version of the DLOQ was used for the study, and the reliability was calculated for each dimension - namely Cronbach's alpha. Except for dimension four, all dimensions met the lowest value of 0.7 [4]. The value of dimension four (0.683) can be considered acceptable because of its close proximity to the lowest required value.

The study focused on small and medium-sized enterprises in the Czech Republic. Small enterprises, employing 1–9 employees, were included in the study because of the small number of companies meeting these conditions. After the analysis, it can be argued that the inclusion of micro-enterprises in the study does not distort its results in any way, as the responses of employees in these enterprises are consistent with the responses in small enterprises and there is no significant difference between these enterprises (p = 0.843).

Overall, the study participants were around 70% men and approximately 30% women. This result was expected with respect to the field chosen for the study and is in line with the reported male/female statistics in the IT sector [13]. A large representation of executives in a study may be due to the fact that the questionnaire was sent to contact addresses of companies, and it can be assumed that correspondence from the contact e-mail will be captured primarily by senior staff or the secretariat. When comparing the average rating of individual dimensions, it's obvious that a higher rating of all dimensions in the case of executives is evident. There is a statistically significant difference (p = 0.004) at the significance level $\alpha = 0.01$ between the average score of the individual dimensions in relation to the work position. Individuals can rank worse by individual staff because they may not fully understand the learning and competence development strategy or prevent changes in the organisation [7]. At the same time, the rankings of senior workers may negatively affect their possible lack of interest in further development of the organisation. Leaders can explain a larger assessment of the dimensions of their coaching functions in the development of education and the creation of a learning climate, and therefore a greater understanding of processes essential to the learning organisation concept. By comparing the learning time of senior and senior executives, it's clear that executives train more than regular staff members. Increased leadership education is probably directly related to their higher assessment of the learning organisation's individual dimensions (Table 3).

6   Conclusion

Based on the survey results, it can be argued that there has been a shift in applied human resources development models in Czech IT organisations towards a learning organisation. The relationship between the size of the organisation and the average assessment of the dimensions of the learning organisation hasn't been confirmed.

Although the topic of the learning organisation is supported by the European Union, there is still a lack of deeper studies in the Czech Republic that would deal with learning organisations. The topic is needed to be dealt further within a European context.

When assessing the individual dimensions of the learning organisation, the differences between managers and staff workers were observed, in the follow-up research, it would be appropriate to analyse several small and medium-sized organisations to look for an opinion of larger sample of both management as well as staff workers. At the same time, it would be useful to compare DLOQ results across the various fields of action.

Acknowledgement. The paper was written with the support of the specific project 6/2018 grant "Determinants of Cognitive Processes Impacting the Work Performance" granted by the University of Hradec Králové, Czech Republic and thanks to help of students Majid Ziaei Nafchi.

References

1. Adamec, J.: Základní principy koncepce učící se organizace a jejich přijímání (2010). http://emi.mvso.cz/EMI/2010-02/07%20Adamec/Adamec.pdf
2. Albertina for business and marketing (2018). http://www.albertina.cz/?gclid=Cj0KCQiAzr TUBRCnARIsAL0mqcz2seJjjxmISfi7QlvHHAwN-ZnZrWpd4Botnujmtq08Zio1vx0BfBMaAu-bEALw_wcB
3. Birdthistle, N.: Family Businesses and the Learning Organisation: A Guide to Transforming the Family Business into a Learning Organisation. VDM Verlag Dr. Müller Aktiengesellschaft & Co. KG, Saarbrücken (2009)
4. Cígler, H.: Jak na postojové škály: Tvorba položek a jejich zpracování. Masarykova Univerzita (2016). https://is.muni.cz/www/175803/pedf2016/pedf_skaly.pdf
5. Czech Statistical Office: Malé a střední podniky (jejich místo a role v české ekonomice) (2005). https://www.czso.cz/csu/czso/cri/male-a-stredni-podniky-jejich-misto-a-role-v-ceske-ekono mice-2005-rhybfgzbj0

6. Czech Statistical Office: Malé a střední firmy v ekonomice ČR v letech 2003 - 2010 (2013). https://www.czso.cz/documents/10180/20534676/116111a.pdf/9c378e0f-d77a-4f21-bf3e-e4ed35cb1122?version=1.0

7. Dymock, D., McCarthy, C.: Towards a learning Organisation? Employee Perceptions. Learn Organ **13**, 525–537 (2006). https://doi.org/10.1108/09696470610680017

8. Institute for Digital Research and Education: What does Cronbach's alfa mean? (2017) https://stats.idre.ucla.edu/spss/faq/what-does-cronbachs-alpha-mean/

9. Jamali, D., Sidani, Y., Zouein, C.: The learning organisation: tracking progress in a developing country. A comparative analysis using the DLOQ. Learn Organ **16**, 103–121 (2009). https://doi.org/10.1108/09696470910939198

10. Marquardt, M.J.: Building the Learning Organisation. Davies-Black Publishing, Palo Alto (2002)

11. Marsick, V.J., Watkins, K.E.: Demonstrating the value of an organisation's learning culture: the dimensions of the learning organisation questionnaire. Adv. Dev. Hum. Resour. **5**, 132–151 (2003). https://doi.org/10.1177/1523422303251341

12. NACE: 62.0 Činnosti v oblasti informačních technologií (2018). http://www.nace.cz/nace/62-0-cinnosti-v-oblasti-informacnich-technologii/

13. National centre for women and information technology (2018). https://www.ncwit.org/

14. Norashikin, H., Safiah, O., Fauziah, N., Noormala, A.: Learning organisation culture, organisational performance and organisational innovativeness in a public institution of higher education in malaysia: a preliminary study. Procedia Econ. Financ. **37**, 512–519 (2016). https://doi.org/10.1016/S2212-5671(16)30159-9

15. Saadat, V., Saadat, Z.: Organisational learning as a key role of organisational success. Procedia Soc. Behav. Sci. **230**, 219–225 (2016). https://doi.org/10.1016/j.sbspro.2016.09.028

16. Srivastava, K.B.L.: Knowledge management in learning organisations. Int. J. Adv. Comput. Manag. **1**, 43–48 (2012)

17. Šuleř, O.: Manažerské techniky II. Rubico, Olomouc (2003)

18. Tichá, I.: Učící se organizace. Alfa Publishing, Praha (2005)

19. Watkins, K.E., Marsick, V.J.: Sculpting the learning organisation: lessons in the art and science of systematic change. Jossey-Bass, San Francisco (1993)

20. Yadav, S., Agarwal, V.: Benefits and barriers of learning organisation and its five discipline. IOSR - JBM **18**, 18–24 (2016). https://doi.org/10.9790/487X-1812011824

21. Zubr, V., Mohelska, H., Sokolova, M.: Factors with Positive and Negative Impact on Learning Organisation. Double-blind peer-reviewed proceedings of the International Scientific Conference Hradec Economic Days 2017 980–985. University of Hradec Kralove, Hradec Kralove (2017)

Economic Aspects of Corporate Education and Use of Advanced Technologies

Libuse Svobodova[✉] and Miloslava Cerna

University of Hradec Kralove,
Rokitanskeho 62, 500 03 Hradec Kralove, Czech Republic
{libuse.svobodova,miloslava.cerna}@uhk.cz

Abstract. The paper focuses on two areas: on employee's skills in the use of modern technologies and on economic aspects of corporation training. National statistics shows that the use of modern technologies has a steadily increasing trend. Individuals in the Czech Republic use most often the Internet. A text processor followed by a table processor and a presentation software are most frequently used office tools. Indicators from the Network readiness index that are evaluated by World Economic Forum are used to gain a global ranking view. Results that relate to network readiness index correspond to results on the computer skills and usage of technologies by individuals in the Czech Republic.

Utilization of information technologies by employed people in the Czech Republic and development of their computer skills within hybrid learning concept are discussed in this paper. Individuals use modern technologies as a main trendy communication tool in various fields, including educational purposes. Companies incorporate into their portfolio various kinds of training materials in the electronic form. These materials are offered in off-line version, on-line version, in LMS, within web-portals or within groups in social networks. Factors influencing the issue of education in the business environment and ways of its financing are described.

Keywords: Economics aspects · Education in corporation · Hybrid learning
Network readiness index · Technologies

1 Introduction

Nowadays ICT (Information and Communication Technologies) and ICT competencies of individuals play an irreplaceable role in the process of education. Among ICT technologies that fruitfully deal with education are web portals with a specific topic, learning management systems, forums, blogs and other websites. Face-to-face training courses can be and are often connected with use of technologies and elements of hybrid learning. Significant increase in utilization of modern technologies in the Czech Republic can be seen since 1993.

The indisputable ICT boom has got reflected in the corporation training, as well. New ways and new approaches to further education corresponding to current ICT potential are being developed [1, 2]. There are huge investments into ICT in the European Union countries connected with the expansion of modern technologies,

© Springer Nature Switzerland AG 2018
T. Hao et al. (Eds.): SETE 2018, LNCS 11284, pp. 117–126, 2018.
https://doi.org/10.1007/978-3-030-03580-8_13

growing need for getting information quickly and fast processing of operations. The ICT has brought not only a rise in overall efficiency and productivity, but it is also contributing to GDP growth.

Within 25 years, the situation in ICT utilization by the individuals in the Czech Republic has crucially changed. Computer literacy has become nearly an inseparable part of private and professional life [3]. Gaining information from various fields, processing information, reading on-line news, booking accommodation, etc. are no exceptional skills. According to official statistics, sharing information and communication with others via social networks represent main reasons why people use the Internet and technologies on various devices like a computer, a notebook or a mobile phone [4].

The authors have been engaged in utilization of technologies, computer literacy of various target groups for a long time within their academic projects [5–11].

Individual states rate their competitiveness with other countries. The World Economic Forum has made comparisons of states all over the world since 2001 [12]. Issue of readiness has also been discussed by Jong-Wha [13], Lin et al. [14], Moorhouse [15], Parasuraman [16], Peltier et al. [17], Richey et al. [18], Scholleová [19] and others.

The paper focuses on two areas: on student's or employee's skills in the use of modern technologies and on the economic aspects of corporation training. In daily life it looks like that the generation of students and people working in the managerial positions or in the offices nowadays are considered to be familiar with digital and electronic technology. Therefore, further education is supposed to be run on the basis of e-learning or hybrid learning. "A hybrid approach to course delivery combines face-to-face classroom instruction with online activities. This approach reduces the amount of seat time in a traditional face-to-face course and moves more of the course delivery online. During classroom instruction time, students can be engaged in authentic, collaborative learning experiences. The online components can include multimedia-enhanced content and channels for ongoing discussion" [20].

2 Methodology and Goal

Presented paper aims to analyze selected issues of current Network Readiness Index of the Czech Republic. A following part is devoted to official statistics from the Czech statistical office focused on the students and individuals 18+. Another discussed category is the level of education of the analyzed group of people. It can be expected that people who have completed high school would like to continue their studies and will be interested in further studies more than people without school-leaving examination. It can also be assumed that people who have reached higher level of education will work in middle or higher management and this is the group we are targeting at. Middle managers are responsible for implementing the top management's policies and plans whereas top management translates the policy into goals, objectives, and strategies, and projects a shared-vision of the future. Therefore, both groups are supposed to be flexible in gaining information, organizing and managing people and processes and to be ready to make instant decisions; all that is nearly impossible without technology support and technology competence.

The discussed topic on the utilization and role of modern technologies with the focus on the students and hybrid learning will be solved in the paper.

Research questions follow:

- Can students and individuals use modern technologies? – (Do students and individuals manage the modern technologies)?
- What type of technologies do they prefer?
- Do they have internet access to share materials?
- What software do they use?
- What are their computer competencies, what skills do they have?

These questions are essential in the preparatory phase of selecting and designing study materials and in deciding which form of education or which approach will be the most convenient for individual groups of potential attendees of computer trainings.

The paper brings an analysis of the technological competitiveness and network readiness of the Czech Republic for the 2012–2016 period and the use of modern technologies for study purposes and hybrid learning by the student's population and population 18+.

The article is based on secondary sources. The secondary sources provide information about network readiness index, professional literature, and information collected from professional press, web sites, discussions and previous participation at professional seminars and conferences related to the chosen subject. Most of the information was gained from the World Economic Forum and the Czech Statistical Office. It was then necessary to select, classify and update accessible relevant information from the numerous published materials that provide the basic knowledge about the selected topic.

One of key terms used in this paper is Network Readiness Index. The World Economic Forum's Networked Readiness Index (NRI), also referred to as Technology Readiness, measures the propensity for countries to exploit the opportunities offered by information and communications technology (ICT). It is published in collaboration with INSEAD (The business school for the world), as part of their annual Global Information Technology Report (GITR). The report is regarded as the most authoritative and comprehensive assessment of how ICT influences the competitiveness and well-being of nations [22].

3 Results

This chapter consists of two parts. Firstly, a global view on the Network Readiness Index in the Czech Republic is provided. Then statistics data and results relating to a selected group of people are presented.

3.1   Global Information Technology Report

Global Information Technology Report reports Network readiness index (NRI) [20]. The Global Information Technology Report 2016 features the latest iteration of the NRI, which assesses the factors, policies and institutions that enable a country to fully leverage (ICTs) for increased competitiveness and well-being. Under the theme Innovating in the Digital Economy, the Report also examines the role of ICTs in driving innovation [21]. Network readiness index consists of 4 sub-indices and 10 pillars that relate to individual topics. Basic construction of NRI is:

- Sub-index A: Environment sub-index
  - 1st pillar: Political and regulatory environment
  - 2nd pillar: Business and innovation environment
- Sub-index B: Readiness sub-index
  - 3rd pillar: Infrastructure and digital content
  - 4th pillar: Affordability
  - 5th pillar: Skills
- Sub-index C: Usage sub-index
  - 6th pillar: Individual usage
  - 7th pillar: Business usage
  - 8th pillar: Government usage
- Sub-index D: Impact sub-index
  - 9th pillar: Economic impacts
  - 10th pillar: Social impacts

Results from selected indicators which encompass business education and utilization of technology are brought in the following part of the paper.

Table 1 visualizes gained results on skills values in the 5th pillar which refers to the education system. Quality of the education system and quality of math and science education reached the similar level in evaluation in 2016. Adult literacy rate in percentages was evaluated only in 2012–2014 in the compared period. There can be seen a positive increasing trend; both analyzed indicators earned better evaluation in 2016 than in 2014. Negative is that quality of the education system was in 2012 and 2013 gained better evaluation than in three following years.

Table 1. 5th pillar – skills value [24–28]

Indicator	2012	2013	2014	2015	2016
Quality of the education system	4.1	3.9	3.7	3.6	3.8
Quality of math and science education	4.1	3.8	4.0	4.1	4.3
Adult literacy rate %	99.0	99.0	99.0	–	–
Total	5.3	5.1	5.3	5.3	5.5

Table 2 illustrates gained data technological equipment, subscription and use of virtual social networks by the individuals. An increasing trend can be seen in all followed areas. The only exception is 2015; there was a slight percentage decrease in the Internet users and households with a personal computer. Mobile-cellular telephone subscriptions/100 pop. reached the highest levels in 2012. The use of virtual social networks decreased slightly by 0.1% in 2016.

Table 2. 6th pillar – individual usage value [24–28]

Indicator	2012	2013	2014	2015	2016
Mobile-cellular telephone subscr./100 pop.	137.2	123.4	126.9	127.7	129.5
Internet users % pop.	68.8	73.0	75.0	74.1	79.7
Households with a personal computer %	64.1	69.9	75.0	73.9	78.5
Households with Internet access %	60.5	66.6	71.0	72.6	78.0
Fixed-broadband Internet subscr./100 pop.	14.5	15.8	16.4.	17.0	27.9
Mobile-broadband subscriptions/100 pop.	43.1	43.4	52.1	52.3	66.7
Use of virtual social networks	5.8	6.0	6.0	6.0	5.9
Total	4.6	5.2	5.3	5.3	5.8

3.2 Computer Skills and Technical Equipment in the Czech Republic

Based on the data gained from the national Czech statistical office, it can be seen that people who are potential further education participants and attendees of various courses have a computer or other device, which is a mobile phone most frequently. This kind of device enables them access to the Internet and further channels to the education [29].

Companies can incorporate into their portfolio various kinds of training materials in the electronic form. These materials might be offered in off-line version, on-line version, in LMS, within web-portals or within groups in social networks [5, 6].

The graph in Fig. 1 shows utilization of a computer (personal computer, notebook or tablet) by individuals in the Czech Republic within a time period 2012 till 2017. Rising trends is clearly visible in the graph. Also linear trend has rising tendency.

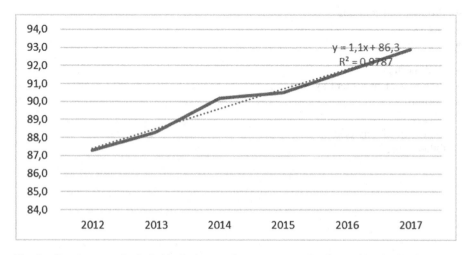

Fig. 1. Computer use by individuals (personal computer, notebook or tablet) in 2012 to 2017

According to [23], individuals in the Czech Republic used mostly mobile tele-phone, notebook and personal computer, as for tablet it was used less frequently. There was recorded a big shift in usage of tablets. In 2012 the level of usage was rather low but it increased by 40%. However, 80.3% students use notebook, which is twice more than use of a tablet. A rise in tablets use was bigger than in notebooks. The reason may be a partial saturation of the market by the notebook technology. Almost all students can transfer files between computers or other devices. Fewer students, to be precise 73.5% of them in 2017 were able to install software or applications and significantly smaller number relates to their skills in programming which reaches only 11.4% [29]. A text processor is the most often used office software followed by a table processor and a presentation software [29].

4   Economic Aspects of Education in the Business Environment

There are various factors influencing the issue of education in the business environ-ment: position of the employee in the company hierarchy, his/her reached level of education, his/her specialization and time when he/she accomplished their studies.

Costs are connected with payment for the education. It is necessary to calculate not only the costs of the course, learning materials, in some case travelling costs but also time of employee that he/she devotes to studying instead of working. Those costs can be also named opportunity costs.

Type of education influences the costs. These types can be categorized as follows: According to time:

- Study in the own (personal) time
- Study in the work time

According to sources:

- Professional journals
- Books
- Websites

- Web portals
- Learning management system
- Forums
- Blogs
- Other social networks
- Other sources

- Face-to-face course provided by a professional organization outside the company in special educational centers
- Face-to-face course at university or other school
- Seminars, conference, shows
- Consultation with experts
- Corporate education

A following table presents proposed solutions to education in the business environment. Solutions are divided on less expensive and more expensive solutions. It is necessary to say that there is no 100% cheapest solution. Due to the fact, that there are many factors influencing the costs, we can only search for optimum solution. It always depends on the concrete situation and conditions in the current time, on the depth and complexity of education, duration and customization. It is possible to state that professional journals, books, web portals, forums, blogs, information on selected websites, which are professionally focused, are basically the less expensive solutions. More costly solutions have precious advantages especially in possibility to be tailored to fit the thoughtfully stated requirements of the company. These solutions include face-to-face courses, courses in learning management system, hybrid learning which combines features and benefits from both educational forms, consultations, seminars, conferences and exhibitions where active involvement of participants plays a vital role [5].

Table 3. Education in business environment and its solutions

Less expensive solutions	More expensive solutions
Professional journals	Learning management system
Books	Courses face-to-face
Web portals	Seminars
Forums	Conference
Blogs	Shows and exhibitions
Other social networks like Facebook, YouTube, Instagram etc.	Consultation with experts
Other websites	

Ways of financing of corporation educations follows. If companies decide to pay for training, they can use the 3 basic and most used options to include training in company accounts. They are:

- Subsidies
- Tax deductible expenses (costs)
- Social fund

Subsidies can be obtained from many listed (offered) training programs not only from the Czech Republic but also from the European Union. Their advantage is that they are generally the most cost-effective for the company because they either cover the full amount or 85% of the eligible expenses. The tax expenditures for the education of employees according to § 24 section (2) j item 3 of the Income Tax Act the expenses (costs) for education are considered to be tax expenditures, if they are related to the subject of the employer's activity or the employment of an employee. Revenue can therefore be reduced by Expenses (costs) incurred to achieve, secure and maintain taxable income. Professional training in the field in which the entrepreneur or company operate and where acquired knowledge is used to achieve (or maintain or secure) income is a wholly legitimate tax-deductible expense. Expenditures are not limited (but it is assumed that entrepreneurs will behave economically and the price and quality of the training corresponds to business opportunities). Tax expenditures may also include wage compensation for work allowances, or study allowance provided under a special regulation (Decree No. 140/1968 Coll., On Work and Economic Security for Students at Employment, as amended by Act No. 188/1988 Coll. Decree No. 197/1994 Coll.). Among these expenses rank also the costs for participation in the training and study of the employee at work in order to widen and improve the qualification for the performance of the work. To fund training, the Social Fund can be used as a motivational element. Disadvantage of the use of Social Fund, however, is that this kind of financing doesn't affect the economic outcomes, and companies can not then reduce the income tax base to pay for training. This makes it less advantageous for entrepreneurs from the point of view of financing and taxes.

5 Conclusion and Discussion

10 indicators from Network Readiness Index were evaluated in the article. Two indicators, which were Quality of the education system and Mobile-cellular telephone subscriptions, reached slightly worse values in 2016 than in 2012. Results show that the Czech Republic is steadily getting better in skills and usage of technologies by individuals in the last five years.

Data from the Czech Statistical Office showed that employed people are prepared to use modern technologies. Hybrid learning is currently widely used approach in further education and it also fits requirements of companies.

As for financing, the company can report its costs on training in various ways. There is a widely applied option to use a social fund that is a kind of an employees' benefit. Employees can get their holidays, sport activities, trainings, etc. payed from this fund. However, it is up to the company, the company sets the rules, which benefits will be promoted [5]. That is why there are such differences among companies in financing employee's activities including educational trainings.

The Department of Human Resources is responsible for the training in bigger companies. However, as for smaller companies training as a specific activity is unfortunately quite often neglected.

Acknowledgement. This paper is supported by specific project No. 2103 "Investment evaluation within concept Industry 4.0" at Faculty of Informatics and Management, University of Hradec Kralove, Czech Republic.

References

1. Pikhart, M.: Implementing new global business trends to intercultural business communication. Proc. Soc. Behav. Sci. **152**, 950–953 (2014)
2. Pikhart, M.: Current intercultural management trends in the global world: knowledge transfer and competitiveness. Hradec Economic Days 2013 - Economic Development and Management Region, Hradec Kralove, Gaudeamus (2013)
3. Cerna, M.: Development of acceptance and utilization of social software applications in higher and further education-case study. In: 8th International Technology, Education and Development Conference INTED 2014, Valencia, Spain, pp. 4300–4307 (2014)
4. Llorente-Barroso, C., Vinaras-Abad, M., Sancher-Valle, M.: Internet and the elderly: enhancing active ageing. Comunicar **45**, 29–36 (2015)
5. Cerna, M., Svobodova, L.: Insight into social networks with focus on corporation setting. Hradecké ekonomické dny 2013, pp. 24–30. Hradec Králové, Gaudeamus (2013)
6. Cerna, M., Svobodova, L.: Current social media landscape. In: Efficiency and Responsibility in Education, Prague, pp. 80–86 (2013)
7. Cerna, M., Manenova, M.: Utilization of web portals and their services: a case study. In: Proceedings of the 9th European Conference on E-learning, Porto, vol. 1, pp. 140–145 (2010)
8. Cerna, M., Poulova, P.: Role of social media in academic setting awareness, utilization and willingness. In: 11th IEEE International Conference on Emerging Elearning Technologies and Applications, Stara Lesna, pp. 59–62 (2013)
9. Svobodová, L.: Technology readiness of the Czech Republic. In: Hradecké ekonomické dny 2010, pp. 126–130. Hradec Králové, Gaudeamus (2010)
10. Svobodová, L.: Technology readiness of the Czech Republic, international days of statistics and economics 2015. In: Proceedings of the 9th International Days of Statistics and Economics, (MSED), pp. 1518–1527 (2015)
11. Svobodova, L., Hedvicakova, M.: Technological readiness of the czech republic and the use of technology. In: Themistocleous, M., Morabito, V. (eds.) EMCIS 2017. LNBIP, vol. 299, pp. 670–678. Springer, Cham (2017). https://doi.org/10.1007/978-3-319-65930-5_53
12. Word Economic Forum, Research, online. (2018). http://www.weforum.org/reports/
13. Jong-Wha, L.: Education for technology readiness: prospects for developing countries. J. Hum. Dev. **2**(1), 115–151 (2001)
14. Lin, C., Shih, H.Y., Sher, P.J.: Integrating technology readiness into technology acceptance: the TRAM model. Psychol. Mark. **24**(7), 641–657 (2007)
15. Moorhouse, D.J.: Detailed definitions and guidance for application of technology readiness levels. J. Aircr. **39**(1), 190–192 (2002)
16. Parasuraman, A.: Technology readiness index (TRI) a multiple-item scale to measure readiness to embrace new technologies. J. Serv. Res. **2**(4), 307–320 (2000)
17. Peltier, J.W., Zhao, Y., Schibrowksy, J.A.: Technology adoption by small businesses: an exploratory study of the interrelationships of owner and environmental factors. Int. Small Bus. J. **30**, 406–431 (2012)
18. Richey, R.G., Daugherty, P.J., Roath, A.S.: Firm technological readiness and complementarity capabilities impacting logistics service competency and performance. J. Bus. Logistics. **28**(1), 195–228 (2007)
19. Scholleová, H.: Czech Republic innovations evaluated by summary innovation index. In: Hradecké ekonomické dny, pp. 203–210. Universita Hradec Králové, Hradec Králové (2009)

20. What is Hybrid Learning? http://sites.psu.edu/hybridlearning/what-is-hybrid/. Accessed 10 Feb 2018

21. Top management. http://www.businessdictionary.com/definition/top-management.html. Accessed 10 Feb 2018

22. Network readiness index. http://reports.weforum.org/global-information-technology-report-2016/networked-readiness-index. Accessed 10 Feb 2018

23. The global information technology report. https://www.weforum.org/reports/the-global-information-technology-report-2016. Accessed 10 Feb 2018

24. Network readiness index Czech Republic (2016). http://reports.weforum.org/global-information-technology-report-2016/economies/#indexId=NRI&economy=CZE. Accessed 10 Feb 2018

25. Network readiness index Czech Republic (2015). http://reports.weforum.org/global-information-technology-report-2015/economies/#economy=CZE. Accessed 10 Feb 2018

26. Network readiness index Czech Republic (2014). http://reports.weforum.org/global-information-technology-report-2014/#section=countryeconomy-profiles-czechrepublic. Accessed 10 Feb 2018

27. Network readiness index Czech Republic (2013). http://reports.weforum.org/global-information-technology-report-2013/#section=countryeconomy-profiles-czechrepublic. Accessed 10 Feb 2018

28. Network readiness index Czech Republic (2012). http://reports.weforum.org/global-information-technology-2012/#section=countryeconomy-profiles-czechrepublic. Accessed 10 Feb 2018

29. Information society in figures – (2017). https://www.czso.cz/csu/czso/information-society-in-figures-2014–2016. Accessed 10 Feb 2018

Investigating the Validity of Using Automated Writing Evaluation in EFL Writing Assessment

Ying Xu[⊠]

School of Foreign Languages, South China University of Technology,
Guangzhou 510641, China
xuying@scut.edu.cn

Abstract. This study aims to follow an argument-based approach to validation of using automated essay evaluation (AWE) system with the example of *Pigai*, a Chinese AWE program, in English as a Foreign Language (EFL) writing assessment in China. First, an interpretive argument was developed for its use in the course of College English. Second, three sub-studies were conducted to seek evidence of claims related to score evaluation, score generalization, score explanation, score extrapolation and feedback utilization. Major findings are: (1) *Pigai* yields scores that are accurate indicators of the quality of a test performance sample; (2) its scores are consistent across tasks in the same form; (3) its scoring features represent the construct of interest to some extent, yet problems of construct under-representation and construct-irrelevant features still exist; (4) its scores are consistent with teachers' judgments of students' writing ability; (5) its feedback has a positive impact on students' development of writing ability, but to some extent. These results reveal that AWE can only be used as a supplement to human evaluation, but can never replace the latter.

Keywords: *Pigai* · Automated essay evaluation · Writing assessments

1 Introduction

With the technology boom in the recent years, automated writing evaluation (AWE) has developed rapidly because it can provide immediate feedback on students' essays to a large EFL writing class. However, the traditional approach to AWE validity mainly focuses on the system's psychometric properties while classroom users' responses and perceptions are neglected [1]. The typical way to validating an AWE system is to calculate the correlation between machine scores and human scores. To date, almost all vendor-sponsored research claim a high correlation coefficient for systems such as *PEG*, *IEA*, and *E-rater* [2]. As a response to Warschauer's call for more independent research, a handful of researchers try to introduce the latest

This work was supported by the Ministry of Education, P. R. China (Number 17YJC740102) and the Fundamental Research Funds for the Central Universities (Number 2018PY22).

© Springer Nature Switzerland AG 2018
T. Hao et al. (Eds.): SETE 2018, LNCS 11284, pp. 127–137, 2018.
https://doi.org/10.1007/978-3-030-03580-8_14

development in test validity to the field of AWE. For example, Xi [3] raised ten fundamental questions for automated scoring systems. On its basis, a framework for evaluation and use of automated scoring was built [4], which clarifies inferences in terms of explanation, evaluation, extrapolation, generalization, and utilization within an argument-based validity. Given that this framework requires various categories of data, empirical studies which have adopted the framework are scanty.

In China, *Pigai* (www.pigai.org) was developed specifically to assess Chinese EFL learners' writing [5]. At the time of writing, it was reported that *Pigai* was used by over 1,000 universities in China. The scoring engine, calibrated against a large corpus of human-scored essays, can generate a score and feedback for a new essay by measuring the distance between features within the essay produced and a corpus of pre-scored essays, using an algorithm. If there is no record of a prompt in the corpus, the system will evaluate essays with a default scoring formula [6]: Total score = Vocabulary (43%) + Sentence (28%) + Structure (22%) + Content relevance (7%). However, there is no information about the rater identity and the scoring algorithm. After submitting an essay, *Pigai* can generate feedback containing three parts: (1) a holistic score; (2) general comments in terms of vocabulary, sentence, structure, and content relevance, and uses a bar graph to show the strength of the essay; (3) an analysis of linguistic features at the sentence level including errors, warnings, learning tips, and suggested usage. Despite its widespread use, there is little research on the validity evidence for improving writing ability. Therefore, this study aims to addresses this gap by adopting the framework for evaluation and use of AWE.

2   A Working Framework

A working framework of interpretive argument (Fig. 1) was developed to evaluate validity of using *Pigai* in the EFL writing assessment.

Three studies are conducted to collect evidence for assumptions in the validity argument. Two issues are worth mentioning here. First, as CET4 is the largest language test in China [7], the CET4 writing rubric was used because of its familiarity with students. Second, as *Pigai* doesn't reveal its scoring engine as *E-rater* does, we have to infer text features adopted by the system by analyzing its feedback.

3   Study 1

3.1   Research Purpose

This study aims to collect evidence of evaluation and explanation in the interpretive argument. Two research questions are raised: (1) What is the reliability of *Pigai* scores? (including A1, A2 and A3 in Fig. 1) (2) Does the *Pigai* feedback include text features described in the CET4 rubric? (including C1 and C2).

Inference: Warrant   Assumptions (numbered under each warrant)

E. Utilization: *Pigai's* feedback helps to promote students' writing ability.

    1. Students hold positive views of using *Pigai* in writing assessment.

    2. Students are willing to use *Pigai* in their writing process.

    3. Teachers consider *Pigai* useful to promote students' writing ability.

    4. Teachers are willing to let students use *Pigai* in their writing process.

D. Extrapolation: *Pigai* score is consistent with independent measures of students' writing ability.

    1. *Pigai* score is consistent with teachers' rankings of students' writing ability.

C. Explanation: *Pigai* score reflects curriculum requirements of writing ability.

    1. *Pigai* feedback contains rubric-relevant text features.

    2. *Pigai* feedback does not contain rubric-irrelevant text features.

B. Generalization: *Pigai* score is consistent across various instances of the same error.

    1. There is no significant difference between *Pigai* scores given to the same students with different tasks.

A. Evaluation: *Pigai* is accurate to score students writing performance.

    1. *Pigai* score distributes consistently with the criterion score.

    2. *Pigai* score correlates significantly with the criterion score.

    3. *Pigai's* severity. internal consistency and bias against students are acceptable.

Fig. 1. Inferences, warrants, and assumptions in the validity argument for using *Pigai* in writing assessment

3.2   Method

Materials and Instruments

CET4 writing adopts a holistic 15-point rubric including five score bands [7]. It describes four constructs including coherence, topic relevance, comprehensibility, and accuracy. It uses five scores (2-, 5-, 8-, 11-, and 14-point) to anchor raters' mental representation. In practice, the range finders (i.e., five benchmark essays provided by National College English Testing Committee (NCETC) to anchor raters' judgment) would be provided to guide rating training. 70 range finders between 2007 and 2014 were used because they were calibrated with preset scores by NCETC. After inputting these essays to the system, *Pigai* scores and feedback can be obtained.

Data Analysis

First, the Multi-faceted Rasch Model (MFRM) analysis for the ratings was conducted in FACETS version No. 3.58 [8]. Since CET4 essay rating adopts a holistic scale, then a two-facet mathematic model was built, where candidates and raters (including *Pigai* and the Criterion) were specified as facets.

$$Log\left(P_{ijk}/P_{ijk-1} = B_i - C_j - F_k\right) \tag{1}$$

P_{ijk} is the probability of examinee (i) being awarded a rating of (k) when rated by rater (j); P_{ijk-1} is the probability of examinee (i) being awarded a rating of (k − 1) when rated by rater (j); B_i represents the ability of examinee (i); C_j represents the severity of rater (j); and F_k represents the step difficulty of being awarded a rating of (k) relative to (k − 1) along the rating scale.

Second, feedback generated by *Pigai* was first segmented into independent "idea units" [9], then coded following guidelines of Grounded Theory [10]. In total, the feedback was segmented into 347 idea units. As a reliability check, all data were coded by a research assistant and the author separately. The inter-coder reliability reached 95.10%. Disagreements were resolved through negotiation.

3.3   Results

Evidence of Score Evaluation

Table 1 shows the descriptive results of *Pigai* and Criterion scores.

Table 1. Descriptive results of *Pigai* scores

	M	SD	Frequency				
			2-point band	5-point band	8-point band	11-point band	14-point band
Pigai score	7.86	3.16	3	20	28	4	15
Criterion score	8.00	4.27	14	14	14	14	14

As shown in Table 1, *Pigai* scores distribute more concentrated than Criterion scores, particularly in the 5-point and 8-point bands, suggesting the existence of central tendency. The inter-rater reliability was measured by the Spearman rank correlation coefficient as scores are not normally distributed. The result ($\rho_s = 0.865$, n = 70, $p < .001$) suggests that *Pigai* score has a fairly high inter-rater reliability.

MFRM results show that first, *Pigai's* severity (0.02 logits) is near to the Criterion score (−0.02 logits). Both rater separation ratio and reliability of rater separation index reached 0.00. The chi square test value ($\chi^2 = .2$, df = 1, $p > .05$) also shows no significant difference between two groups in terms of severity. Second, the infit value of the *Pigai* score and the Criterion score reached 0.91 and 0.92 respectively, showing that *Pigai* has a good level of internal consistency. Last, the bias analysis revealed that *Pigai* has two biases towards essays, accounting for 1.43% of the total interactions (140) between raters and essays, which is acceptable [11].

Evidence of Score Explanation

Table 2 shows the frequency of each code in *Pigai's* feedback.

According to Table 2, most codes are related with language, such as accuracy (19), variety (17), and cohesion (15), and no code with content, suggesting that *Pigai* focuses on language form. The four text features including coherence, topic relevance, comprehensibility, and accuracy in CET4 writing rubric are the de-facto intended constructs. It was found that rubric-related features only accounts for 33.43% in *Pigai's* feedback, implying the existence of construct irrelevance in *Pigai's* scores.

Table 2. Frequency of codes in the *Pigai's* feedback

Main category	Category	2-point band	5-point band	8-point band	11-point band	14-point band	Total
General impression	Fluidity	1	3	3	1	1	9
Structure	General evaluation	2	2	3	1	0	8
	Paragraphing reasonableness	5	2	2	5	0	14
	Convergence	4	1	0	1	1	7
	Compactedness	5	4	4	2	9	24
Language	Variety	17	16	17	15	9	74
	Complexity	10	20	18	24	26	98
	Appropriateness	1	1	3	0	1	6
	Accuracy	19	16	5	9	5	54
	Cohesion	15	11	8	9	10	53

Nonetheless, *Pigai's* feedback covers three kinds of rubric-related features, showing that *Pigai* scoring features represent the construct of interest to some extent. As *Pigai* adopts a heavy percentage of form-related features, issues like whether students would adopt certain form-dominated writing strategy are worth analyzing.

4   Study 2

4.1   Research Purpose

This study aims to collect evidence of generalization and utilization. Two research questions are raised: (1) Can *Pigai* score be generated to different tasks? (including B1) (2) What are students' attitudes towards *Pigai's* feedback? (including E1 and E2).

4.2   Method

Participants
Sixty-one EFL learners, and one EFL teacher participated in the study. These students, aging between 17 and 19, were from two intact classes (Class A and Class B) at a university in China. They were first-year undergraduate students and were enrolled in a freshman College English course. Class A has 16 males and 15 females, and Class B 14 males and 16 females. They were taught by one EFL teacher with over ten years' experience in teaching English as a foreign language.

Materials
Two writing tasks (Appendix 1 and 2) were selected as after-class assignment. They are typical CET4 writing tasks, which require students to write an argumentative essay with no less than 150 words.

Procedure

The study adopted a counter-balanced design across two weeks to control the order effect. Class A finished Task 1 in Week 1 and Task 2 in Week 2, while the order of tasks was reversed for Class B. At the end of research, a semi-structured interview was arranged on an individual basis. Two students (one male and one female) from each class were purposively chosen because of their willingness to participate. S1 to S4 were used to preserve their anonymity. The following questions were designed to guide students: (1) What effect does *Pigai* feedback have on your writing? (2) Are you willing to receive *Pigai* feedback in the future? Why?

Data Analysis

As the interval between two tasks is just one week, it could be operationally argued that students' writing ability does not change. Therefore, quantitative analysis was first conducted to determine descriptive statistics of *Pigai* scores for the two tasks, and the correlation coefficient between them. Then, a paired-sample t-test was conducted to test whether the means of *Pigai* scores for two tasks are equal. Finally, the interview protocols were analyzed thematically [12].

4.3   Results

Evidence of Score Generalization

Results of descriptive analysis suggest that *Pigai* scores of Task 1 (M = 12.61, SD = 0.56) is close to Task 2 (M = 12.52, SD = 0.65). The Kolmogorov-Smirnov test result ($p > .05$) shows that the two sets of scores are normally distributed. Pearson correlation coefficient between the two sets of scores reached .443 (n = 61, $p < .001$). Results of the paired-sample t-test (t = 1.00, df = 60, $p > .05$) suggest that there is no significant difference between the two tasks.

Evidence of Feedback Utilization (Students' Attitudes)

Pigai's feedback was deemed useful particularly in the three aspects. First, it helps students identify errors quickly. For example, the following quote from S1 suggests that students appreciate *Pigai's* ability to detect errors. *"Pigai's feedback really helps, because I can quickly know errors in my essay, such as spelling error, phrase error and grammatical error."* (S1). Second, *Pigai* provides information of highly scored essays, which improve students awareness of how to score high. In one example, S2 shared such experience. *"Pigai feedback is illuminating because it indicates clearly which expression is key to scoring high. I remember that Pigai pointed out that 'have … confidence' is a common collocation and appeared 7,096 times in the corpus'. Since then, I began to use the structure."* (S2) Last, *Pigai's* provision of referenced synonyms is deemed beneficial to enlarge students' vocabulary size. S4's comment below shows clearly that this information helps students vary their expressions. *"In Task 1, Pigai told me that 'prepare for' can be replaced by 'brace for' in that context, which was useful to improve the lexical capacity."* (S4)

Nonetheless, the interviewees also queried the effectiveness of *Pigai's* feedback. First, *Pigai's* benefit is quite limited as it is not able to provide any information about content. A common disadvantage is pointed out by S1. *"Pigai's feedback focuses on language form such as spelling and collocation, while ignores other writing components like content, layout, and logic."* (S1) Second, the most common negative perception is being too general to act upon. S4 commented clearly below. *"Pigai commented that my article does not read fluidly and advised me to use more linking words. However, it didn't specify the position. I was left puzzled."* (S4)

Moreover, all students expressed their willingness to receive *Pigai's* feedback in the future because *"It can enhance my collocation ability"* (S2), *"I know some techniques how to achieve a good score"* (S3), *"I cannot receive such abundant and timely feedback from my teacher."* (S4), and *"I can promote my lexical ability"* (S1).

5 Study 3

5.1 Research Purpose

This study aims to collect evidence of extrapolation and utilization. Two questions are raised: (1) What is the correlation coefficient between *Pigai's* scores and teachers' rankings of student writing ability? (including D1) (2) What are teachers' attitudes towards *Pigai's* feedback? (including E3 and E4).

5.2 Method

Participants
722 EFL learners and their seven EFL teachers (T1 to T7) participated in the study. These students, ranging in age from 17 to 19, were from 14 intact classes at a university in China. They were first-year undergraduate students and were enrolled in the same course like Study 2. Each teacher taught two classes. After writing on *Pigai* for one year, students and teachers were well informed of the *Pigai's* feedback.

Materials and Instruments
First, students' writing texts in the course exam of the first year were obtained. The task prompt can be found in Appendix 3. Second, teachers' rankings of these students' writing ability were solicited. Last, a questionnaire (Appendix 4) was administered to the seven teachers.

Data Analysis
First, the Spearman rank correlation coefficient was calculated to determine the relationship between *Pigai's* scores and teachers' rankings. Second, the quantitative part of teachers' response to the questionnaire (mainly Question 1 and 3) was analyzed descriptively. Last, the qualitative part of teachers' response to the questionnaire (mainly Question 2) was analyzed following Grounded Theory [10]. As a result, teachers' responses can be segmented into 62 idea units. Those codings for and against using *Pigai's* feedback amount to 33 and 29 respectively. The coding reliability between the research assistant and the author reached 93.55%, suggesting the creditability of coding results.

5.3   Results

Evidence of Score Extrapolation

It was found that the Spearman rank correlation coefficients between *Pigai's* scores and teachers' rankings for each class ranged between 0.39 ($p < .01$) and 0.70 ($p < .01$), which suggested that *Pigai* scores have substantial relationship with teachers' rankings. This result was also cross-validated by teachers' responses to Question 1 in the questionnaire, where all teachers considered that *Pigai* score was largely consistent with their observations of students' writing ability.

Evidence of Feedback Utilization (Teachers' Attitudes)

Teachers' attitudes toward using *Pigai* in the classroom can be summarized with Table 3. All teachers expressed their willingness to let students receive *Pigai's* feedback as far as Question 3 in the questionnaire is concerned.

Table 3. The coding framework of teachers' attitudes

Code	Example
Advantage	
1. Able to identify errors	"*Pigai* is able to diagnose some spelling errors." (T1)
2. Enrich assessment methods	"As teachers can set sample essays for students' reference, and students can realize their disadvantages during the revising process, *Pigai* thus enriches the assessment method." (T5)
3. Improve vocabulary	"*Pigai's* feedback on synonyms is quite useful." (T3)
4. Develop the habit of revising	"Writing on *Pigai* can help students revise their own performances from time to time, which is good to form a good habit." (T7)
5. Stimulate interest	"Students become more interested in writing." (T4)
6. Facilitate learning by revising	"A student revised the essay over 70 times on *Pigai*. He knows his writing problems more deeply in the process, which cannot be achieved by relying on teachers' corrective feedback." (T7)
7. Enable to write more	"Students have more chances to write, as compared with the traditional writing instruction." (T2)
Disadvantage	
1. Difficult to understand	"*Pigai's* feedback on grammar is sometimes puzzling." (T6)
2. Difficult to act upon	"Students have no idea how to revise based on *Pigai's* feedback because some of them are too general and ambiguous." (T2)
3. Inaccurate judgment	"Some grammar feedback contains erroneous information." (T6)
4. Narrow down the construct	"*Pigai* feedbacks only on form-related features, which are just part of writing ability." (T2)
5. Limited to boost learning	"Relying solely on *Pigai's* feedback can have a limited effect to promote students' writing." (T4)

6 Discussion and Conclusion

The main findings of the research are summarized below:

First, *Pigai* yields scores that are accurate indicators of the quality of a test performance sample (including Assumptions A1, A2, and A3), *Pigai* yields scores that are sufficiently consistent across tasks in the same form (including B1), and *Pigai* yields scores that are consistent with teachers' judgments of students' writing ability (including D1). However, *Pigai* scores tend to be more centralized and distribute more narrowly than the criterion scores. There are some possible reasons. First, *Pigai's* scoring features are predictive of scores awarded by human raters. As *Pigai* derived the score of an essay based on a large corpus of human-scored essays, the scoring algorithm can help *Pigai* extract distinctive features and ensure its reliability. Second, the task prompts used in this study are with similar genre and structure, which helps *Pigai* achieve a good reliability across prompts. Finally, as CET4 writing rubric emphasizes language rather than content, students would give priority to producing texts with accurate language. Under the context where all AWE system can only judge surface features, *Pigai's* scoring reliability would be improved.

Second, *Pigai* scoring features represent the construct of interest to some extent, yet problems of construct under-representation and construct-irrelevance still exist. As *Pigai's* feedback is deemed general and opaque by most users, its effect on improving students' writing ability is doubtful. It would be better for *Pigai* to develop both general and prompt-specific modeling for scoring. In addition, *Pigai* is suggested to provide clear definition and specific example of certain text features in the feedback, such as "convergence" and "compactedness" in Table 2.

Finally, *Pigai* generates feedback that helps students' development of writing ability, but to some extent (including E1 and E4). The root cause may lie in the feedback explanation of *Pigai*. Fundamentally, a computer cannot score essays in the same way like a human rater. It generates scores by devising certain algorithm using natural language processing and so on, rather than drawing on certain learning theory or writing theory. Therefore, there are still a number of doubts and oppositions against its application to L2 writing assessment [1]. As conceptualization of the writing construct is narrowed down using an AWE system, students may develop a primarily formalist approach to writing, i.e. writing to a machine rather than writing to a human. In that case, the authenticity of writing instruction and assessment would be seriously violated. Considering that AWE can never replace the role of human in the writing assessment, students should be trained to conduct other forms of assessment such as peer assessment and self-assessment for their writing.

There are several limitations. First, all inferences focus on scores except utilization, which are concerned with feedback. Therefore, investigating *Pigai's* feedback in terms of evaluation, generalization, explanation and extrapolation is warranted. Second, as all the task prompts are with the same genre (i.e. argumentative), the study should be replicated with different text types. Last, none of the sub-studies provided the result related to the system's effectiveness on affecting students' writing performance, which should be investigated further in the future.

Appendix 1: Task 1 (A Technological Invention)

Write an essay of no less than 150 words about a technological invention. Your writing should include four points: 1. An introduction of the invention. 2. Its positive impact on peoples' life. 3. Its negative impact on people's life. 4. Your opinion.

Appendix 2: Task 2 (Fame – Good or Evil?)

Write an essay of no less than 150 words on the topic "Fame-Good or Evil?" Your paper should cover the following points: 1. The advantages of being famous. 2. The disadvantages of being famous. 3. Your attitude towards fame.

Appendix 3: The Internet and Our Daily Lives

Write an essay of no less than 150 words on the topic "The Internet and Our Daily Lives". Your paper should include: 1. Internet is important in our daily lives. 2. Internet has also disadvantages. 3. What shall we do to make better use of Internet?

Appendix 4: A Questionnaire of Teachers' Attitudes Towards *Pigai*

1. Is *Pigai* score consistent with your observation of students' writing ability?
   A. Consistent B. Largely consistent C. Largely inconsistent D. Inconsistent
2. Is *Pigai's* feedback beneficial to improve students' writing ability? Why?
3. Would you like to let students receive *Pigai's* feedback in the future? (Yes/No).

References

1. Warschauer, M.: Automated writing evaluation: defining the classroom research agenda. Lang. Teach. Res. **10**, 1–24 (2006)
2. Valenti, S., Neri, F., Cucchiarelli, A.: An overview of current research on automated essay grading. J. Inf. Technol. Educ. Res. **2**, 319–330 (2003)
3. Xi, X.: Automated scoring and feedback systems: where are we and where are we heading? Lang. Test. **27**, 291–300 (2010)
4. Williamson, D.M., Xi, X., Breyer, F.J.: A framework for evaluation and use of automated scoring. Educ. Meas.: Issues Pract. **31**, 2–13 (2012)
5. Zhang, Z.: Student engagement with computer-generated feedback: a case study. ELT J. **70**, 1–12 (2016)

6. Bai, L., Hu, G.: In the face of fallible AWE feedback: how do students respond? Educ. Psychol. **37**, 67–81 (2017)

7. Zhang, J.: Same text different processing? Exploring how raters' cognitive and meta-cognitive strategies influence rating accuracy in essay scoring. Assessing Writ. **27**, 37–53 (2016)

8. Linacre, J.M.: A User's Guide to FACETS: Rasch-Model Computer Programs. MESA Press, Chicago (2005)

9. Green, A.: Verbal Protocol Analysis in Language Testing Research: A Handbook. Cambridge University Press, Cambridge (1998)

10. Glaser, B.G., Strauss, A.L.: The Discovery of Grounded Theory: Strategies for Qualitative Research. Aldine de Gruyter, Chicago (1967)

11. McNamara, T.F.: Measuring Second Language Performance. Longman, London (1996)

12. Miles, M.B., Huberman, A.M.: Qualitative Data Analysis: An Expanded Sourcebook. Sage, Thousand Oaks (1994)

Emerging Technologies and Assessment Preferences in Learning English Through CLIL/EMI

Ivana Simonova[✉]

University of Jan Evangelista Purkyne, Pasteurova 3544/1,
40096 Usti nad Labem, Czech Republic
ivana.simonova@ujep.cz

Abstract. Results of research on students' assessment preferences reflecting their learning styles are presented in the article. The research was conducted at the Faculty of Informatics and Management, University of Hradec Kralove, Czech Republic. Totally, 203 students enrolled in Applied Informatics, Information Management, Financial Management and Tourism Management study programmes participated in the research. The main objective was to discover whether there exist correlations between the preferred assessment format and student's learning style. The latest version of LMS Blackboard was exploited to enhance the process of learning English which was conducted via Content and Language Integrated Learning and English as Medium of Instruction approaches. Totally 18 assessment formats were considered by the students; special attention was paid to those enhanced by technologies. Two research tools were exploited to reach the objective: Learning Combination Inventory and Assessment Format Questionnaire. Collected data were processed by multiple regression and ANOVA analyses. Statistically significant correlations between the preferred format of assessment and individual learning style were discovered in two assessment formats: essay writing on the pre-defined topic and group discussion on the problem using the critical analysis, evaluation, application of students' previous knowledge and experience. Results close to significance were found in several other assessment formats. Finally, the results were discussed in relation to findings published within the world context.

Keywords: Assessment · Learning style · Preference · Higher education
English · CLIL · Content and Language Integrated Learning · EMI
English as Medium of Instruction

1 Introduction

Emerging technologies and devices [1] have become widely spread and common tools enhancing the process of learning which is firmly connected to assessing newly gained knowledge. As generally known, students differ in preferences regarding the style of teaching/learning [2]. Latest technologies provide both designers and teachers with such tools which enable them to create learning strategies which meet most of learner's individual needs and preferences. Teachers' task is to exploit the potential of

© Springer Nature Switzerland AG 2018
T. Hao et al. (Eds.): SETE 2018, LNCS 11284, pp. 138–148, 2018.
https://doi.org/10.1007/978-3-030-03580-8_15

technologies effectively. Virtual learning environments (VLE) work as 'all in one' content and software package as they provide tools for displaying the learning content, practising and applying new information, assessment and self-assessment, and administration of the whole process. Within the years of exploitation, both the advantages, barriers/limits relating to technology-enhanced learning have been presented and discussed, starting from the quality and reliability of technological tools and finishing with the contributions to individualized teaching/learning [3]. If students are not provided appropriate space and ways to show what they learned, they might be strongly frustrated and definitely not motivated to further studies. In technology-enhanced learning, his condition is even more important because the student/teacher face-to-face contact during the course may be minimized, e.g. in distance learning through VLE. And, students with different preferences definitely have different ways in mind how to present their knowledge.

Reflecting the above mentioned, the research question is whether there exists any correlation between individual learning style and preference to selected assessment format/s in learning English so as learners could show the teacher what they learned to maximum extent.

2   Theoretical Background

Fast development of ICT affords innovations also in the field of education. Learning, widely understood as a cognitive process of acquiring knowledge and/or skills through studying theory and collecting practical experience, emphasizes the importance of assessment. Technology-enhanced learning suits best to those learners who are independent, able to learn without face-to-face interaction with teachers and other students, using the guiding directions only. They are often lack of time but self-motivated and well-organized, particularly in terms of time, and have good IT skills and appropriate technological equipment. Based on the individual learning styles, students apply various learning strategies, which include not only acquiring new knowledge but they also result in showing the teacher what they learned.

Several well-known theories of learning styles were created, e.g. by Felder [4]; Honey [5]; Mitchell [6], but also less-known ones, e.g. 'Unlocking the will to learn' by Johnston [7] etc. Their reflections in the process of instruction were applied during last few decades so as to maximize the learning results. Either accepted, or rejected by other scientists, as analyzed e.g. by Coffield [3] or Mitchell [6], the learning style theories were applied in teaching various subjects, including foreign languages. Following the Comenius' approach [8], all four phases of the process of instruction, i.e. motivation to learning, explanation the learning content, fixing new knowledge and assessing its increase were under the focus of learning style theories. So as to make the process of learning easier for the learners [9], individual learning preferences should be accommodated. It mostly means that various sources of information and types study materials are used to present the learning content, as well as different teaching methods and activities to fix the new knowledge and apply it in practice [10, 11]. To reach this target, various technology-enhanced tools and (mobile) applications might help, Honey proved [4]. However, this approach has not been applied for assessing learners' knowledge to a larger extent. Moreover, the process of assessment stayed rather unchanged, i.e. identical for all learners, so as to create the same conditions for each learner with the aim to be 'fair'. In practice, such an approach is very 'unfair', as it does not reflect individual learners' preferences [12]. Leither proved that if students were given the possibility to choose an assessment format, the experimental group where assessment preferences were reflected, reached significantly higher test scores compared to the control group [12:417]. Whereas Leither conducted the research in political science, we applied her approach to learning English – this was the only difference between the two research designs.

3   Technology-Enhanced Learning of English and Ways of Assessment at FIM

Having more than 2,500 students, the Faculty of Informatics and Management (FIM), University of Hradec Kralove (UHK), Czech Republic, prepares them in bachelor (Applied Informatics, Financial Management, Tourism Management), master (Information Management) and doctoral (Knowledge Management, System Engineering) study programmes. English is taught in all study programmes within various subjects. Content and Language Integrated learning (CLIL) and/or English as Medium of Instruction (EMI) approaches are applied in all of them. The process of instruction is enhanced by LMS Blackboard, i.e. each subject is supported by one course as minimum.

Applied Informatics (AI), Financial Management (FM) and Information Management (IM) students attend English for Specific Purposes (ESP) for four semesters. Online courses in LMS support the face-to-face instruction, particularly they are used for presenting information, practising and assessing new knowledge, reading, listening, writing, discussing the professional topics etc. Each ESP subject consists of four six-hour blocks per semester, i.e. 24 h, which are taught face-to-face and are mainly devoted to the development of speaking skills.

In ESP1 and ESP3 credits are required for graduation from the subjects – students' knowledge is assessed by written formats, e.g. online multiple-choice test with one correct answer, writing professional CV and a letter responding to an advertisement. For graduation from ESP2 and ESP4 the credit and exam are required; identically to ESP1 and ESP3 credits can be reached through written assessment formats, e.g. writing an essay on pre-defined topic. For oral exam in ESP2 the reading a professional text and discussing the content with teacher is the assessment format, and designing and performing a presentation on a selected professional topic is required for ESP4.

In the Tourism Management (TM) study programme the language knowledge and skills are developed so as the students were able to reach the C1 level of knowledge according to Common European Framework of Reference for Languages [13], e.g. following subjects are taught: English grammar in practice (six semesters); Culture of English-speaking countries (four semesters); History, Geography, Tourism and Sights of English-speaking countries (six semesters); Conversation in English with native speakers (six semesters); Translation and interpretation in practice (three semesters); ESP seminars with special focus on tourism and management (six semesters);

Academic Writing (two semesters); Business English (two semesters); and elective subjects German, Spanish, Italian, Chinese languages, Business Russian (six semesters each).

Students' knowledge for gaining credits is assessed through various written formats, e.g. multiple choice, Yes/No, True/False tests, essays etc. For exams oral assessment formats are exploited (presentation, discussion, open answers to questions from the pre-defined or unknown list of items etc.).

Considering the fact that any of these compulsory assessment formats might not be preferred or accepted by single students regarding to their individual learning style preferences, some formats could be even rejected, which definitely limits the presentation of knowledge, students of all study programmes were addressed to submit their own proposal of assessment formats which (they thought) would enable them to show what they learned to maximum extent. Partial research in this field was conducted in 2016 [14] which focused on three assessment formats (written translation, oral dialogue and oral/written presentation). Consequently, learners expressed their preferences to other 15 assessment formats, both oral and written, individual and group ones. All researched formats are listed in Table 1.

Table 1. Types of assessment formats.

AF	F	Description of assessment format
O1	I	Student is asked a question from the pre-defined list
O2	I	Student is asked a question from the unknown list
O3	I	Student provides answer, teacher listens to the student
O4	I	Teacher-student dialogue starting with question 'What were you most interested in within this subject?', teacher listens to student's answer without interruptions
O5	I	Teacher-student dialogue starting with question 'What were you most interested in within this subject?', teacher asks additional questions to the topic
O6	I	Teacher-student dialogue starting with question 'What were you most interested in this subject?', teacher asks questions to relating topics
O7	G	Students sit at the round table, each answers his/her question
O8	G	Students sit at the round table, each answers his/her question, other students add the answer
O9	G	Students sit at the round table, they answer the same question - each student adds something new to previous student's answers (first-come first-choice principle), several rounds of answers are recommended
O10	G	Students sit at the round table, they focus on the same question (problem) using critical analysis, evaluation, application of previous knowledge and experience etc
W11	I	A question (problem, topic) from pre-defined list is set for essay writing
W12	I	A question (problem, topic) from unknown list is set for essay writing
W13	I	Multiple-choice test with 1 correct answer

(continued)

Table 1. (*continued*)

AF	F	Description of assessment format
W14	I	Multiple-choice test with 2+ correct answers
W15	I	Yes/no test
W16	I	True/false test
W17	G	Students introduce results of the project they worked on during the semester; topic was set at the beginning of the semester
W18	G	Students introduce results of the project they worked on during the exam day; a topic is selected from the unknown list

AF: assessment format; O: oral; W: written; F: form of assessment; I: individual; G: group

4 Research Design

4.1 Research Objective and Hypotheses

The main objective of the research was to discover correlations between individual learning styles and 18 selected assessment formats displayed in Table 1. So as to reach the research objective, the following main hypothesis was set to be tested:

H: There exists the significant correlation between student's individual learning styles and assessment format preference so as new knowledge could be presented to maximum extent

Consequently, 18 partial hypotheses were set (H1 – H18) relating to single assessment formats, e.g.

H1:   There exists the significant correlation between student's individual learning style pattern and preference of O1 individual assessment format (answer to a question from the pre-defined list). ....

H18:   There exists the significant correlation between student's individual learning style pattern and preference of W18 group assessment format (students introduce results of the project they worked on during the exam day; a topic is selected from the unknown list)

4.2 Research Methods and Tools

Reflecting the research objective, two tools were applied: (1) standardized Learning Combination Inventory (LCI) and non-standardized Assessment Format Questionnaire (AFQ).

The LCI was created by Johnston to determine students' learning preferences through 28 statements. Respondents' agreement/disagreement to single statement was expressed on the five-point Likert scale (1 – never ever, 2 – almost never, 3 – sometimes, 4 – almost always, 5 – always). The statements were followed by three open-answer questions; the second one mapping the assessment preferences: Question 1 – What makes assignments frustrating for you?; Question 2 – If you could choose, what would you do to show your teacher what you have learned?; Question 3 – If you were the teacher, how would you have students learn? The final LCI score determines the individual learning style pattern consisting of four approaches to processing informa- tion [7:51–54]: sequential type (applying the step-by-step approach), precise type (focusing on information details), technical type (preferring concrete numbers, figures, diagrams) and confluent type (not following any common way/s but emphasizing student' creativeness and 'marching to a different drummer').

The AFQ was based on Question 2 of LCI, targeting to discover what students' preferences to single assessment formats are. The AFQ was designed in three phases: (1) before the beginning of the research, approximately 300 students in AI, IM, FM and TM study programmes were asked to expressed their opinions in the open-answer format on Question 2 of the LCI (return rate was 84%), (2) their answers were analyzed and a list of 18 assessment formats was set, (3) the list was piloted by another group of 48 FIM students (not a single student piloting the AFQ was included in the research group described below); unclear items were changed and the tool was finalized. Var- ious assessment formats were included – oral and written, individual, pair and team, pre-defined, unknown and their combinations (Table 1). The student's preference to each of these 18 formats was evaluated by listing them in such an order, where a stronger preference came first, i.e. two separate orders were created within oral and written formats (O1 – O10, W11 – W18). The collected data were processed by SPSS statistic software using the multiple regression and ANOVA analyses.

4.3   Research Sample

At the beginning, approximately 300 FIM students enrolled in the study programmes mentioned above. However, from various reasons, finally, only 203 of them completed the whole process of research.

The research sample consisted of 40% of female and 60% of male respondents structured into five age groups (<20 years: 2%; 20–24 years old: 71%; 25–29 years old: 13%; 30–39 years old: 11%; 40+: 3%), studying in the part-time (60%), or full-time form (40%); in four study programmes (AI: 41%; IM: 22%; FM: 10%; TM: 27%).

The learning style preferences are displayed in Table 2.

Table 2. Research sample: learning style preferences according to study programmes and age.

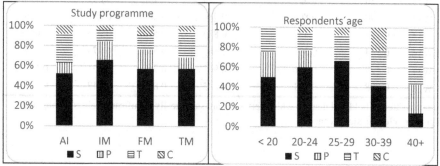

As clearly seen from the figures in Table 3, the sequential type is more or less prevailing within all four criteria compared to precise, technical or confluent information processors. The only exception is the group of 40+ year old respondents where more than 50% of them are of technical type, followed by precise processors and sequential ones; not a single respondent belongs to the confluent processors.

5   Research Results

Data collected by LCI and AFQ were processed by the SPSS statistic software by the method of multiple regression of four variables (i.e. types of processors – sequential, precise, technical, confluent) and 18 types of assessment formats. The multiple correlation coefficient (R) was calculated which describes how tight the correlation between learning style and assessment format is. R reaches values $<-1;1>$; the higher the value, the tighter the correlation. Results are presented in Table 3.

Table 3. Research results.

AF	R	Sig: ANOVA	Sig.: Coefficients			
			Sequential	Precise	Technical	Confluent
O1	0.153	0.324	0.447	0.322	0.515	0.327
O2	0.158	0.293	0.565	0.833	0.094	0.898
O3	0.119	0.595	0.600	0.769	0.349	0.608
O4	0.180	0.170	0.936	0.107	0.960	0.249
O5	0.212	0.062	0.256	0.122	0.268	0.209
O6	0.191	0.122	0.634	0.073	0.068	0.522
O7	0.181	0.165	0.501	0.486	0.365	0.210
O8	0,135	0.458	0.189	0.149	0.282	0.912
O9	0.131	0.491	0.262	0.537	0.932	0.476
O10	0.227	**0.034***	**0.011***	0.313	0.465	0.435
W11	0.177	0.184	0.964	0.145	**0.038***	0.817
W12	0.073	0.904	0.674	0.605	0.367	0.777
W13	0.136	0.459	0.214	0.706	0.801	0.477
W14	0.090	0.809	0.984	0.266	0.961	0.949
W15	0.136	0.457	0.835	0.592	0.236	0.091
W16	0.144	0.396	0.660	0.583	0.073	0.165
W17	0.179	0.176	0.967	0.767	0.304	0.128
W18	0.098	0.761	0.645	0.859	0.847	0.277

Values written in bold and marked with asterisk (*) are statistically significant; values highlighted in grey are close to significance.

In our research all R values were low, which shows low correlation between the learning style and preferred assessment format (see Table 3, column R). The statistical significance, then, could not be clearly proved. Therefore, the ANOVA analysis was conducted (Sig. < 0.05) for all learners (column ANOVA) and separately for each group (column Coefficients). The significant values were discovered:

- with all learners in O10 assessment format (Students sit at the round table, they focus on the same question or problem using critical analysis, evaluation, application of previous knowledge and experience etc.; 0.034; column ANOVA);
- with technical processors in W11 format (A question, problem, topic from pre-defined list is set for essay writing; 0.038; column Coefficients – Technical);
- with sequential types of processors in O10 assessment format (Students sit at the round table, they focus on the same question or problem using critical analysis, evaluation, application of previous knowledge and experience etc.; 0.011; column Coefficients – Sequential).

Moreover, some results were rather close to the Sig. < 0.05:

- in O5 assessment format (Teacher-student dialogue starting with question 'What were you most interested in within this subject?', teacher asks additional questions to the topic) the value of 0.062 for ANOVA was calculated; however, this result was not reflected in single types of processors;
- in O6 assessment format (Teacher-student dialogue starting with question 'What were you most interested in this subject?', teacher asks questions to relating topics) the value of 0.073 was discovered with precise processors and 0.068 with technical processors;
- in O2 (Student is asked a question from the unknown list) the value of 0.094 was calculated with technical processors;
- in W15 (Yes/No test) the value of 0.091 was found out with confluent processors;
- in W16 (True/False test) another close value of 0.073 was discovered also with technical processors.

Reflecting the statistic results displayed in Table 3, we can conclude that two hypotheses were verified:

H10:   There exists the significant correlation between student's individual learning style pattern and preference of O10 individual assessment format (*Students sit at the round table, they focus on the same question/problem using critical analysis, evaluation, application of previous knowledge and experience etc.*) for students of all types (0.034), and particularly for sequential students (0.011).

H11:   There exists the significant correlation between student's individual learning style pattern and preference of W11 group assessment format (*A question, problem, topic from pre-defined list is set for essay writing*) for technical students (0.038)

6   Conclusions

Either expected, or not, the results discovered that the only assessment format was preferred by all learning style learners – i.e. group oral assessment format, when students focus on the question/problem using critical analysis, evaluation, application of previous knowledge and experience etc. (O10); within this result, the strong preference of sequential processors is reflected. For technical students, the group written assessment format of essay on a question, problem, topic from pre-defined list (W11) was preferred. Further on, some (non-significant) preference was given to the assessment formats based on learners' interests (O5; O6) with precise and technical processors. Moreover, technical processors expressed their preference to questions from unknown lists (O2) and written True/False tests (W16). Confluent processors preferred written Yes/No tests (W15), which is rather surprising preference from creative processors who 'march to a different drummer'.

From the view of assessment formats required for gaining credits and exams, the received results are in accord to some extent. Consensus was discovered in writing on a pre-defined topic (CV, letter responding to advertisement; W11), individual (not group) discussion on the professional topic the student read about – the topic was randomly selected from a list of approximately 200 topics by the teacher at the beginning of exam (O2), Yes/No (W15) and True/False (W16) tests. However, presentations required from the students were not preferred, as well as students' interests (O5, O6) were not considered within required assessment formats. At the same time, we expected that e.g. the work on projects (W17, W18) would belong to preferred assessment formats, at least with the confluent processors. However, students seem to give preference to answering questions from pre-defined lists over being creative and applying new knowledge within the exam, providing a new solution and defending it. It means, unfortunately, they give preference to memorizing (by heart) of what they learned over the creative thinking and solving problems at the site. Because of the total amount of respondents, of course, we are aware that these findings cannot be generalized over the whole population; they are valid for the research group only. Despite this, we expected other formats would be preferred by the students, particularly those which were required for developing competences of the 21century learners, as defined by European and Czech educational documents, e.g. [15, 16].

As for the CLIL and EMI approaches which are applied in teaching all English-relating subjects, the discussion on findings within the world context is not easy, as publications dealing with assessment preferences reflecting individual learning styles *and* CLIL and/or EMI are rather rare. Scholars researching CLIL and EMI mainly focus on the internationalization of higher education, not on the individualization of this process and adjusting its assessment to learners' preferences. Emerging technologies can play this role, e.g. interactive applications enhancing learners' interest, active learning etc. as proved e.g. by Chuang [17]. And, mobile technologies/devices can serve as tools of assessment, which is preferred or accepted (not rejected) by students of most learning style patterns [14].

The lack of research works in the field of assessment preferences *and* CLIL/EMI approaches leads us to conclusion that despite CLIL and EMI are gaining/have gained popularity in some countries, further research activities are highly needed, e.g. such as [18], or those conducted by Berbero nad Maggi [19]. The research should particularly focus on the field of didactics/educational science so as to reach real internationalization and multi-culturalization, including the final success on the global labour market, which is the objective hidden behind all the innovations within the higher education. Thus the research topic on assessment preferences reflecting individual learning styles in CLIL/EMI is open.

Acknowledgments. The article is supported by the IGA project 2018 "Technologies in Learning English", Faculty of Education, University of Jan Evangelista Purkyne.

References

1. Emerging technologies. BusinessDictionary.com. WebFinance, Inc. http://www.business dictionary.com/definition/emerging-technologies.html. Accessed 18 May 2018
2. Felder, R.M., Brent, R.: Understanding student differences. J. Eng. Educ. **94**(1), 57–72 (2005)
3. Coffield, F., Moseley, D., Hall, E., Ecclestone, K.: Learning Styles and Pedagogy in Post-16 Learning: A Systematic and Critical Review. Learning and Skills Research Centre, London (2004)
4. Felder, R.M.: Are learning styles invalid? (hint: no!) (2010). http://www4.ncsu.edu/unity/lockers/users/f/felder/public/Papers/LS_Validity(On-Course).pdf. Accessed 1 Mar 2018
5. Honey, P.: Learning styles – the key to personalised e-learning (2010). www.bbmatters.net/bb_matters…/Learning%20styles_peter%20honey.pdf. Accessed 18 Feb 2018
6. Mitchell, D.P., et al.: Learning Style: A Critical Analysis of the Concept and Its Assessment. Kogan Page, London (2004)
7. Johnston, C.A.: Unlocking the Will to Learn. Corwin Press Inc., Thousand Oaks (1996)
8. Comenius, J. A.: The Gate of Languages Unlocked, or, a Seed-Plot of All Arts and Tongues. T.R. and N.T. for the Company of Stationers, London (1946)
9. Simonova, I., Poulova, P.: Learning Style Reflection in Tertiary e-Education. WAMAK, Hradec Kralove (2012
10. Simonova, I.: Multimedia in the teaching of foreign languages. JoLaCE – J. Lang. Cult. Educ. **1**(1), 112–121 (2013)
11. Simonova, I.: Mobile-assisted ESP learning in technical education. JoLaCe – J. Lang. Cult. Educ. **1**(3), 3–25 (2015)
12. Leither, A.: Do student learning styles translate to different "testing styles?". J. Polit. Sci. Educ. **7**(4), 416–433 (2011)
13. Common European Framework of Reference for Languages (CEFR): Cambridge assessment. http://www.cambridgeenglish.org/exams-and-tests/cefr/. Accessed 11 Mar 2018
14. Simonova, I.: Assessment preferences and learning styles in ESP. JoLaCe – J. Lang. Cult. Educ. **4**(3), 142–153 (2016)
15. Partnership for 21st century skills. 21st century skills assessment (2007). http://www.p21.org/storage/documents/21st_Century_Skills_Assessment_e-paper.pdf. Accessed 22 Feb 2018
16. Teaching and assessing 21 century skills. Cambridge assessment. http://www.cambridgeas sessment.org.uk/insights/teaching-and-assessing-21st-century-skills/. Accessed 22 Feb 2018
17. Chuang, Y.T.: MEMIS: a mobile-supported English-medium instruction system. Telemat. Inform. **34**(2), 640–656 (2017)

18. Tsou, W., Kao, S.-M.: Overview of EMI development. In: Tsou, W., Kao, S.-M. (eds.) English as a Medium of Instruction in Higher Education. ELE, vol. 8, pp. 3–18. Springer, Singapore (2017). https://doi.org/10.1007/978-981-10-4645-2_1. https://www.springer.com/la/book/9789811046445. Accessed 4 Mar 2018
19. Berbero, T., Maggi, F.: Assessment and evaluation in CLIL. In: Marsh, D., Meyer, O. (eds.) Quality Interfaces. EAP, Eichstaett Academic Press, Eichstatt (2011)

Assessment Framework of English Language Proficiency for Talent Seeking Platforms at Pearl River Delta Region

Xiaojing Weng[1], Haoran Xie[1], and Yi Cai[2(✉)]

[1] Department of Mathematics and Information Technology,
The Education University of Hong Kong,
New Territories, Hong Kong SAR
[2] School of Software Engineering, South China University of Technology,
Guangzhou, China
ycai@scut.edu.cn

Abstract. English language is becoming more and more important in the 21st century while the trend of globalization is getting increasingly obvious in the worldwide. Since one of the essential missions of education is to cultivate qualified professionals and satisfy the talent demand from the economic market, many universities and technical schools have taken English as their compulsory course in the curricula. However, due to the gap of language assessment between universities and industrial companies, English language teaching and learning in higher education has not reached its goal to provide satisfying human resources for the employers. Therefore, our research takes the effort to contribute in proposing a preliminary unified assessment framework for English Language Proficiency (ELP), which fills the gaps among the higher education sectors, industrial companies and talent seeking platforms by examining heterogeneous data sources from various talent seeking platforms. Then we will apply the model in the context of Pearl River Delta Region to guide fresh graduates when they are looking for jobs. This framework can assist different stakeholders including students, companies and educational institutions in developing talent for the society.

Keywords: ELP · Talent · Language assessment

1 Background

English as the lingua franca is taking a dominant position in modern society. 75% of the world's TV programs are using English, 3/4 of the emails in the world are written in English [1], and any conference, if it is an international one, would choose English as its official language. Besides, there are numerous governmental activities, documents and communications are conducted in English. In the business world, English is being regarded as the standard language, particularly in foreign trade communications, international etiquettes, correspondences and telecommunications, import and export documents, and bank documents. The Internet industry is built on the basis of English, medicine, architecture, and literature fields all have great relevance with English. Furthermore, English language and literature have been set up as an official major in

© Springer Nature Switzerland AG 2018
T. Hao et al. (Eds.): SETE 2018, LNCS 11284, pp. 149–155, 2018.
https://doi.org/10.1007/978-3-030-03580-8_16

most countries' higher education [2]. Take China as an example, more than 100 universities or colleges have English majors or English related majors. ELP is critical for the 21st century.

Market is the wind vane as well as the final tester of education practice. According to the statistics of the Human Resources and Social Security in China, during the period of 2001 to 2009, which was the first decade after China's participation of WTO and the time when China hosted its first Olympic Games, English major graduates have never failed the top 10 positions in terms of their employment rates, none English major graduates who were capable of English can win satisfying works without much difficulties. This positive market signal changed to the opposite where there was a dramatic drop in language students' competitiveness in the market since the year 2010 [3]. Based on Zhou and Sun's research, elements including the expansion of college enrollment, the adoption of the traditional English pedagogy in higher education, and students' perceptions on their career paths are responsible for the decline [4].

Measures have been taken to address the information asymmetry problems between industry companies and education institutions. For instance, intern program is compulsory for the senior students in higher education, influential entrepreneurs are invited to deliver lectures to students in the colleges. But according to the research conducted by Dai, these practices are facing many challenges [5]. As graduation time is usually close to the intern, there is no space for students to make huge changes even if they have realized their weaknesses. Also, individual person's stories have their uniqueness and are not convincing enough for students to take as the sign of their future directions. Hence, actions should be made throughout students' ELP gaining process in a formal approach.

No commonly used English language proficiency assessment framework, both for education sectors and industrial companies, has been proposed to help delete the mismatch mentioned above. In fact, both of the two areas are taking assessment measures to facilitate their goals, whether for students' performance growth or talent cultivation [6]. Current ELP assessment practices like CET 4/CET 6 examinations in colleges have proved to be useful in improving students' academic performance [7], but limitations are existing as these assessments ignore the significance of taking employers' purposes into consideration.

In this study, therefore, we attempt to design a Dual Purposes ELP Assessment (DPEA) framework in the talent seeking platforms which can be shared for education sectors and industrial companies to equip graduates when they are learning English for job hunting.

2   The DPEA Framework

Functional linguistics is the theoretical foundation for the DPEA framework. When we come back to the essence of languages, communication becomes our focus of attention. Functional linguistics emphasizes that the purpose of language is communication [8], and it stresses meaning-based language use and regards language context and social purposes important elements for language development [9]. This social oriented linguistic view reflects the demand to improve language learners' proficiency both for their college education and career preparation.

The DPEA framework is human-centered. Education sectors and industrial companies are defined as two parties who are training and using talents respectively. Talent seeking platforms are scaffolded by technologies to bridge graduates and enterprises. Although this medium has saved social cost and increased employee satisfaction in matching talent demand and supply, there are gaps in the existing operating systems. Our DPEA framework aims to conceptualize the current situations of ELP assessment among all the stakeholders and their gaps, it could be presented in the following diagram (see Fig. 1).

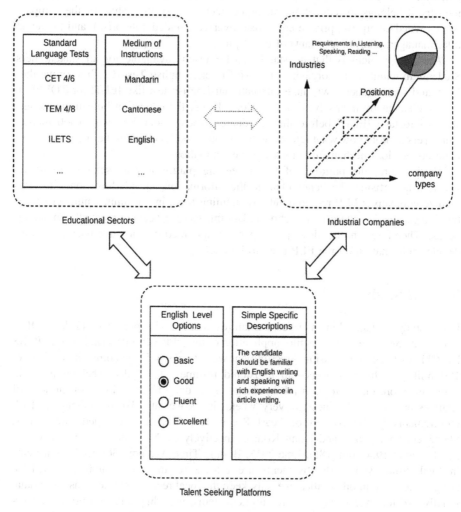

Fig. 1. Concept map of DPEA framework.

For the same group of people, they are students when studying in educational institutions. After that, they are potential employees from the corporates' perspective. It is assumed that when graduates enter the job market, they should already be adequate in ELP for their ideal positions. But in fact, students in schools are following their own training systems which are independent of the economic world. There are gaps among educational sectors, industrial companies and talent seeking platforms.

First of all, different regions apply different instructional languages. For instance, in the Pearl River Delta Region, Mandarin is adopted in the higher education institutions in Guangdong province, while Hong Kong uses English due to the historical reasons. But it is challenging for employers to put out a uniform language standard for their potential staff. Because every position has its uniqueness which is decided by the industry it belongs to (education, medicine, technology), the nature of the company (state-owned enterprise, private enterprise, overseas-funded enterprise), and the actual title (manager, analyst, assistant) of the application.

Another problem is that no standard ELP test is available for all stakeholders. Students in mainland are organized to take College English Test (CET) to prove their ELP, and some students will take international English test like IELTS or TOEFL as the supplement by themselves. But in Hong Kong, the education bureau encourages students to take IELTS before they graduate. When students flow into job market, employers do not know what reference they should take to maintain fairness since there is no conversion mechanism among these examinations.

Furthermore, the building of talent seeking platforms may set constraints for vocation advertising. To better manage the information, the platform tends to standardize company's ELP requirements by defining them into a limited number of distinctive groups for enterprises to choose. But this category cannot meet all companies' needs. Therefore, in the description part of the recruitment advertisement, some detailed information on the ELP need to be added.

3   Case Study

In this study we take China's largest human resources service provider, Nasdaq: JOBS, as our data resource to have a pilot application of the DPEA framework. Nasdaq: JOBS has China's leading professional recruitment website: www.51job.com, which has over 100 million individual users and registered resumes. This talent seeking platform maintains more than 5 million job openings in the daily base, and tens of millions of resumes are sent to businesses every week via its website. To investigate the ELP requirements in the context of Pearl River Delta Region, we typed three cities, Shenzhen, Guangzhou and Hong Kong respectively as the location choice at www.51job.com at 19:44 pm, 18th, June 2018, Beijing Time. We got 536 recruitment items in total. Since some advertisements are off-site recruitments, candidates will be assigned to work in other cities, we only keep the local recruitment items as valid data. Finally, we totally received 492 recruitment items, including 219 recruitment advertisings from Shenzhen, 271 job advertisements from Guangzhou and 2 pieces of vocation information from Hong Kong. Among these recruitment advertisings, 210 of them, which occupies 42.7% of the whole market, have ELP requirements.

10% of the employers require their vocation applications to have basic English skills. The majority of the companies, which takes 73% of the sample, however, think that graduates should have fluent English proficiency to be competent for their tasks. The rest 17% of the enterprises have high expectations for their staff, proficient English is compulsory for them. The distribution of the three ELP requirements is presented in the Fig. 2.

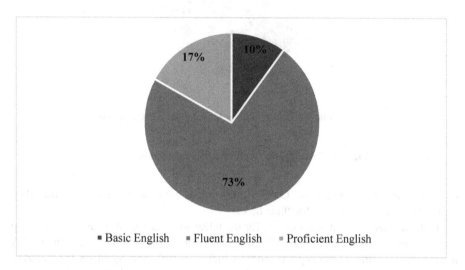

Fig. 2. Distribution of the three ELP requirements.

ELP is not the only requirement from the employers in the post description, some of them have multiple requirements including other language skills and professional skills. We coded the description into four groups in respect to the DPEA framework to better illustrate the requirements. Group one, ELP is the only language requirement, which occupies 58% of all the items; group two, ELP and other language proficiency (Mandarin, Cantonese) are required, this group takes 10% of the sample; group three, ELP and professional skills are required, 28% of the advertisements have this feature; group four, both ELP, other language proficiencies, and professional skills are required, it only accounts 4% of the recruitment. The classification result is shown in the Fig. 3.

4   Conclusion

There is the urgency to match fresh graduates' ELP with the need for human resources in the society. The current common practice is that education sectors are taking the ELP assessment criteria which are designed by the national education department to guide their talent training plan [10]. While, the employers are longing for job applications who can be defined as capable in English under their companies' language proficiency standards. As a result, on the one hand, although graduates have matched the language proficiency requirements from their schools, it is still challenging for them to get the

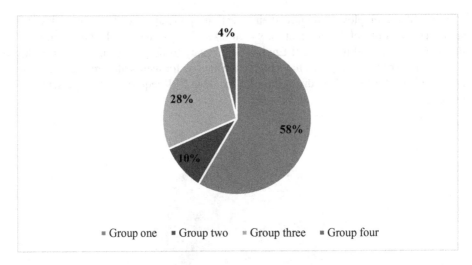

Fig. 3. Classification result of company's requirements.

positions they are targeting at. On the other hand, employers are fretting that they cannot find the right person for their tasks.

Language assessment is important for the talent/job seeking, at meanwhile, the gap between universities and industrial companies have not been filled. Our DPEA framework is a unified conceptual model which is established based on the different assessment criteria required by both industrial companies and higher education sectors. DPEA framework can help bringing some insights to bridge the gaps among these three parties. For our future research directions, we plan to develop a mapping function component in the proposed assessment framework to fill the gaps and verified the mapping function by collecting more data from various job seeking platforms and surveys on the educational sectors and industrial companies.

Acknowledgement. The research described in this article has been supported by the Innovation and Technology Fund (Project No. GHP/022/17GD) and the Internship Programme (Ref: InP/015/18) from the Innovation and Technology Commission of the Government of the Hong Kong Special Administrative Region, and the Science and Technology Planning Project of Guangdong Province (No. 2017B050506004).

References

1. Crystal, D.: English as a Global Language. Cambridge University Press, Cambridge (2012)
2. Nelson, G., Greenbaum, S.: Comparing English Worldwide: The International Corpus of English. Clarendon Press, Oxford (1996)
3. Weihe, Z., Weiwei, W., Enmou, W.: Language-in-education planning from the perspective of national foreign language capacity building. Chin. J. Lang. Policy Plan. **5**, 45–51 (2016)
4. Shutao, Z., Yu, S.: Employment-based training model for English majors. Youth Soc. **2**, 213 (2014)

5. Lisheng, D.: Research on the problems of educational practice of English majors in normal colleges. Educ. Vocat. **3**, 167–169 (2007)
6. Singh, R.K., Murty, H.R., Gupta, S.K., Dikshit, A.K.: An overview of sustainability assessment methodologies. Ecol. Indic. **2**(9), 189–212 (2009)
7. Yan, J., Huizhong, Y.: The English proficiency of college and university students in China: as reflected in the CET. Lang. Cult. Curric. **19**(1), 21–36 (2006)
8. Halliday, M.A.: Language as Social Semiotic. University Park Press, London (1978)
9. Schleppegrell, M.J.: The Language of Schooling. A Functional Linguistics Perspective. Routledge, London (2004)
10. Abedi, J.: The no child left behind act and English language learners: assessment and accountability issues. Educ. Res. **33**(1), 4–14 (2004)

Study of Future EFL Teachers' ICT Competence and Its Development Under the TPCK Framework

Xiaojun Wang and Jiří Dostál[✉]

Palacký University Olomouc, Zizkovo Nám. 5, 771 40 Olomouc,
Czech Republic
{xiaojun.wang02, j.dostal}@upol.cz

Abstract. In a technology-rich society, Information and Communication Technology (ICT) can have a great influence on the educational system. Numerous studies have indicated that ICT can benefit the outcome of teaching and learning. Many schools and universities have been equipped with ICT tools such as the Internet, computers, projectors, multimedia players, etc. This creates a need for a new type of teacher competence. This study focuses on future English Foreign Language teachers' ICT competence and its development in the context of the Czech Republic and Slovakia. We employ documentary analysis (curriculum analysis of future English Foreign Language teachers), questionnaires and semi-structure interviews to collect data. Respondents are college and university teachers, future English Foreign Language teachers in university, lower secondary school English Foreign Language teachers. Gaining information about the current ICT competence of future English Foreign Language teachers will provide information to teaching faculties and education policymakers for their efforts to design a training program designed to develop stronger ICT competence in these future teachers. The findings in the study will also show implications for future study of the professional development of English Foreign Language teachers.

Keywords: ICT competence · English Foreign Language · TPCK framework

1 Introduction

It is universally acknowledged that technology has greatly changed our life. In a digital society, nearly everything we do is closely related to technology. For instance, we use mobile phone to communicate with families and friends; we use computers to facilitate our learning and search for life information; we use electronic cards to pay fees, etc. There is no doubt that education system has also been affected in this environment. In fact, education is facing more than a little change. It has undergone unprecedented changes evidenced by changes in teaching environment, teaching forms, teaching

Paper presented at the Doctoral Consortium SETE-ICWL 2018.

© Springer Nature Switzerland AG 2018
T. Hao et al. (Eds.): SETE 2018, LNCS 11284, pp. 156–165, 2018.
https://doi.org/10.1007/978-3-030-03580-8_17

materials and frequency of interactivity between students and teachers. With the help of ICT, students in remote or rural areas can also listen to class lectured by prestigious professors whom usually only famous universities can afford to employ. This cannot be realized without digital technology. ICT can also support individual learning. For instance, Augmented Reality-Based learning system can improve learning experience [1]; flipped class can provide flexible time for students to study before and after class [2]. Nowadays, it is not uncommon that many students use mobile phones to learn English vocabulary. There are various kinds of educational software downloadable onto phones, enabling students to learn via online courses. Students can learn at their own pace and time. And most educational software combines audio and visual technology, presenting vocabulary in a vivid way before students. Many studies have indicated that ICT can facilitate active classroom teaching and benefit the outcomes of teaching and learning [3–6]. Due to this, countries from all over the world have invested substantial funds in the form of technologies, in the belief that if technology is introduced to the classroom, it will be used; and if it is used, it will transform schooling [7]. However, we are suffering from the fact that nowadays although schools are rich with digital technology such as computers, projectors, CDs, DVDs, language laboratories, multimedia players, digital networks, the classroom teaching in many schools is still dominated by traditional teaching mode characterized by using textbooks, chalk, and blackboards [8]. Or teachers just use ICT for subject content delivery. Dostál [9] conducted an investigation into the extent of teachers' use of ICT tools for experiments. 260 basic and secondary school teachers were involved. The study showed that 47% of teachers did not use computers for experiments, and 27% of teachers used them insufficiently. The result also indicated that most teachers did not use computers for experiments even in the science-based subjects in which ICT should have been used for teaching. Hansen [10] found out that search systems are mainly viewed as tools for retrieving online content to satisfy information needs, however search system are able to be used for many other functions as well. Chaaban and Ellili-Cherif [11] examined English Foreign Language teachers' use of technology in classroom. The respondents include 263 English Foreign Language teachers in Qatari Independent Schools. The result showed that the vast majority of English Foreign Language teachers use technology for instructional delivery (92.4%) and/or preparation (88.2%). Studies conducted in Saudi Arabia, Greece, Vietnam, USA, Jordan also indicated similar findings [12–16]. Although there exist various factors affecting the unsuccessful and ineffective use of ICT in classroom teaching, studies have found out that teachers' ICT competence is an important factor. Helgesson [17] found out that the main reason why teachers do not use new media in the EFL classroom is a lack of knowledge on how to use new media in the EFL classroom. This finding is consistent with Holmberg's [18] conclusion that teachers need knowledge of technical know-how. The lack of competence of teachers in using the entire didactic potential of modern ICT hinders the process of informatization of education in general, and the intensification of teaching specific subjects in particular [19]. The process of using technology to improve learning is never solely a technical matter, concerned only with properties of educational hardware and software, rather, it is closely related to teachers' digital competence [20]. Thus, studying teachers' ICT competence is important.

English has become the main international language and has been included as a mandatory subject in many schools and universities worldwide. The big challenge of learning English is a lack of an authentic English speaking environment, which is very important for language learning. With the ICT, a real authentic environment can be created, in which students can watch videos and communicate with native speakers.

This study attempts to study the future English Foreign Language teachers who are being trained to teach at the lower secondary school level after they graduate. The research has been conducted in the Czech Republic and Slovakia. This study is designed to answer the following questions:

1. How competent are the future English Foreign Language teachers at using ICT tools?
2. How to develop future English Foreign Language teachers' ICT competence?

2 Literature Review

2.1 TPCK Framework

The Technological Pedagogical Content Knowledge (TPCK) Framework was proposed by Koehler and Mishra [21]. It is a framework for teacher knowledge. The framework is shown in Fig. 1. The TPCK framework includes three aspects of knowledge: Technological Knowledge (TK), Pedagogical Knowledge (PK), Content Knowledge (CK). It argues that, in a digital –rich society in which technology has dramatically influenced teaching and learning, developing good content requires a thoughtful interweaving of the above mentioned three sources of knowledge [22]. Compared to the traditional view of what knowledge teachers need to know, which emphasizes mainly CK and PK, the TPCK framework adds a new element called TK into the traditional framework. According to the TPCK framework, all subjects of teachers need to be equipped with the TPCK for most efficient teaching. This means that English Foreign Language teachers also need knowledge of how to use technology in teaching besides other essential knowledge. In other words, ICT competence constitutes one of the integral components of English Foreign Language teachers' professional competence.

2.2 Related Works of English Foreign Language Teachers' ICT Competence

ICT competence has been studied by many researcher home and abroad. Its definition is described in different term such as digital literacy, ICT literacy, technology literacy, e-competence, etc. But the basic definition is the integrated ability of the individual to use Information and Communication Technologies competently and responsibly [23].

European Commission issued a document'Common European Principles for Teacher Competence and Qualification', in which three broad areas of competence are mentioned as teacher competence and qualification: working with others; working with

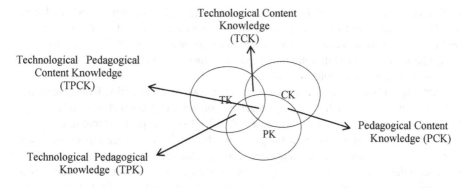

Fig. 1. TPCK framework and elements

knowledge, technology and information; working in and with society. We can see ICT competence is listed as one of core competence of teachers [24].

Sysoyev and Evstigneev [25] defined the foreign language teacher's ICT competence as the ability to use Web-based educational resources, Web 2.0 social networks and other Information and Communication Technologies in order to create language skills and to develop students' verbal abilities in learning foreign language and culture. He said that the foreign language teacher's ICT competence includes the following five interrelated components: value-motivational, cognitive, operational, communicative and reflective components.

Malinina [26] studied foreign language teachers' ICT competence in the context of Russia. Respondents are primary, secondary and high school foreign language teachers. Questionnaire, interview and observation were employed in the research to collect data. The results indicated that foreign language teachers have above basic or intermediate level of knowledge of ICT competence.

AL Khateeb [27] examined in-service English Foreign Language teachers' digital competence in the context of Saudi Arabia. The research employed questionnaires to collect data. The findings showed that the majority of teachers are basic users, just over a third indicated they were intermediate users, and advanced users accounted for just over a quarter.

Røkenes and Krumsvik [28] investigated how secondary student teachers are educated to teach with ICT through an English as a Second Language (ESL) didactics course offered at a teacher education program in Norway. Data were collected through surveys, participant observations, and semi-structured interview. Five suggestions were proposed for the development of student teachers' ICT competence: modeling didactical ICT-use for student teachers; scaffolding student teachers' learning experiences with ICT; teacher educator linking theory and practice; raising student teachers' awareness through reflection; providing student teachers with access to resources and support.

Some other researches focus on the ICT competence of student teachers in various fields. For example, Elstad and Christophersen [29] studied factors influencing Norwegian student teachers' ICT competence. Still some researches are about teachers'

ICT competence. It is suited for teachers of all subjects. For instance, Gudmundsdottir and Hatlevik explored how newly qualified teachers are prepared to use ICT in their initial teacher education in Norway. Questionnaires were used in the study to obtain data. The results showed that the initial teacher education did little contribution to their professional digital competence [30].

Although ICT competence in education has drawn much attention from researchers, when it comes to English Language teachers' professional competence, ICT competence is rarely mentioned in some studies. Zein [31] studied professional development needs of primary English Foreign Language teachers only from three aspects: language (e.g., speaking, pronunciation), knowledge (e.g., children's learning style and strategies, knowledge of child psychology), and pedagogy (e.g., error correction, lesson planning). ICT competence is not mentioned in the research. In the same vein, McGraner and Saenz [32] summarized core competence for English Language teachers are as follows: (1) sociocultural and political foundations for teaching ELL students, (2) foundations of second-language acquisition, (3) knowledge for teaching academic content to ELL students, (4) effective instructional practices for teaching academic content to ELL students, (5) assessment practices and accommodations for ELL students. Yükse [33] examined pre-service English Language teachers' teaching competence from five domains: classroom management, instructional strategies, pedagogical content knowledge, student engagement, and content knowledge. And in some countries, such as China, ICT competence is not included in professional qualification requirements, which are mainly determined by language skills (writing, listening, reading and speaking) and other knowledge [34]. In conclusion,many countries still have a long way to go before ICT competence is held in high regard.

From the analysis of related works in this area, we found out that most previous studies were concerned with the following aspects: in-service foreign language teachers ICT competence, student teachers' ICT competence (for all subjects), teachers' ICT competence (for all subjects). In addition, most studies focus on knowledge and skills teachers need to possess with little attention to how to develop theses competence. There are very few studies on future English Foreign Language teachers' ICT competence and its development. Since English Foreign Language teachers' ICT competence is different than other subjects' and future English Foreign Language Teacher will become English Foreign Teachers after their graduation and their ICT competence will affect the quality of teaching, this research tries to study future English Foreign Language Teachers' ICT competence in the context of the Czech Republic and Slovakia.

3 Methodology

A mixed methodology is employed to collect data. In other words, both qualitative and quantitative methods are used since quantitative methodologies focus on measurable factors in a wide range of sampling, they usually only reflect the effects of the variables operationalized in the research design and qualitative methodologies, on the other hand, have the potential to provide a rich and multifaceted insight into multi-dimensional perspectives and values, but do not easily facilitate with any degree of certainty provable generalization from data [35]. The qualitative methods we will use are interviews, documentary analysis and the quantitative methods we will use are questionnaires. To state specifically, we use documentary analysis, questionnaires and semi-structure interviews to answer the first question presented in the introduction. We use questionnaires and interviews to answer the second question presented in the introduction. Qualitative data collected will be analyzed by Nvivo [36] and quantitative data will be analyzed by Statistical Package for Social Science (SPSS) [37]. Approximately, the study samples in our research consist of 350 future English Foreign Language teachers, 35 college and university teachers, and 45 English Foreign Language teachers at the lower secondary school level.

Documentary analysis is realized by analyzing the curriculum for future English Foreign Language teachers from Czech Republic universities and Slovakia universities. The future English Foreign Language Teachers refer to current graduate students majoring in English. They will become lower secondary school English Foreign Language teacher after their graduation.

There are three sets of questionnaire for college and university teachers, teachers of English at lower secondary schools, and future English Foreign Language teachers respectively. A calculation of Cronbach's coefficient alpha is used to verify the reliability of our questionnaires. The questionnaire for the first group consists of three parts. The first part is about their view of how well the preparation of future English Foreign language teachers' ICT competence is. The second part is about their view of which ICT training courses related to teaching English should be added into the current curriculum for the development of future English Foreign Language Teachers' ICT competence. In other words, this part concerns about the development of future English Foreign language teachers' ICT competence. The participants will be required to respond to each item on a five-point scale ranging from (5) strongly agree to (1) strongly disagree. According to their opinions, ICT training courses will be suggested to develop future English Foreign Language teachers' ICT competence. Samples of ICT training courses are given below:

(a) Training in using ICT for motivating students
(b) Training in using ICT for introducing new learning materials
(c) Training in using ICT for the fixation of knowledge

The third part of the questionnaire for college and university teachers is about personal information including age, gender, years of teaching experience.

The questionnaire for future English Foreign Language teachers is designed to test their ICT competence. It includes their mastery of basic ICT skills and other ICT tools for future teaching, their attitudes towards using ICT in teaching English in the future.

The questionnaire for lower secondary school teachers of English aims to understand if they feel that they should have more ICT courses related to English teaching when they were students, and how they evaluate the ICT courses they had as a student, if there had any, for their preparation of ICT competence.

Semi-structure interview is used for collecting in-depth information from participants. The interviews last about 30 min each and are audio-recorded.

4 Results

At present, the search that has been done for this study is just a beginning, so now only preliminary results can be provided. Documentary analysis constitutes a part of our research because curriculum can be an indicator of the extent of the preparation of future English Foreign Language teachers' ICT competence. As stated previously, documentary analysis is actualized by analyzing current curriculum for future English Foreign Language teachers from Czech Republic universities and Slovakia universities. Findings from documentary analysis showed that there are very few course concerning using ICT in teaching exclusively for future English Foreign Language teachers. For example, by studying the curriculum for future English Foreign Language teachers from the Faculty of Education, Constantine the Philosopher University in Nitra, we found out that there is no courses related to using ICT tools in teaching English for bachelor degree students, and there is only one course called 'Multimedia in Teaching Foreign Language' for master degree students majoring in English. In this course, students will learn pedagogy in new millennium; CALL; pedagogical theories and CALL; Internet in English language teaching/ learning; blended learning; using multimedia in teaching listening, reading, speaking, and writing skills, etc. Another case is from Faculty of Education, Palacky University Olomouc. Consistent with the above finding, from analysis of the curriculum for future English Foreign Language teachers, we again found out that there are just two courses related to using ICT in teaching English for bachelor degree students. One is 'Methodology of teaching English pronunciation, spelling and punctuation by means of ICT'. This course aims to increase the competency of students in three areas of English language (English pronunciation, spelling, and punctuation) and to increase students' computer literacy in order to enable them to work with and by means of different types of information technology. Another one is 'ICT for ELT (ICT for English Language Teachers)'. In this course, students will get to know online dictionaries and web of portals for teachers of English; will learn how to create interactive exercises for their pupils; will create their own blog; will create online and offline presentations for their lessons; will create study materials using pictures and graphics, etc. However, these two courses are selective courses, not mandatory ones. And there are no ICT courses for teaching English offered to master degree students. In a word, documentary analysis shows that the preparation of English Foreign Language teachers' ICT competence is inadequate.

Our next step of research is to carry out questionnaires and interviews to see if the findings are consistent with the results from documentary analysis.

5 Conclusion and Study Limitation

Digital technology has greatly influenced teaching and learning, and many studies have shown that it can benefit the outcomes of education. The trend of integrating ICT in educational field is irreversible. The use of technology in education requires new competence of teachers [38]. Teachers are being required to be able to use digital technology in teaching. Without skills in using digital technologies, it is difficult to meet our needs. Just as it would be of no help if we had a smartphone available but we were not able to use the applications designed for communication [39]. The study focuses on English foreign language teachers' ICT competence and its development. The findings from our research will give insights to teacher educators and policy makers to make better decisions.

The main limitation of this study is its sample size of teachers. Further studies need to include larger samples of teachers at all the levels of foreign language instruction, in order to ensure a more complete understanding of the current situation and analysis of what work still needs to be done. Furthermore, there are many factors influencing the inadequate ICT competence of future English Foreign Language teachers. This study does not cover all other factors. It only concerns curriculum improvement as a method for the development of future English Foreign Language teachers' ICT competence. Future study should be carried out to investigate other ways for the development of future English Foreign Language teachers' ICT competence.

References

1. Xiao, J., Xu, Z., Yu, Y., Cai, S., Hansen, P.: The design of augmented reality-based learning system applied in U-learning environment. In: El Rhalibi, A., Tian, F., Pan, Z., Liu, B. (eds.) Edutainment 2016. LNCS, vol. 9654, pp. 27–36. Springer, Cham (2016). https://doi.org/10.1007/978-3-319-40259-8_3
2. Zang, X.:The application of flipped classroom in English grammar teaching in second high school. In: The International Conference on Arts, Design and Contemporary Educatio, pp. 1430–1433. Atlantis Press (2016)
3. Barak, M., Watted, A., Haick, H.: Motivation to learn in massive open online courses: examining aspects of language and social engagement. Comput. Educ. **94**, 49–60 (2016)
4. Barrs, K.: Fostering computer-mediated L2 interaction beyond the classroom. Lang. Learn. Technol. **16**(1), 10–25 (2012)
5. Blattner, G., Fiori, M.: Facebook in the language classroom: promises and possibilities. Instr. Technol. Distance Learn. (ITDL) **6**(1), 17–28 (2009)
6. Wang, B.T., Teng, C.W., Chen, H.T.: Using iPad to facilitate english vocabulary learning. Int. J. Inf. Educ. Technol. **5**(2),100–104 (2015)
7. Cuban, L.: Oversold and Underused:Computers in the Classroom. Harvard University Press, Cambridge (2001)
8. Wang, X., Dostál, J.: An analysis of the integration of ICT in education from the perspective of teachers' attitudes. In: EDULEARN 2017, pp. 8156–8162 (2017). ISBN 978-84-697-3777-4
9. Dostál, J., Wang, X., Nuangchalerm, P.: Experiments in education supported by computer use: teachers' attitudes towards computers. In: Proceedings of the 9th International Conference on Computer Supported Education (CSEDU2017), vol. 2, pp. 248–254 (2017)
10. Hansen, P., Rieh, S.Y.: Editorial: recent advances on searching as learning: an introduction to the special issue. J. Inf. Sci. Feb. **42**, 3–6 (2016). https://doi.org/10.1177/0165551515614473
11. Chaaban, Y., Ellili-Cherif, M.: Technology integration in EFL classrooms: a study of Qatari independent schools. Educ. Inf. Technol. **22**(5), 2433–2454 (2017). https://doi.org/10.1007/s10639-016-9552-3
12. Alenezi, A.: Influences of the mandated presence of ICT in Saudi Arabia secondary schools. Int. J. Inf. Educ. Technol. **5**(8), 638–644 (2015)

13. Alzaidiyeen, N.J., Mei, L.L., Fook, F.S.: Teachers' attitudes and levels of technology use in classrooms: the case of Jordan schools. Int. Educ. Stud. **3**(2), 211–218 (2010)

14. Nikolopoulou, K., Gialamas, V.: Barriers to the integration of computers in early childhood settings: teachers' perceptions. Educ. Inf. Technol. **20**(2), 285–301 (2015)

15. Peeraer, J., Van Petegem, P.: Integration or transformation: looking in the future of information and communication technology in education in Vietnam. Eval. Program Plann. **48**(8), 47–56 (2015)

16. Shapley, K.S., Sheehan, D., Maloney, C., Caranikas-Walker, F.: Evaluating the implementation fidelity of technology immersion and its relationship with student achievement. J. Technol. Learn. Assess. **9**(4), 69 (2010)

17. Helgeson, J.: English in the digital era: Swedish grades 4–6 teachers' use of pupil's extramural English experience of new media. Degree thesis, Dalarna University (2018)

18. Holmberg, J.: Applying a conceptual design framework to study teachers' use of educational technology. Educ. Inf. Technol. **22**(5), 2333–2349 (2017). https://doi.org/10.1007/s10639-016-9536-3

19. Sysoyev, P.V., Evstigneev, M.N.: Foreign language teachers' competency and competence in using information and communication technologies. Soc. Behav. Sci. **154**, 82–86 (2014)

20. Bransford, J., Brown, A.L., Cocking, R.R.: How People Learn: Brain, Mind, Experience, And School, Expanded edn. National Academy Press, Washington (2000)

21. Koehler, M.J., Mishra, P.: Teachers learning technology by design. J. Comput. Teach. Educ. **21**(3), 94–102 (2005)

22. Mishra, P., Koehler, M.: Technological pedagogical content knowledge: a framework for teacher knowledge. Teach. Coll. Rec. **108**(6), 1017–1054 (2006)

23. Demchenko, I.: Forming of future teachers ICT-Competence: Canadian experience. Comp. Prof. Pedagogy **6**(1), 54–60 (2016) https://doi.org/10.1515/rpp-2016-0008

24. Caena, F.: Teachers' core competences : requirements and development. European Commission (2011)

25. Sysoyev, P., Evstigneev, M.: Foreign language teacher's competency and competence in using information and communication technologies. In: The XXV Annual International Academic Conference, Language and Culture. Procedia – Social and Behavioral Sciences, vol. 154. pp. 82–6 (2014). https://doi.org/10.1016/j.sbspro.2014.10.116

26. Malinnina, I.: ICT competencies of foreign languages teachers. In: 4th World Conference on Educational Technology Researches, WCETR, Procedia-Social and Behavioral Sciences (2015)

27. Al Khateeb, A.A.M.: Measuring digital competence and ICT literacy: an exploratory study of in-service english language teachers in the context of Saudi Arabia. Int. Educ. Stud. **10**(12), 38 (2017)

28. Røkenes, F.M., Krumsvik, R.J.: Prepared to teach ESL with ICT? a study of digital competence in Norwegian teacher education. Comput. Educ. **97**, 1–20 (2016)

29. Elstad, E., Christophersen, K.A.: Perceptions of digital competency among student teachers: contributing to the development of student teachers' instructional self-efficacyin technology-rich classrooms. Educ. Sci. **7**(1), 27 (2017)

30. Gudmundsdottir, G.B., Hatlevik, O.E.: Newly qualified teachers' professional digital competence: implications for teacher education. Eur. J. Teach. Educ. **41**(2), 214–231 (2017). https://doi.org/10.1080/02619768.2017.1416085

31. Zein, M.S.: Professional development needs of primary EFL teachers: perspectives of teachers and teacher educators. Prof. Dev. Educ. **42**(3), 423–440 (2016). https://doi.org/10.1080/19415257.2016.1156013

32. McGraner, K.L., Saenz, L.: Preparing teachers of English language learners. National Comprehensive Center for Teacher Quality, Washington (2009). http://www.tqsource.org/publications/issuepaper_preparingELLteachers.pdf
33. Yüksel, H.G.: Teachers of the future: perceived teaching competences and visions of pre-service English language teachers. Int. J. Hum. Sci. **11**(2), 27–39 (2014). https://doi.org/10.14687/ijhs.v11i2.2920
34. Mak, B.: Professional qualifications of teachers for English for primary and secondary education – a brief comparison between Hong Kong and China. J. Pan-Pacific Assoc. Appl. Linguist. **20**(2), 19–29 (2016)
35. Guo, R.X.: Information and communication technology (ICT) literacy in teacher education: a case study of the University of British Columbia. Doctoral dissertation, The University of British Columbia (2006)
36. Bazeley, P., Jackson, K.: Qualitative Data Analysis with NVivo. Sage, Los Angeles (2013)
37. Tolmie, A., Muijs, D., McAteer, E.: Quantitative Methods In Educational and Social Research Using SPSS. Open University Press, Maidenhead (2011)
38. Zhu, C.: Teacher roles and adoption of educational technology in the Chinese context. J. Educ. Res. Online **2**(2), 72–86 (2010)
39. Dostál, J., Wang, X., Steingartner, W., Nuangchalerm, P.: Digital intelligence- new concept in context of future of school education . In: ICERI 2017, pp. 3706–3712. Seville (2017)

UMLL (International Symposium on User Modeling and Language Learning)

A Bibliometric Analysis of the Research Status of the Technology Enhanced Language Learning

Xieling Chen[1], Juntao Hao[2], Junjie Chen[3], Songshou Hua[4],
and Tianyong Hao[5(✉)]

[1] College of Economics, Jinan University, Guangzhou, China
shaylyn_chen@163.com
[2] Xuchang Computer Applied Engineering Research Center, Xuchang, China
jun_419@126.com
[3] Software College, Northeastern University, Shenyang, China
martinorudo@gmail.com
[4] Department of Computer Science,
Liaoning Vocational College of Light Industry, Dalian, China
mmc_hua@163.com
[5] School of Computer, South China Normal University,
Guangzhou, China
haoty@126.com

Abstract. The integration of technology into language learning has demonstrated great success and drawn much attention from academia in recent years. Using publications retrieved from Web of Science, this study reveals the research status and development trend of the field from a bibliometric and systematic perspective. The analysis is conducted from publication statistical characteristics, geographical distribution, and collaboration relations. Analysis techniques include a bibliometric method, a geographic visualization method, and a social network analysis method. This analysis of the technology enhanced language learning field presents a global view on the research evolution over time, current research interests, and potential opportunities and challenges.

Keywords: Technology · Language learning · Bibliometric analysis

1 Introduction

The rapidly developed and well-established technologies have enabled a fast growth of learning resources such as online learning communities, open course videos, and other learning materials available for language learning. Therefore, instructors are encouraged to alter their teaching strategies or adjust their teaching activities to effectively utilize such resources [1]. Technological innovations in language learning can benefit learners in increasing interests, enhancing motivations, encouraging interactions, developing writing/thinking connections, facilitating cross-cultural awareness, etc. Moreover, it provides instructors with efficient means to organize course content and interact with multiple students.

© Springer Nature Switzerland AG 2018
T. Hao et al. (Eds.): SETE 2018, LNCS 11284, pp. 169–179, 2018.
https://doi.org/10.1007/978-3-030-03580-8_18

Consequently, technology enhanced language learning research field has attracted more and more interests from academia given the continuing growth of publications. Some representative works are as follows. Based on learner location, learning time, individual English vocabulary abilities and leisure time, Chen and Li [2] presented a personalized context-aware ubiquitous learning system for English vocabulary learning. Hsu et al. [3] focused on personalized recommendation-based mobile language learning. Aiming at engaging students in self-initiated use of technology for language learning, Lai and Gu [4] investigated the usage of technology to self-regulate language learning outside the class-room for students from the University of Hong Kong. Hu et al. [5] applied a deep neural network trained acoustic model and transfer learning based logistic regression classifiers for mispronunciation detection. Their experiment demonstrated a significant improvement in detection performance of the proposed method. Liu et al. [6] applied an electroen-cephalogram technique to investigate the potential of inhibition advantage in modulating different language switches, regardless of the time spent on second language learning.

Bibliometrics has been considered as an effective statistical method for evaluating scientific publications, and has been widely applied in various fields such as natural language processing [7], diabetes [8], and cardiovascular magnetic resonance [9]. Especially, it has also been applied in interdisciplinary research fields, e.g., natural language processing in medical research [10], natural language processing empowered mobile computing [11], and corporate social responsibility in supply chain management [12]. The results from bibliometric analysis can help researchers better choose their potential research fields, recognize future academic collaborators, and identify appropriate affiliations for conducting joint research [13].

Therefore, this study focuses on the bibliometric analysis of the technology enhanced language learning filed, to analyze the current research status by summarizing existing research publications. Firstly, a statistical descriptive method is used to investigate the latest research status and trend, including publications and citations, dominant subjects and journals, prolific authors and affiliations. Secondly, geographic visualization analysis is applied to investigate geographical distributions of the publications. Finally, scientific collaborations are measured using collaboration degrees and are further visualized using social network analysis.

2   The Statistical Approach

Web of Science was used as the data source for retrieving research publications. A list of relevant search words were determined by a domain expert. 807 publications in "Article" type during the period 2008–2017 were obtained. Citations counted to April 30th, 2018 were considered for each publication. The key elements, e.g., title, journal, subject category, author keywords, abstract, and author address of the publications were extracted. 805 publications were identified to be relevant to the research field through manual verification. Author address information was further processed to identify corresponding affiliations and countries/regions. Key terms were extracted from author keywords, keywords-plus, title and abstract.

In addition to basic statistical analysis, methods used in this paper include: geo-graphic visualization, collaboration degree analysis, and social network analysis.

Geographic visualization is a set of techniques such as image processing and virtual reality for the analysis of geospatial data. As Tobler's First Law of Geography shows, everything is related to everything else, and near things are more related than distant things. Through geographic visualization with location as the key index variable, we are able to get related information which is previously unfound. Geographic visualization can be used throughout the process of problem-solving in geographical analysis, from the development of initial hypotheses to knowledge discovery, analysis, presentation and evaluation. In this study, geographic visualization analysis is applied to investigate geographical distributions of publications.

The collaboration degree is used for measuring scientific research's connective relations to the level of authors, affiliations, and countries with Eq. (1) [14].

$$C_{Ai} = \frac{\sum_{j=1}^{N} \alpha_j}{N}, C_{Ii} = \frac{\sum_{j=1}^{N} \beta_j}{N}, C_{Ci} = \frac{\sum_{j=1}^{N} \gamma_j}{N} \tag{1}$$

C_{Ai}, C_{Ii}, and C_{Ci} are the author, affiliation and country's collaboration degrees of the i year. α_j, β_j, and γ_j represent the number of authors, affiliations and countries for each publication. N indicates the annual number of publications in the research field.

This paper uses the social network analysis method to investigate the collaboration relations among countries/regions, affiliations, and authors. Social network analysis is a process of exploring social structures using networks and graph theory to quantify the relations among actors in the social network [15]. In the network, each country, affiliation or author is presented as a node with node size representing publications and node color denoting the continent/country that it belongs to. The line thickness indicates collaboration strength between two countries, affiliations or authors. By accessing to the dynamic networks, users can explore collaboration relations for specific countries/regions, affiliations, or authors by simply clicking the nodes.

3   Results and Discussions

3.1   Publications and Citations

The statistics result of total publications, total citations, and average citations from 2008 to 2017 is presented as Fig. 1. The publication exhibits an overall upward trend in fluctuation (from 46 publications in 2008 to 100 publications in 2017). The research sees a sudden increase in number in year 2016 with 143 publications compared with 99 publications in the previous year. The highest total citation count is 1477 and average citations per publication is 21 in 2009. However, the highest average citation count is 188 in 2016. Among the total publications, papers by Flöel et al. [16] and Yang [17] have the highest citations as 203 and 167, respectively.

0.50% of the publications have more than 100 citations, and 2.36% have more than 50 citations. 12.92% and 25.84% of the publications have more than 20 and 10 citations, respectively. About half of publications, i.e. 44.35%, have more than 5 citations. Of the total publications, 20.37% have no citations at all, most of which come from 2017.

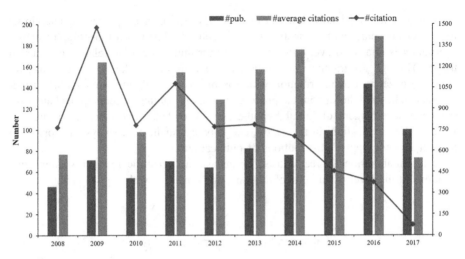

Fig. 1. Total publications, total citations, and average citations of the publications

3.2 Journals and Subjects

The technology enhanced language learning field is not limited to *Education* or *Linguistics*, but covers over 67 Web of Science categories. This indicates wide applications of technologies in language learning fields. Figure 2 shows the top 10 subjects ranked by the quantities of publication and citation, respectively. *Education & Educational Research* is the largest category with nearly one-third of the total publications and citations. The followings are *Linguistics* and *Language & Linguistics*, each with a sharing of 25.30% and 13.80% publications, as well as 25.94% and 14.71% citations, respectively. This reflects a high influence and quality of the publications in the three subjects. In addition to *Education* and *Linguistics* related categories, the publications are also found to be widely appeared in *Computer Science*, *Acoustics*, *Psychology*, and *Audiology* related categories.

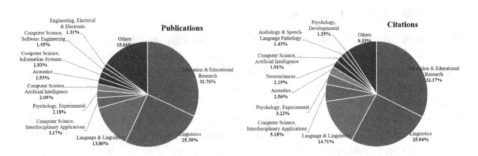

Fig. 2. Top subjects ranked by publication and citation quantities

242 SCIE/SSCI-indexed journals have published relevant research work. Among them, *Computer Assisted Language Learning* is the largest one with 93 publications and the highest h-index, followed by *Language Learning & Technology* (83 publications) and *ReCALL* (42 publications). Table 1 lists the top 11 publication outlets in the field. These top journals account for nearly half (46.21% for publications and 57.78% for citations) of the total investigated publications, implying their dominant positions and wide influences in the field. It is worth noting that *Computers & Education* has the highest average citations per publication although with only 15 publications.

Table 1. Top 11 contributing journals in the research field

Rank	Journals	TP	%P	TC	ACP	H	≥ 10
1	*Computer Assisted Language Learning*	93	11.55%	987	10.61	17	30
2	*Language Learning & Technology*	83	10.31%	764	9.20	16	22
3	*ReCALL*	42	5.22%	619	14.74	15	19
4	*Educational Technology & Society*	28	3.48%	391	13.96	9	9
5	*System*	26	3.23%	92	3.54	5	2
6	*Speech Communication*	23	2.86%	335	14.57	11	11
7	*Modern Language Journal*	19	2.36%	349	18.37	11	12
8	*Computers & Education*	15	1.86%	381	25.40	11	12
9	*Foreign Language Annals*	15	1.86%	119	7.93	7	3
10	*Computers in Human Behavior*	14	1.74%	62	4.43	4	3
11	*Interactive Learning Environments*	14	1.74%	101	7.21	4	1

Note: TP: total publications; %P: percentage of publications; TC: total citations; ACP: average citations per publication, calculated as TC/TP; H: h-index; ≥ 10: publication number with citations ≥ 10.

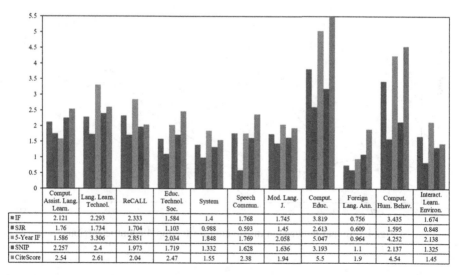

	Comput. Assist. Lang. Learn.	Lang. Learn. Technol.	ReCALL	Educ. Technol. Soc.	System	Speech Commun.	Mod. Lang. J.	Comput. Educ.	Foreign Lang. Ann.	Comput. Hum. Behav.	Interact. Learn. Environ.
IF	2.121	2.293	2.333	1.584	1.4	1.768	1.745	3.819	0.756	3.435	1.674
SJR	1.76	1.734	1.704	1.103	0.988	0.593	1.45	2.613	0.609	1.595	0.848
5-Year IF	1.586	3.306	2.851	2.034	1.848	1.769	2.058	5.047	0.964	4.252	2.138
SNIP	2.257	2.4	1.973	1.719	1.332	1.628	1.636	3.193	1.1	2.137	1.325
CiteScore	2.54	2.61	2.04	2.47	1.55	2.38	1.94	5.5	1.9	4.54	1.45

Fig. 3. Comparisons of the top 11 productive journals on five metrics for the year 2016

The competency of the top productive journals are further compared using 5 assessment indicators, for the year 2016. As shown in Fig. 3, *Computers & Education* and *Computers in Human Behavior* have the relative high IF, 5-Year IF, and CiteScore. The SJR scores of *Computers & Education* and *Computer Assisted Language Learning* are higher than others, while *Computers & Education* and *Language Learning & Technology* have higher SNIP. It is clear that as for all the 5 indicators, *Computers & Education* has the highest values.

3.3   Geographical Distribution

Through the analysis of geographical distributions of the publications, the USA dominates in the field, accounting for 26.96% of the total publications, followed by Taiwan with 116 publications. Other productive countries/regions include China, UK, Turkey, Japan, Spain, Australia, Canada, and Germany. The 10 countries/regions have contributed mainly on *Education & Educational Research* and *Linguistics* subjects. They serve as first authors in more than 70% of their publications except Germany.

Figure 4 shows the annual publication numbers of top 4 productive countries/regions. The USA ranks at the top 1 for the period 2008–2017. A sudden increase takes place in 2016. Taiwan ranks at the top 2 since 2009, but falls behind China in 2017. The publication numbers for Taiwan and China are on the whole presenting upward trends in fluctuation, and they both experience sharp increases in 2011. As for UK, the publication number increases slightly with years.

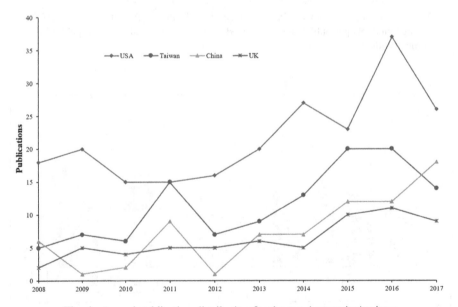

Fig. 4. Annual publication distribution for the top 4 countries/regions

3.4   Affiliations and Authors

741 affiliations perform technology enhanced language learning research, where 242 affiliations participate in more than one publications. *Nanyang Technological University* from Singapore and *National Taiwan Normal University* from Taiwan lead with 17 publications each, followed by *The University of Hong Kong* from Hong Kong with 14 publications. Table 2 lists the details of the top 14 most prolific affiliations. Among them, 5 organizations locate in Taiwan, confirming that Taiwan is active in technology enhanced language learning research. The 14 affiliations publish studies centering most on subjects *Education & Educational Research* and *Linguistics*. It is worth noting that *Iowa State University* has the highest citations although with only 10 publications, thus it receives the highest average citations per publication as 20.4. This indicates the high influence and quality of its publications.

Table 2. The most prolific affiliations in the research field

R	Name	C/R	TP	TC	ACP	H	FP(%)	CP(%)
1	*Nanyang Technological University*	SG	17	141	8.29	7	41.18	76.47
2	*National Taiwan Normal University*	TW	17	144	8.47	7	41.18	70.59
3	*The University of Hong Kong*	HK	14	124	8.86	6	42.86	100.00
4	*National Central University*	TW	12	68	5.67	5	41.67	66.67
5	*National Cheng Kung University*	TW	12	118	9.83	7	58.33	66.67
6	*The Open University*	UK	11	162	14.73	6	54.55	72.73
7	*Iowa State University*	USA	10	204	20.40	6	60.00	60.00
8	*Michigan State University*	USA	10	71	7.10	4	40.00	30.00
9	*Radboud Universiteit Nijmegen*	NL	9	93	10.33	4	44.44	100.00
10	*Arizona State University*	USA	8	103	12.88	5	62.50	62.50
11	*Islamic Azad University*	IR	8	37	4.63	4	50.00	100.00
12	*Macquarie University*	AU	8	65	8.13	3	37.50	87.50
13	*National Taiwan University of Science and Technology*	TW	8	110	13.75	3	37.50	37.50
14	*National Tsing Hua University*	TW	8	69	8.63	4	50.00	87.50

Note: C/R: Country/Region; TP: total publications; TC: total citations; ACP: average citations per publication; H: h-index; FP(%): publication percentage as first affiliation; CP(%): collaboration percentage.

In total, 1,707 authors are acknowledged for their contributions although 11.19% of these authors contribute only one publication. Table 3 lists the top 14 most productive authors including their respective publication numbers and h-indexes. The most prolific author is *Lai, Chun* from Hong Kong with 8 publications, followed by *Cucchiarini, Catia* and *Strik, Helmer* from Netherlands (each with 7 publications). In case of Taiwan and the USA, *Wu, Wen-Chi Vivian* and *Chapelle, Carol A.* are the most productive authors. From the perspective of h-index, *Wong, Lung-Hsiang* form Singapore has the highest h-index as 6. It is worth noting that *Chapelle, Carol A.* has the highest citations although with only 6 publications, thus he receives the highest average citations per

Table 3. The most prolific authors in the technology enhanced language learning research field

R	Name	C	TP	TC	ACP	H	FP(%)	LP(%)	CP(%)
1	*Lai, Chun*	HK	8	105	13.13	5	100.00	25.00	75.00
2	*Cucchiarini, Catia*	NL	7	65	9.29	4	0.00	14.29	100.00
3	*Strik, Helmer*	NL	7	65	9.29	4	14.29	28.57	100.00
4	*Wong, Lung-Hsiang*	SG	7	73	10.43	6	85.71	28.57	71.43
5	*Chapelle, Carol A.*	USA	6	134	22.33	4	66.67	66.67	50.00
6	*Wu, Wen-Chi Vivian*	TW	6	15	2.50	3	33.33	66.67	100.00
7	*Blake, Robert J.*	USA	5	83	16.60	3	80.00	100.00	20.00
8	*Chen, Chih-Ming*	TW	5	99	19.80	3	100.00	0.00	100.00
9	*Huang, Yueh-Min*	TW	5	37	7.40	4	0.00	40.00	100.00
10	*Lee, Gary Geunbae*	KR	5	32	6.40	3	0.00	80.00	100.00
11	*Lee, Kyusong*	KR	5	32	6.40	3	20.00	0.00	100.00
12	*Meurers, Detmar*	DE	5	45	9.00	3	0.00	60.00	100.00
13	*Noh, Hyungjong*	KR	5	32	6.40	3	20.00	0.00	100.00
14	*Warschauer, Mark*	USA	5	66	13.20	3	20.00	80.00	80.00

Note: LP(%): publication percentage as last author; other abbreviations are the same to Table 2.

publication as 22.33, demonstrating the high influence and quality of his publications. The 14 authors publish studies centering most on subjects *Education & Educational Research, Linguistics, Language & Linguistics, Computer Science, Information Systems, Computer Science*, and *Software Engineering*.

3.5 Collaboration Relationship

The collaboration degrees at the country, affiliation and author levels in the research field are shown in Fig. 5. The collaboration in the three levels are experiencing slow growth. Compared with the collaborations between countries and affiliations, the auctorial collaboration degree is much higher. This finding suggests that the authors tend to collaborate more with those within the same affiliation or country. The three average degrees are 2.49, 1.59 and 1.19, respectively. That is to say, 2.49 authors, 1.59 affiliations and 1.19 countries participate in one publication averagely.

Furthermore, the collaborations among countries, affiliations, and authors are visualized using network analysis. 37 of the 47 affiliations with publications ≥ 5 and 40 of 61 authors with publications ≥ 3 involve in publication collaborations. The collaboration among affiliations is as Fig. 6.

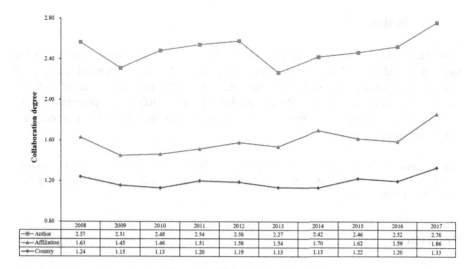

	2008	2009	2010	2011	2012	2013	2014	2015	2016	2017
—■— Author	2.57	2.31	2.48	2.54	2.58	2.27	2.42	2.46	2.52	2.76
—▲— Affiliation	1.63	1.45	1.46	1.51	1.58	1.54	1.70	1.62	1.59	1.86
—◆— Country	1.24	1.15	1.13	1.20	1.19	1.13	1.13	1.22	1.20	1.33

Fig. 5. Collaboration degrees in the field

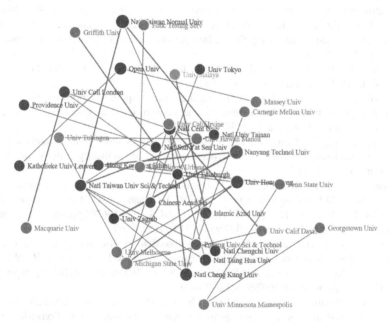

Fig. 6. Collaboration network of 37 affiliations with publications $\geq$ 5, accessed via http://www.zhukun.org/haoty/resources.asp?id=UMLL2018_affiliation

4   Conclusion

This study presents a comprehensive overview and an intellectual structure of the technology enhanced language learning research field from the period 2008–2017 through bibliometric analysis. The literature characteristics are revealed through statistics description and geographical visualization. The findings can potentially assist researchers especially newcomers in systematically comprehending the status and development of the field.

Acknowledgements. This work was supported by National Natural Science Foundation of China (No. 61772146) and Innovative School Project in Higher Education of Guangdong Province (No. YQ2015062).

References

1. Golonka, E.M., Bowles, A.R., Frank, V.M., Richardson, D.L., Freynik, S.: Technologies for foreign language learning: a review of technology types and their effectiveness. Comput. Assist. Lang. Learn. **27**(1), 70–105 (2014)
2. Chen, C.M., Li, Y.L.: Personalised context-aware ubiquitous learning system for supporting effective english vocabulary learning. Interact. Learn. Environ. **18**(4), 341–364 (2010)
3. Hsu, C.K., Hwang, G.J., Chang, C.K.: A personalized recommendation-based mobile learning approach to improving the reading performance of EFL students. Comput. Educ. **63**, 327–336 (2013)
4. Lai, C., Gu, M.: Self-regulated out-of-class language learning with technology. Comput. Assist. Lang. Learn. **24**(4), 317–335 (2011)
5. Hu, W., Qian, Y., Soong, F.K., Wang, Y.: Improved mispronunciation detection with deep neural network trained acoustic models and transfer learning based logistic regression classifiers. Speech Commun. **67**, 154–166 (2015)
6. Liu, H., Liang, L., Zhang, L., Lu, Y., Chen, B.: Modulatory role of inhibition during language switching: evidence from evoked and induced oscillatory activity. Int. J. Bilingualism **21**(1), 57–80 (2017)
7. Chen, X., Chen, B., Zhang, C., Hao, T.: Discovering the recent research in natural language processing field based on a statistical approach. In: Huang, T.-C., Lau, R., Huang, Y.-M., Spaniol, M., Yuen, C.-H. (eds.) SETE 2017. LNCS, vol. 10676, pp. 507–517. Springer, Cham (2017). https://doi.org/10.1007/978-3-319-71084-6_60
8. Chen, X., Weng, H., Hao, T.: A data-driven approach for discovering the recent research status of diabetes in China. In: Siuly, S., Huang, Z., Aickelin, U., Zhou, R., Wang, H., Zhang, Y., Klimenko, S. (eds.) HIS 2017. LNCS, vol. 10594, pp. 89–101. Springer, Cham (2017). https://doi.org/10.1007/978-3-319-69182-4_10
9. Khan, M.S., Ullah, W., Riaz, I.B., Bhulani, N., Manning, W.J., Tridandapani, S., Khosa, F.: Top 100 cited articles in cardiovascular magnetic resonance: a bibliometric analysis. J. Cardiovasc. Magnet. Reson. **18**(1), 87 (2017)
10. Chen, X.L., Xie, H.R., Wang, F.L., Liu, Z.Q., Xu, J., Hao, T.Y.: A bibliometric analysis of natural language processing in medical research. BMC Med. Inf. Decis. Making **18**(Suppl 1), 14 (2018)

11. Chen, X.L., Ding, R.Y., Xu, K., Wang, S., Hao, T.Y., Zhou, Y.: A bibliometric review of natural language processing empowered mobile computing. Wirel. Commun. Mob. Comput. (in press)
12. Feng, Y., Zhu, Q., Lai, K.H.: Corporate social responsibility for supply chain management: a literature review and bibliometric analysis. J. Cleaner Prod. **158**, 296–307 (2017)
13. Geng, Y., Chen, W., Liu, Z., Chiu, A.S., Han, W., Liu, Z., et al.: A bibliometric review: energy consumption and greenhouse gas emissions in the residential sector. J. Cleaner Prod. **159**, 301–316 (2017)
14. Wei, Y.M., Mi, Z.F., Zhang, H.: Progress of integrated assessment models for climate policy. Syst. Eng.-Theor. Pract. **33**(8), 1905–1915 (2013)
15. Otte, E., Rousseau, R.: Social network analysis: a powerful strategy, also for the information sciences. J. Inf. Sci. **28**(6), 441–453 (2002)
16. Flöel, A., Rösser, N., Michka, O., Knecht, S., Breitenstein, C.: Noninvasive brain stimulation improves language learning. J. Cogn. Neurosci. **20**(8), 1415–1422 (2008)
17. Yang, S.H.: Using blogs to enhance critical reflection and community of practice. J. Educ. Technol. Soc. **12**(2), 11–21 (2009)

Evaluation of Cooperative Learning in Graduate Course of Natural Language Processing

Ruifeng Xu[✉] and Zhiyuan Wen

Harbin Institute of Technology (Shenzhen), Shenzhen 518055, China
xuruifeng@hit.edu.cn, wenzhiyuan2012@gmail.com

Abstract. As a new collaborating teaching approach, cooperative learning has attracted more and more educational research interests. In this study, taking the teaching characteristics of graduate course of natural language processing into consideration, we apply cooperative learning based on Blackboard platform to improve the conventional graduate teaching. Through two years of teaching practice, we evaluate the effect of cooperative learning in the learning of course content and project development. The evaluation results show that cooperative learning approach improves the teaching effectiveness on course contents. Especially, this approach improves the cooperation among students in the project development effectively.

Keywords: Cooperative learning · Graduate teaching
Natural language processing course

1 Introduction

The main purpose of graduate education is helping graduate students to grasp cutting-edge knowledge in their professional field through systematic teaching and training. Meanwhile, graduate education emphasizes the capacity establishment to comprehensively use cutting-edge technologies to solve practical engineering problems [1]. At present, based on our education experiences, we think that the graduate teaching are puzzled by four difficulties. Firstly, with the increasing of the number of graduate students, it is difficult for the lectures to organize effective discussions during the classroom teaching. Secondly, the graduate students need to learn the frontier theory and technologies, however, it is difficult to completely cover these contents in the classroom teaching. Thirdly, due to the knowledge basis of the graduate students are diversity, the effect of unified teaching is insufficient. Finally, the examination based teaching evaluation criterion is too simple to evaluate the learning effect objectively.

Natural language processing (NLP) is an area of computer science and artificial intelligence concerned with the interactions between computers and human (natural) languages, in particular how to program computers to fruitfully process large amounts of natural language data[1]. In recent years, natural language processing research attracts

---

[1] https://en.wikipedia.org/wiki/Natural-language_processing.

© Springer Nature Switzerland AG 2018
T. Hao et al. (Eds.): SETE 2018, LNCS 11284, pp. 180–189, 2018.
https://doi.org/10.1007/978-3-030-03580-8_19

much interests from both academic research and industry applications. However, on one hand, natural language processing research involve many subjects such as computational linguistics, machine learning, and sociology. On the other hand, the research in NLP area is active which leads to the emerging of new method and technologies. These lead to many difficulties in the teaching of NLP courses for graduate students [1]. The teaching effect is unsatisfactory. Therefore, we consider to introduce cooperative learning approach to improving the teaching effectiveness and quality.

Cooperative learning is a type of educational approach which aims to organize classroom activities into academic and social learning experiences[2]. Cooperative learning approach arranges the students into groups, and it has been described as "structuring positive interdependence." The students must work in groups to complete tasks collectively toward academic goals. Unlike individual learning, which can be competitive in nature, students learning cooperatively can capitalize on one another's resources and skills such as asking information, evaluating ideas and monitoring work among the group members. Everyone succeeds when the group succeeds. From the point of view from lectures, their role changes from teaching information to facilitating students' learning [2]. The education evaluation results show that cooperative learning achieved better learning effects compared to individual learning and classroom learning [3].

In this study, based on Blackboard platform, we introduced cooperative learning approach to the teaching of graduate course of natural language processing. We encourage the deep discussion and project cooperative research and development among the students. During the teaching practice in two years, we evaluate the effectiveness of cooperative learning on course content learning and project development, respectively. The evaluation results show that cooperative learning improve teaching quality effectively, especially on the group cooperation in project development.

2   Related Work

2.1   Cooperative Learning

Cooperative learning emphasizes the communication and interaction during the learning process. Generally speaking, cooperative learning approach include synchronous cooperative learning and asynchronous cooperative learning [4]. Synchronous cooperative learning is a type of tightly coupled learning. It is usually conducted through face-to-face after class discussion. Asynchronous cooperative learning is a type of loosely coupled cooperative learning. The learners needn't gathering for face-to-face discussion. The asynchronous cooperative learning normally relies on some online platform [5]. Prey et al. adopted the cooperative learning in undergraduate computer science curriculum. In the final closed laboratory course, the students are shown benefits of working/helping their peers [6]. Chase et al. combined cooperative learning and peer instruction in introductory computer science teaching

---

[2] https://en.wikipedia.org/wiki/Cooperative_learning.

and obviously lower the WDF rate (i.e. percentage of students receiving a grade of "D" or "F", or withdrawing from the course) [7]. Trytten et al. progressed conventional small group work to cooperative learning in group programming of computer science course [8]. Their experiences shown promising preliminary results, from both the student and the professor's perspective, through creating positive cooperative learning experiences. In China, Chen et al. proposed a resource-based Computer Supported Cooperative Learning (CSCL) scheme for computer science education [9]. Li et al. investigated the security issues in cooperative learning based virtual community and proposed a threshold proxy signature based security scheme [10]. The existing experiences has shown cooperative learning are helpful to online learning, but they cannot fully meet the needs of lectures and students, especially the graduate students. To improve the effectiveness of asynchronous cooperative learning, a more professional, full-function, flexible online platform is desired.

2.2   Blackboard Platform

Blackboard platform is developed by the United States Blackboard Company [11]. Blackboard platform provides an online platform for millions of lectures and students in thousands of universities and education institutes. This network education platform, with teaching, communication and sharing as the core goal, provides a complete set of optimized solutions for educator. It is well received by teachers and learners.

The Blackboard platform consists of seven major modules: lecture introduction, course notification, course document distribution, interactive communication between lectures and students, course groups, course assignments distribution and submission, and course tools. The lecture may flexibly use these seven modules to meet the requirement of course teaching. The seven modules constitute the three major functions of Blackboard platform:

1. Resource management functions. It is the core function of the Blackboard platform. The lecture may use this function to distribute, manage and organize the teaching materials. The students may access the teaching resources at anytime and anywhere.
2. Interaction and communication function. This function takes students as the core. It helps the students to communicate and discuss freely. Meanwhile, it supports the question and answering, experiences sharing and discussions between lecture and students. In addition, group learning and discussion are also supported.
3. Evaluation function. The evaluation function aims to help the lecture to conduct comprehensive evaluation of learning effects of the students, including assignment, online quiz, self-assessment and course participation statistics collection.

With the development of network technology and modern education technology, Blackboard network teaching platform has been adopted by many schools at home and abroad. At present, most China universities use this platform only for resource sharing. They have not integrated the Blackboard platform with conventional teaching to explore the new teaching mechanisms [12].

3   Our Cooperative Learning Design

The conventional classroom teaching approach has shown its shortages in natural language processing education at graduate level, which requires to meet the growing needs of the cooperative development of production, education and research. Besides the conventional classroom teaching, current graduate course of NLP desires the self-study of the frontier of theory and technology which are not included in the textbook. Establishing the solid theoretical foundation, practical development capability and group development experiences are the three major targets of this course. Aims to three targets, based on Blackboard platform, the cooperative learning for natural language processing course is designed.

The overall framework of curriculum consists of five major components, namely student collaborating, course design, project design, cross scoring and course grading, as shown in Fig. 1.

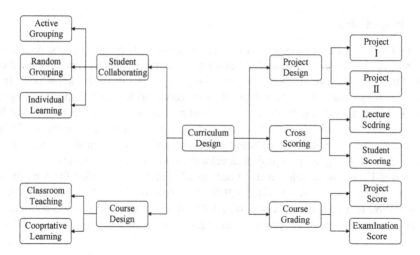

Fig. 1. Overall framework of curriculum design based on cooperative learning

3.1   Student Collaborating

Cooperative learning emphasizes the communications, discussions and cooperation among the students. Thus, grouping students is the first step to cooperative learning. Here, we firstly divided the students into cooperative learning groups and individual learning groups. Next, the cooperative learning groups are further divided into active collaborating students and random collaborating students. Each group has two or three student members. Here, active collaborating means that the students are actively and freely grouped. Normally, the team member is familiar to each other. Random collaborating means that the students are randomly assigned to groups by the lecture.

Through the establishment of student groups and subsequent group learning, we expect that the group members can deepen their understanding and complement each other, establish a cooperative learning vision and stimulate students' learning. In addition, the two collaborating strategies are designed to evaluate the effect of active collaborating to cooperative learning.

3.2 Course Design

We divided the course teaching into two parts: one is the conventional classroom teaching and the other one is online cooperative learning on Blackboard platform. Classroom teaching mainly teaches NLP knowledge to help students systematically master the relevant knowledge framework and mainstream techniques. Cooperative learning mainly uses Blackboard platform to support learning resources sharing and the discussions and communications between lecturer and the students. The students are expected to play a more active role in the process of learning. Meanwhile, the students are encouraged to learn the latest research technologies spontaneously.

3.3 Project Design

Natural Language Processing is one of the research hotspots in recent years. As a result, new models and methods are updated quickly. Meanwhile, this field is very practical. Therefore, for graduate students, they not only expect to learn the knowledge from textbooks only. They are expected to establish good self-learning ability to grasp the state-of-the-art knowledge in the field. More important, they are expected to establish the capability that uses learned knowledge to solve practical engineering problems. This is one of the key differences between undergraduate and graduate study. Thus, in this course, we designed two project development tasks for the students.

Project I aims to develop a document level sentiment classifier for Sina Weibo (Chinese twitter) text. We provided 5,000 annotated Weibo text as training dataset, 5,000 Weibo text as testing dataset and 10,000 Weibo text as developing dataset. The Weibo text are classified into positive and negative. Two instances are show in Table 1.

Table 1. Instances of Project I: Sentiment Classification for Weibo Text

ID.	Label	Text
1	Positive	王总的手机好牛, 苹果三星什么的都弱爆了 *Mr. Wang's mobile phone is perfect, and Apple and Samsung mobile phones are too weak*
2	Negative	今天的头条新闻太颓了 *Today's headlines are so decadent*

Each student is required to build their own machine learning based classifier. The performances of the classifiers are evaluated on the testing dataset. Attribute to the informal languages in twitter, such a sentiment classification task is difficult.

Project II aims to develop a system for identifying and classifying the relation between two persons. It consists of two subtasks: the person entity identification and the relation classification. Two instances are illustrated in Table 2. Each time, two entities are extracted from the text, the system is required to determine the relationship category among a total 19 types between two persons. In the case that the relation between two person match current relation type, the output label is TRUE. Otherwise, FALSE.

Table 2. Instances of Project II: Identify and Classify Person Relations

Realtion	Entity 1	Entity 2	Text	Label
偶像 idol	舒马赫 Schumacher	天亮 Tianliang	天亮崇拜舒马赫 Tianliang adore Schumacher	TRUE
同居 cohabit	黄晓明 Huang Xiaoming	张翰 Zhanghan	郑爽张翰同居杨颖劈腿黄晓明 Zheng Shuang and Zhang Han cohabitation. Yang Ying cheat Huang Xiaoming	FALSE

Generally speaking, these tasks covers many issues in NLP including word segmentation, entity identification, text classification, sentiment classification, and relation extraction. The student is encouraged to develop their systems using the knowledge learned from classroom teaching, self-learning and cooperative learning.

3.4 Cross Scoring

In addition to the performance-based scoring in the two projects, we introduced cross scoring for project evaluation. Each student group is required to perform an oral presentation for their developed systems. After that, each group cross scored the systems based on the innovations and technologies. We expected such cross scoring scheme further strengthen the cooperative learning in the groups, so that the students in each group work hard for their common goals. Furthermore, cross scoring is helpful to enable students to play the role of lecture for increasing the interaction and participation among the students.

3.5 Course Grading

The course grading is divided into two parts. One is the final written examination for each individual student. It aims to evaluate the understanding of the knowledge from textbook. Another one is the project score which is related to the group results that the student belongs to. It aims to evaluate the application of knowledge and team work.

4 Evaluation Results

To evaluate the effectiveness of cooperative learning in graduate natural language processing course, we conducted two-year education experiments. 50 and 52 students participated this education experiment in 2016 and 2017, respectively. They are camped into 18 groups each year while 2 or 3 students constituted one group. As discussed, 12 groups are based cooperative learning, in which 6 groups are based on active collaborating and 6 groups are based on random collaborating. The remaining students did not participate cooperative learning, but they were also grouped into 6 groups during project development. They are based on conventional self-learning and face-to-face discussions. We evaluate the effects of cooperative learning based on the scores on written examination and project development, respectively.

4.1 Written Examination Scores

The scores of written examinations in two years are listed in Table 3. In this table, CL (Active) denote the active grouped student following cooperative learning, CL (Random) denote the randomly grouped students following cooperative learning, and Conventional denote the students following conventional self-learning and face-to-face discussions. It is observed that the examination scores of the students following cooperative learning are obviously higher than the students following conventional mode. The average improvement is 4.685 points in 2016 and 3.146 in 2017. The students who exchange their understandings and question and answering on the blackboard platform achieved higher score. It means that cooperative learning are effect to improve the knowledge understanding in the classroom teaching. Furthermore, we evaluate the examination scores between active grouped students and randomly grouped students. It is observed that their differences are minor. The average gap is only 0.3268, indicating that the influence of grouping strategy is not significant.

Table 3. Scores of written examination.

Year	CL (Active)	CL (Random)	Conventional
Year 2016	78.278	78.265	73.586
Year 2017	78.167	78.833	75.354

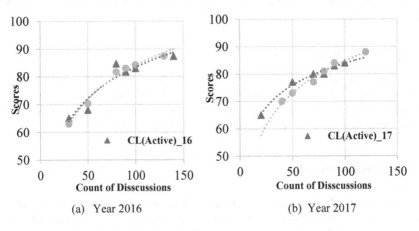

(a) Year 2016   (b) Year 2017

Fig. 2. Examination scores vs. the number of discussions

Next, we estimate the influence of online discussion quantity to the examination scores. Since the discussions are performed on Blackboard system, only the students following cooperative learning are estimated here. Figure 2 shows the examination scores vs. count of discussions for each group. It is observed that count of discussions has shown clear positive correlation with examination scores as a whole. Meanwhile, active collaborating and randomly grouping have not shown obvious impact.

4.2   Project Development Scores

Table 4 lists the project development scores. It is observed that the project development scores of the groups following cooperative learning are obviously higher than the conventional groups. For Project I, the average improvement are 8.758 in 2016 and 9.534 in 2017, respectively. For Project II, the average improvement are 6.697 in 2016 and 5.608 in 2018, respectively. It clearly shown that cooperative learning are effective to improve the practical project development performance. Meanwhile, the improvement on project development scores are higher than examination scores. It indicates that the contribution of cooperative learning on project development, which relies on more discussions and group cooperation, are higher than examination which more relies on individual learning. The observation also shown that the score differences between CL (Active) and CL (Random) are minor. The average gap is 0.116 in Project I and 0.824 in Project 2, respectively, indicating that the influence of active collaborating and random collaborating is not significant. It partially attributes to the fact that the group members become familiar during the project development even they are randomly grouped.

Table 4. Scores of project development

	CL (Active)	CL (Random)	Conventional
Project I 2016	82.092	82.509	73.542
Project II 2016	85.098	84.705	78.204
Project I 2017	83.106	82.456	73.247
Project II 2017	85.598	84.342	79.362

Next, we estimate the influence of the count of online discussions to the project development scores. Since the discussions are performed on Blackboard system, only the students following cooperative learning are estimated here. Figure 3 shows the project development scores vs. the count of online discussions for each group. In which, (a) and (b) are for Project I in 2016 and 2017, respectively; (c) and (d) are for Project II in 2016 and 2017, respectively. It is shown that the count of online discussions have shown strong positive correlation with project development scores. It shows that the discussions and cooperation on Blackboard platform are helpful to the student for sharing their new ideas, removing the bugs and group developing, which is essential to practical project development. Meanwhile, active collaborating and randomly grouping didn't lead to obvious differences on project development scores.

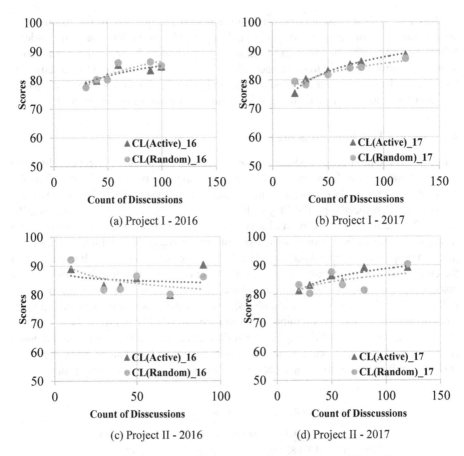

Fig. 3. The scores of project development vs. the number of discussions.

5   Conclusion

In this study, we applied cooperative learning based on Blackboard platform to the teaching of graduate course of natural language processing. Accordingly, we re-design the curriculum including student grouping, course design, project design, cross scoring and course grading to meet the requirement of group based cooperative learning. The evaluation on two-year education experiments show that the cooperative learning is effective to enhance the interest, participation and cooperation of the students in the curriculum. It leads to the obvious improvements on both course content learning and cooperative project development. At present, cooperative learning is shown more effective for engineering-oriented graduate courses. In the future work, we will applied cooperative learning to other fundamental graduate courses.

Acknowledgements. This work was supported by Course Construction Project No. JGYJ-201541, Harbin Institute of Technology, Shenzhen Graduate School, Key Technologies Research and Development Program of Shenzhen JSGG20170817140856618, Shenzhen Foundational Research Funding 20170307150024907.

References

1. Bontcheva, K., Cunningham, H., Tablan, V., et al.: Using GATE as an environment for teaching NLP. In: Proceedings of the ACL-02 Workshop on Effective Tools and Methodologies for Teaching Natural Language Processing and Computational Linguistics, vol. 1, pp. 54–62. Association for Computational Linguistics (2002)
2. Johnson, D.W., Johnson, R.T., Smith, K.A.: Active Learning: Cooperation in the College Classroom. Academic Achievement, 140 (1991)
3. Kaufman, D., Sutow, E., Dunn, K.: Three approaches to cooperative learning in higher education. Can. J. High. Educ. **27**(2/3), 37–66 (2017)
4. Millis, B.J., Cottell Jr., P.G.: Cooperative Learning for Higher Education Faculty. Series on Higher Education. Oryx Press, Phoenix (1997)
5. Ahn, B., Nelson, M.: Assessment of the effects of using the cooperative learning pedagogy in a hybrid mechanics of materials course. Int. J. Mech. Eng. Educ. (2018). https://doi.org/10.1177/0306419018759734
6. Prey, J.C.: Cooperative learning and closed laboratories in an undergraduate computer science curriculum. ACM SIGCUE Outlook **24**(1–3), 23–24 (1996)
7. Chase, J.D., Okie, E.G.: Combining cooperative learning and peer instruction in introductory computer science. ACM SIGCSE Bull. **32**(1), 372–376 (2000)
8. Trytten, D.A.: Progressing from small group work to cooperative learning: a case study from computer science. In: Frontiers in Education Conference. IEEE (1999). 2001:13A4/22-13A4/27
9. Chen, Y., Xie, S., Lin, X., et al.: Design of cooperative learning network teaching system based on resources. Audio Video Educ. Res. **9**, 42–45 (2007). (in Chinese)
10. Li, F., Qi, Y., Xue, Q.: Research on the security of virtual learning community in the perspective of big data - discussions on collaborative learning system based on threshold proxy signature. J. Distance Educ. **31**(4), 76–82 (2013). (in Chinese)
11. Wang, R., Huang, X.: Exploration of excellent courses based on the Blackboard platform. Chin. Distance Educ. **19**, 83–85 (2011). (in Chinese)
12. Kubiszyn, T., Borich, G.: Educational Testing and Measurement. Wiley, Hoboken (2015)

Protein Complex Mention Recognition with Web-Based Knowledge Learning

Ruoyao Ding[1], Xiaoyi Pan[1], Yingying Qu[2(✉)], Cathy H. Wu[3],
and K. Vijay-Shanker[3]

[1] School of Information Science and Technology, Guangdong University
of Foreign Studies, Guangzhou, Guangdong, China
ruoyaoding@outlook.com, 13724019961@163.com
[2] School of Business, Guangdong University of Foreign Studies,
Guangzhou, China
jessie.qu@gdufs.edu.cn
[3] Department of Computer and Information Science, University of Delaware,
Newark, DE 19716, USA
{wuc,vijay}@udel.edu

Abstract. Protein complex plays an essential role in cellular functions and is an important named entity in the biomedical field. Since protein complex –relevant experimental results are usually published in scientific articles, recognizing protein complex mentions from literature is a crucial step of discovering protein complex-related information from existing scientific research studies. In this paper, we propose a method for protein complex mention recognition, which applies knowledge automatically learned from PubMed. Evaluation shows our method achieves a F1-score of 81%, demonstrating its effectiveness in the protein complex recognition task.

Keywords: Named entity recognition · Protein complex
Conditional Random Field

1 Introduction

Most biological experimental results are described in published literature. Researchers need to find the information of their interest from the research literature in order to conduct and interpret their own experiments. However, with the rapid growth of biomedical publications, molecular biology has become an information-saturated field. Manually extracting information from the literature usually is a time consuming and labor-intensive process. As a result, a major focus of bioinformatics research is to automatically extract information from published literature, using text mining techniques.

Protein complex is an important named entity in the biomedical field. It is often defined as a stable set of interacting proteins and where the complex has been shown to exist as an isolated, functional unit in vivo [1]. The need for recognizing protein complex in text stems from their importance in bio-medicine: (1) Proteins often function as components of larger complexes to perform a specific function,

© Springer Nature Switzerland AG 2018
T. Hao et al. (Eds.): SETE 2018, LNCS 11284, pp. 190–197, 2018.
https://doi.org/10.1007/978-3-030-03580-8_20

(2) formation of these complexes may be regulated [2], and (3) some molecules exist only in certain types of complex (e.g., collagen type I, EBI-2325312) [3].

Despite the large body of work [4–11] conducted in the recognition of other types of bio-named entities, as far as we are aware, no work has been done for protein complex mention recognition. This is probably due the fact that the current resources for protein complex are very limited, as a result, some valuable clues for recognizing the mentions may not work effectively. For example, Protein Ontology [12], Complex Portal at IntAct [3] and CORUM [13] are some well-known resources which containing information about protein complexes. There are only 2561 unique protein complex names in these resources. Due to the incomplete of the protein complex dictionary, the value of dictionary lookup may be underestimated.

In this paper, we describe a method to recognize protein complex mentions in literature. When developing the method, we applied knowledges automatically learned from PubMed to tackle the problem of limited resources for protein complex. Our method is the first publicly available method specifically designed for protein complex mention recognition. It can be used to assist in the improvement of the coverage of protein complex in resources such as Complex Portal and CORUM.

2 Methodology

The flow chart of our method is shown in Fig. 1. The input text is broken up into sentences and then into individual tokens. Next, for each token, a set of features is created, with the help of knowledges learned from PubMed. Then, a CRF model is employed to label the tokens in the text. Finally, the s completes the protein complex mention recognition process with several post processing steps.

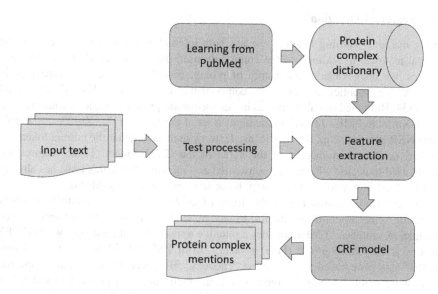

Fig. 1. The flow chart of the proposed method.

2.1 Text Preprocessing

Given abstracts or full-length articles as input, we use an in-house developed tool to split the input text into sentences and then tokenize the sentences. Note that common tokenization method breaks one sentence into either a contiguous block of letters and/or digits or a single punctuation mark. We treat the adjacent words which are c-terms as one token. For example, in the tokenized sentence "Signal transduction by the alpha 6 beta 4 integrin" from PMID 7556090, "alpha 6 beta 4" is treated as one token. The notion of c-term was introduced in [14], it is characterized by the presence of ortho-graphic features such as capital letters, numerals and special prefix symbols, which indicates that the term is not a typical English word but likely to be a name.

2.2 CRF Model Application

It is common to treat the named entity recognition task as a sequence labelling task using the **BIO** model, where each token in the text is labelled as **B**eginning of a named entity, **I**nside a named entity, or **O**utside a named entity. In this work, we also treat the protein complex mention recognition task in this way. For example, in sentence "Endosomal sorting complex required for transport-I is one of three defined protein complexes …", to recognize the protein complex mention "endosomal sorting complex required for transport-I", we will need to assign label "B" to the token with word "Endosomal", assign label "I" to tokens with words "sorting", "complex", "required", "for", "transport-I", and assign the rest of the tokens with label "O".

Conditional Random Field (CRF) [15] is a machine learning technique which is commonly used in the sequence labelling task. We employ CRFsuite [16], an imple-mentation of the CRF, to label the tokens in the text.

2.3 Feature Extraction

As for machine learning features, we use both internal and external features. For the internal features, in addition to the commonly used part-of-speech (POS) and lemma features, we also consider the nature of protein complex names, i.e., some protein complex are mentioned via their components, e.g., "Mis16-Mis18" in PMID 24774534. But noted not all mentions in this format are protein complex mentions, e.g., "Xnr1-Xnr6" in PMID 11934150 mentions a set of genes: "Xnr1", "Xnr2", … "Xnr6". Some NER systems, e.g., BANNER, use features such as whether the current token is a number, or Roman numerals, or the name of the Greek letters. These features are mainly used to decide what can be considered as a mention. Since this issue has already been handled in our tokenization step, these features are not considered.

The external features are in the form of context. Normally, contextual words describing some functions are helpful to recognize the type of bio-named entities. For example, in sentence "EMF1 encodes a putative transcriptional regulator, while EMF2 encodes a Polycomb group (PcG) protein." from PMID 19783648, we can know "EMF1" is a gene based on its context "encodes". However, since protein complexes and proteins can have the same type of function, their contexts can also be similar. For instance, in sentence "Sgk1 phosphorylates Nedd4-2." from PMID 18197893, the gene mention "Sgk1" has the context "phosphorylates". However, complexes such as CK2 can also have this context, as in sentence "We showed that CK2 phosphorylates PU.1" from PMID 16439360.

Therefore, due to the similarity in the descriptions of actions conducted by proteins and protein complexes, we do not learn from context for disambiguation. Instead, we only consider f-terms. The notion of f-term was introduced in [14] and further developed in [17]. An f-term comes from a small list of words which can indicate the type of a named entity, such as gene, disease, and complex. However, we will have to find an exhaustive set of f-terms for protein complexes. For this purpose, we use complex portal to automatically mine protein complex f-terms. Entries in Complex Portal contain terms which describe complex-assembly information, e.g., heterodimer. These terms are collected and used as protein complex f-terms. Table 1 shows a regular expression, which is generated from collected protein complex f-term list, used for identifying protein complex f-terms.

Table 1. Regular expression for identifying protein complex f-terms.

/(complex|dimer|trimer|tramer|hexamer|nonamer|tamer|decamer|octomer|oligomer)$/

Dictionary lookup is helpful to recognize the bio-named entities, thus has been used as a machine learning feature by most of the named entity recognition systems. However, unlike other types of named entities, currently the coverage of the protein complex resources is limited. The value of dictionary lookup feature may be underestimated by a machine-learning method, if the protein complex dictionary is only created based on those resources. Thus, we develop a method to automatically mine protein complex names from Medline abstracts. Details of this mining process is described in Sect. 2.4.

Eventually, we decided to use the following set of features. For a current token, represented as token i below, the following features are used:

1. POS feature. The part of speech tags of tokens $i - 2$, $i - 1$, i, $i + 1$, and $i + 2$.
2. Lemma feature. The lemmas for the words of tokens $i - 2$, $i - 1$, i, $i + 1$, and $i + 2$.
3. c-term feature. Whether the word/words of token i contains a c-term.
4. f-term feature1. The protein complex f-term flag (whether it is a f-term) for word of tokens $i - 2$, $i - 1$, $i + 1$, and $i + 2$.
5. f-term feature2. Whether the headword of token i is a protein complex f-term. The headwords here include: (a) the head of the NP which contains token i, (b) the head of the appositive of token i, (c) the head of the relative clause of token i.
6. Multiple gene names feature. Whether the word/words of token i contain multiples gene names. Gene dictionary lookup is applied on the word/words of token i to see whether it contains multiple gene names. The gene dictionary used here is based on our previous work [18], with gene names from human, mouse, rat, and yeast added.
7. Dictionary lookup feature. Is token i: (a) the beginning of a dictionary match, (b) inside of a dictionary match, or (c) outside of a dictionary match.
8. Feature combinations. Combinations of feature 3 and 4, as well as feature 3 and 5.

2.4   Dictionary Construction Based on Knowledge Learning

We want to extract protein complex names automatically from Medline abstracts and create a protein complex name dictionary. Recall that we have created a list of protein complex f-terms (described in Sect. 2.3). The mining of protein complex names is based on this f-term list, with the following steps:

(1) Search in all Medline abstracts for sentences that contain protein complex f-terms.
(2) Detect the "is_a" relation in the extracted sentences. The detection of the "is_a" relation is handled by in-house developed tool, which basically applies a set of rules based on syntactic dependencies. For each "is_a" relation pair, it outputs two arguments (two NPs).
(3) When one argument ends with a f-term or contains an adjectival form of a f-term (e.g., heterdimeric), then we will extract the other argument as protein complex name if it is a c-term (and hence likely to be a named entity).

Using this method, 3.445 unique protein complex names are extracted. Among them, 1.318 are not in Protein Ontology, Complex Portal, or CORUM.

2.5   Post-processing

To improve the performance of our protein complex mention recognition method, we apply several postprocessing rules to the CRF results: (1) If one mention is recognized as a protein complex, then all the mentions in the same abstract/article which have same name will also be tagged as protein complex. For example, "Arp2/3" in PMID 23354023 sentence 7 is recognized as a protein complex by the CRF model, then all occurrence of "Arp2/3" in this PMID is tagged as protein complex. (2) Abbreviation pairs are extracted using Stanford acronym detection algorithm [19]. Both the full name and the short name will be tagged as a protein complex if either one of them is recognized. (3) Recognized mention which is number or starts with number is removed, e.g., "850-kDa complexes" in PMID 4092036.

3   Evaluation and Results

3.1   Evaluation Setup

As to our knowledge so far, there is no annotated corpus available for protein complex mention recognition, we develop our evaluation corpus in-house. The Gene Ontology (GO) is a resource which provides structured ontologies that describe gene products in terms of their associated biological processes, cellular components and molecular functions. Entries in GO contain names of the GO term, and some of these names are associated with PMID. 200 PMIDs are extracted randomly from entries under Protein complex (GO:0043234) sub-hierarchy, and abstracts are retrieved from PubMed using the 200 PMIDs.

As stated in the introduction section, Complex Portal at IntAct and CORUM are two famous resources for protein complex, Entries in these two resources are associated with PMIDs. Another 100 PMIDs are extracted randomly from these two resources (50 from each).

Protein complex mentions are manually annotated in these 300 abstracts. The annotation is completed by two senior biocurators. Altogether, 745 protein complex mentions (329 unique PMID-protein complex name pairs) are annotated from the first 200 abstracts, and 471 protein complex mentions (191 unique PMID-protein complex name pairs) are annotated from the second 100 abstracts.

We use the first set of 200 abstracts for development, and the second set of 100 abstracts for evaluation. We apply 10-fold cross validation to evaluate the performance of our method. Like the evaluation for other NER tasks, the performance is computed using the standard measures of precision, recall and F1-score. Since our method has a propagation step (If one mention is recognized as a protein complex, then all the mentions in the same abstract/article which have same name will also be tagged as protein complex), the performance is computed based on the PMID-protein complex name pairs, instead of mentions. As far as we are aware of, no previous work has been done for protein complex mention recognition. Thus, there is no alternate method to compare with.

3.2   Results and Discussion

In order to investigate the effectiveness of the postprocessing steps, we compared the performance of our method using CRF model plus postprocessing, as well as the performance using CRF model only. Table 2 shows the average precision, recall and F1-score using 10-fold cross validation. Using the CRF model only achieved a F1-score of 76% (with a precision of 73% and a recall of 79%). Combined with the postprocessing, our method obtained a F1-score of 81% (with a 6.6% increase). Both the precision and recall were also increased to 80% and 82%, respectively.

Table 2. Results of 10-fold cross validation.

	Precision	Recall	F1-score
CRF	73%	79%	76%
CRF + postprocessing	80%	82%	81%

We analyzed the false positives (FNs) and the false negatives (FPs) and found that majority of the FNs were due to the fact that these FNs did not have valid features to be used by the model. For example, in sentence "Ego3 assumes a homodimeric structure similar to ..." from PMID 23123112. The context "homodimeric structure" indicates "Ego3" is a protein complex. However, this clue relies on a semantic structure, and is not captured by the current used machine learning features. Other FNs were because our method failed to detect the actually name of protein complex. For example, in sentence "... interaction with a Rps28p/3'UTR mRNP complex." from PMID 15225542. The actual name of the complex is "Rps28p/3'UTR". However, our method detected "mRNP" as the name. Of course, this type of errors also leaded to FPs. As expected, the postprocessing steps improved both the precision and the recall. This is basically because using of acronym detection and clues based syntactic dependencies contribute more TPs, while the step to filter out invalid names reduce the number of FPs.

When developing our method, many of the features used in the training of the CRF model were manually designed. This is due to the fact that the corpus we were able to obtain for training is not large enough. With a large enough corpus, more data driven approach to feature engineering can be adopted. The dictionary we used in our method is automatically created by extracting protein complex names from the PubMed using high confidence. We believe the same idea can be applied in other situations when a dictionary of names needs to be created.

4   Conclusion

In this paper, we presented a method for recognizing protein complex mentions from literature. The method applies CRF, combined with knowledge automatically learned from PubMed. Evaluation shows our method achieves a F1-score of 81%. The method can potentially provide high confidence text evidence for the protein complex resources such as Complex Portal and assist in the improvement of the coverage in these resources. In the future, we plan to integrate our method of protein complex mention recognition with our previous method of gene mention recognition [18], we will investigate whether this can improve the performance for both methods.

Acknowledgements. This paper is supported by grants from National Key R&D Program of China (2016YFF0204205, 2018YFF0213901) and China National Institute of Standardization (522016Y-4681, 522018Y-5948, 522018Y-5941).

References

1. Gene Ontology Consortium webpage. http://geneontology.org/page/protein-complexes. Accessed 21 May 2018
2. Gingras, A.-C., Aebersold, R., Raught, B.: Advances in protein complex analysis using mass spectrometry. J. Physiol. **563**(Pt 1), 11–21 (2005)
3. Meldal, B.H.M., Forner-Martinez, O., Costanzo, M.C., et al.: The complex portal–an encyclopaedia of macromolecular complexes. Nucleic Acids Res. **43**(Database issue), D479–D484 (2015)
4. Settles, B.: ABNER: an open source tool for automatically tagging genes, proteins and other entity names in text. Bioinformatics **21**(14), 3191–3192 (2005)
5. Leaman, R., Gonzalez, G.: BANNER: an executable survey of advances in biomedical named entity recognition. In: Pacific Symposium on Biocomputing, pp. 652–663 (2008)
6. Torii, M., Hu, Z., Wu, C.H., Liu, H.: BioTagger-GM: a gene/protein name recognition system. J. Am. Med. Inform. Assoc. (JAMIA) **16**(2), 247–255 (2009)

7. Lu, Y., Ji, D., Yao, X., Wei, X., Liang, X.: CHEMDNER system with mixed conditional random fields and multi-scale word clustering. J. Cheminformatics **7**(Suppl 1), S4 (2015). Text mining for chemistry and the CHEMDNER track
8. Liu, H., Torii, M., Hu, Z.Z., Wu, C.: Gene mention and gene normalization based on machine learning and online resources. In: Proceedings of the Second BioCreative Challenge Workshop, pp. 135–140. CNIO (2007)
9. Batista-Navarro, R., Rak, R., Ananiadou, S.: Optimising chemical named entity recognition with pre-processing analytics, knowledge-rich features and heuristics. J. Cheminformatics **7** (Suppl 1), S6 (2015). Text mining for chemistry and the CHEMDNER track
10. Lowe, D.M., Sayle, R.A.: LeadMine: a grammar and dictionary driven approach to entity recognition. J. Cheminformatics **7**(Suppl 1), S5 (2015). Text mining for chemistry and the CHEMDNER track
11. Kaewphan, S., Hakala, K., Ginter, F.: UTU: disease mention recognition and normalization with CRFs and vector space representations. In: SemEval@ COLING, pp. 807–811 (2014)
12. Natale, D.A., Arighi, C.N., Blake, J.A., et al.: Protein Ontology: a controlled structured network of protein entities. Nucleic Acids Res. **42**(Database issue), D415–D421 (2014)
13. Ruepp, A., Waegele, B., Lechner, M., et al.: CORUM: the comprehensive resource of mammalian protein complexes–2009. Nucleic Acids Res. **38**(Database issue), D497–D501 (2010)
14. Fukuda, K., Tamura, A., Tsunoda, T., Takagi, T.: Toward information extraction: identifying protein names from biological papers. In: Pacific Symposium on Biocomputing, pp. 707–718 (1998)
15. Lafferty, J., McCallum, A., et al.: Conditional random fields: probabilistic models for segmenting and labeling sequence data (2001)
16. Okazaki, N.: CRFsuite: a fast implementation of Conditional Random Fields (2007). [2015-03-24]
17. Narayanaswamy, M., Ravikumar, K.E., Vijay-Shanker, K.: A biological named entity recognizer. In: Pacific Symposium on Biocomputing, pp. 427–438 (2003)
18. Ding, R., Arighi, C.N., Lee, J.-Y., Wu, C.H., Vijay-Shanker, K.: pGenN, a gene normalization tool for plant genes and proteins in scientific literature. PLoS ONE **10**(8), e0135305 (2015)
19. Schwartz, A.S., Hearst, M.A.: A simple algorithm for identifying abbreviation definitions in biomedical text. In: Pacific Symposium on Biocomputing, pp. 451–462 (2003)

Towards a Knowledge Management Model for Online Translation Learning

Yuanyuan Mu[1], Lu Tian[2,3(✉)], and Wenting Yang[1]

[1] School of Foreign Studies, Hefei University of Technology, Hefei, China
[2] School of Interpreting and Translation Studies,
Guangdong University of Foreign Studies, Guangzhou, China
ivytianlu@gdufs.edu.cn
[3] Center for Translation Studies, Guangdong University of Foreign Studies,
Guangzhou, China

Abstract. This paper endeavors to build a knowledge management model for translation learning with special reference to an on-line translation teaching platform. The Platform features a computable network of inter-related and hierarchically distributed conceptual representations of the knowledge in this field. The representation utilizes "tag-words" as the knowledge nodes to form a roadmap of navigation and also as the keywords to introduce theory-informed annotations. This knowledge management system of tag-words aims to advance our understanding of how the knowledge of language and use of language can be modeled in the source language context and remodeled in different settings of the target language context. With the help of this knowledge management system, we may explore the ontological representations of translation and provide a navigation roadmap capable of generating effective learning pathways for learners. Facilitated by the platform, learning activities may be designed to investigate the behavioral patterns of knowledge construction in specific translation learning tasks.

Keywords: Knowledge management · Translation learning · Tag-words

1   Introduction

The translation and interpreting industry has witnessed tremendous growth in the past decades, at a rate of 10% to 15% annually [1]. The increasingly prosperous industry and the shortage of qualified translators or interpreters call for rapid development of translation and interpreting courses in universities throughout the world. Take China for instance, since the establishment of BTI (Bachelor of Translation and Interpreting) program in 2006 and MTI (Master of Translation and Interpreting) program in 2007, translation related programs and courses have experienced rapid growth in universities all over China. According to the latest statistics provided by China National Committee for BTI Education on its official website[1] as of 18 July 2017, there are altogether 215 universities in China with MTI programs and 252 with BTI programs (with 86 universities including both BTI and MTI programs), increased by almost 20 universities

---

[1] http://cnbti.gdufs.edu.cn/info/1006/1519.htm.

© Springer Nature Switzerland AG 2018
T. Hao et al. (Eds.): SETE 2018, LNCS 11284, pp. 198–207, 2018.
https://doi.org/10.1007/978-3-030-03580-8_21

on average annually. However, due to lack of professionally trained teachers in the field of translation in China, a large number of the newly added universities with BTI and MTI programs have encountered problems of shortage of qualified teachers. In this regard, our research team design the ClinkNotes Online Platform for the Teaching/ (self-)learning of Translation (hereinafter referred to as "ClinkNotes Online Platform"), aimed at developing a cost-effective educational paradigm in classroom and web-based settings for the training of professional translators and English-Chinese bilingual language users.

The interdisciplinary scope of ClinkNotes Online Platform covers such fields as computer science, translation studies, language acquisition, functional linguistics, and corpus linguistics. It comprises: (1) corpus-construction (including text-annotation, exercises with explanation of answers, and knowledge-based topical boards); (2) the knowledge management system (theoretically-informed investigations to generate a system of glossed "tag-words" as knowledge nodes to identify/describe textual phenomena and translation methods); (3) electronic program design to interconnect all the aforementioned components for inter-module navigation online. The Platform features a variety of genres/subject domains (including news reports, technical texts, government documents, legal documents, literary texts, etc.), and the data are annotated following a system of 198 tag-words generated from research-informed text analyses, representing knowledge nodes indicating translation methods or language rules for learners. To be more specific, the translation corpus includes 1,772 bilingual texts for general reading and 240 bilingual texts with altogether 3,000 pieces of in-depth annotations, each of which contains the description of approximately 200 words to identify and explain language phenomena or translation techniques by using specific tag-words as knowledge nodes. Meanwhile, 3000 exercises in accordance with the tag-word-based knowledge nodes have been designed for learners to practice what can be learnt in the text data annotation, with each exercise accompanied by the explanation of approximately 200 words. In addition, there are 155 pieces of knowledge-based topical boards containing longer versions of detailed explanation to the tag-word-based knowledge nodes that may occur in the texts and annotations, accounting for 230,000 words in total. In this sense, the tag-words, functioning as important knowledge nodes for the description and explanation of language phenomena or translation techniques, form a knowledge management system and also a guideline for translation learning.

2 Literature Review

According to Zhu and Wang's review [2], the number of universities offering fully-fledged undergraduate translation programs is on the rise, not to mention translation courses offered in foreign languages or literatures across China. However, some institutions of tertiary education are found to be in a rather passive position in adapting to the trend, particularly on account of staff shortage. Liao [3] reported in 2004 that in most foreign languages and literature departments, where translation courses were normally provided and translation programs hosted, there were usually no more than two to three staff members who were engaged in teaching or research in translation, not to mention the situation of staff shortage in training schools. In this sense, the internet-based and computer-aided language/translation training paradigm is of great necessity to optimize learning resources and alleviate the pressure of staff shortage/labor-intensive teaching.

Equally unsatisfactory is the pattern and quality of translation teaching. The model dominating translator training in China still follows the tradition, blurring the line between translation teaching and language acquisition. Despite the awareness of using corpora in translation teaching, the current use of corpora in translator education is still limited to data retrieval by such means as concordancing, word frequency modeling, collocation clustering and keyword tracking [4–8]. With the lack of a systematic, knowledge-management based and theory-informed approach, the traditional translation teaching tends to be subjective and impressionistic. More often than not, assessment of learners' translation assignments leaves the them perplexed and unconvinced, and teachers themselves are sometimes trapped in their own intuitive comments. Moreover, traditional classroom teaching of translation usually favors general discussions at lexical and syntactical levels, without a clear guideline for the specific knowledge nodes that learners need to master. Sometimes, isolated sentences used by teachers as teaching examples with no context provided alongside may lead to diversified interpretations, and therefore it is difficult for learners to provide convincing translations supported by systematic knowledge repositories. In this circumstance, the application of a theory-informed and knowledge-management based approach is called for to drag translation teaching back to its role as cross-linguistic text formulation [2] away from the present undue concern with training of fragmented language skills. Indeed, a clarification for translation teaching and learning is needed. The latest literature on language teaching has pointed out "the weakness of exclusively monolingual language teaching" and argued strongly that "translation has an important role to play in language learning – that it develops both language awareness and use, that it is pedagogically effective and educationally desirable, and that it answers student needs in the contemporary globalized and multicultural world" [9]. In this spirit, the relationship between translation learning and bilingual language learning is that of a mutually benefited "symbiosis" [9]. In this regard, we define translation learning as a process of building up a knowledge management system for bilingual language rules and conversion methods between two languages, and therefore the dependence on knowledge-management based model of translation learning is crucial.

3 Knowledge Management Model for Online Translation Learning

The knowledge management model for translation learning on ClinkNotes Online Platform, which focuses on building up a knowledge management system for bilingual language rules and conversion methods between two languages, provides a research-informed and systematic guideline for translation teaching and learning. This model will be more objective and applicable than the simple empiricism of translators or translation trainers which used to take a large role in conventional translation teaching and learning. The core concept of this model is the system of 198 knowledge nodes (called tag-words in the platform) clearly defined based on existing linguistic and translation theories, which are used to summarize and tag the main knowledge points concerning translation methods or bilingual language phenomena as instructed in the text annotations. In fact, the annotations tagged by the knowledge nodes function as learning instructions on how to use specific translation methods or language rules to solve translation problems in various contexts. Such instructions as revealed in the text annotations form teaching contents for learners, while the network of tag-words functions as a roadmap for knowledge construction of translation learning. The knowledge management model for online translation learning can be implemented through the following steps:

- Step 1: Selecting a tag-word from the network of knowledge nodes;
- Step 2: Finding out other tag-word combinations centering on the main knowledge node;
- Step 3: Referring to the text annotations tagged by a set of tag-word combinations for instructions on translation methods or language rules;
- Step 4: Reflecting on the tag-word network that learners have navigated, and summarize the perception of knowledge learning features in translation learning.

3.1   Tag-Word-Based Network of Knowledge Management Model

The tag-word network includes 9 categories of 198 tag-words to constitute a theory-informed knowledge network and act as signposts in on-line navigation. These 9 categories are idiomatic usage, grammar, rhetoric, translation methods, sentence information distribution, inter-sentence connection, intra-paragraph development, inter-paragraph development and cultural background knowledge. The following shows examples of tag-words for the 9 categories:

- Idiomatic Usage: Idioms, Four-characterPhrase, Collocation, Three-characterRhythm, Context, etc.
- Grammar: NounNumber, Article, ModifierTransfer, Adverbial-SubjunctiveMood, Tense-Particle, etc.
- Rhetoric: Pun, Reduplication, Personification, Parallelism, Understatement, etc.
- Translation Methods: Simple-Complex, Passive-Active, Positive-DoubleNegative, Merge, Transfer, etc.
- Sentence Information Distribution: EndFocus, Theme-Rheme, Progression, Sequence, Foregrounding, etc.
- Inter-sentence Connection: Inter-sentence, Connection, Cause-Effect, Condition, Adversative, etc.
- Intra-paragraph Development: Intra-paragraph, Listing, Comparison, Elaboration, Foreshadow, etc.
- Inter-paragraph Development: Inter-paragraph, Introduction, Conclusion, SubjectMatter, Echo, etc.
- Cultural Background Knowledge: BackgroundKnowledge, Intertextuality, SemanticGap, Allusion, Image, etc.

Apart from the tag-word-based network mentioned above, detailed annotations are provided for the original text and its translation at word, phrase, sentence, paragraph or textual levels, based on the explanations of key knowledge nodes involved in specific cases as learning instructions. In this way, tag-word-based network and annotations as learning instructions form the core of knowledge management model. Within the network, different tag-words are interrelated and used as combinations in data annotation, to realize the co-reference and retrieval between text phenomena and translation methods, between text and text, as well as between method and method. As can be seen from the example below, the definition of a tag-word includes the following elements: (1) Definition of tag-word (2) Possible tag-word combinations (3) Relevant tag-words.

As Table 1 shows, the definition of the tag-word "Transfer" refers to other related tag-words that might be combined in particular annotations. For example, after translation, changes might happen to the information structure of the text, either in terms of information sequence or effects conveyed by the text. Another case might be that the theme, or the topic of the source text, becomes the rheme or the focus in the target text, accompanied with the changes in the textual effects produced. This translation phenomenon could be described as Theme-Rheme or Topic-Focus, with the sign "-" implying the concept of "Transfer". Taking into account the interconnection between tag-words in the knowledge network and the manifestations of the interconnection in description and explanation of specific texts, textual phenomena and translation methods, these tag-words, or rather the nodes in the knowledge network, can be combined and form the theoretical framework for data analysis. Figure 1 shows the possible tag-word combinations of "Transfer" that can be found and tagged in the data annotation of the corpus.

Table 1. Definition of tag-word

Tag-word: Transfer
Definition: Transfer focuses on the change of the effects of information delivery or the position of a certain language component in terms of its information structure in the process of translation, with considerations on different communication purposes, for instance, the transfer between topic and focus, the transfer between theme and rheme; the transfer between modifier and the headword, and other lexical or syntactical transferring devices.
Possible Tag-word Combinations: Topics, Focus, Theme, Rheme, Development, etc.
Relevant Tag-words: Shift, Transformation, etc.

The tag-words, stemming from text, textual phenomena and translation methods, form an inter-related knowledge network, and data annotation extracts several related nodes, or rather tag-words, to illustrate the text design or information management, either in ST or TT, and the effects achieved in both texts. Figure 2 demonstrates a knowledge network with 'Transfer' as the projecting node, which can be extracted from the various tag-word combinations existing in the actual data annotations of the corpus as shown in Fig. 1. The combination of these inter-related tag-words has corresponding data annotation examples on the platform. Doubtless the tag-words system is open-ended. With more tag-words and annotated text data added to the platform, this diagram is likely to be more complicated.

Fig. 1. Tag-word and possible tag-word combinations in data annotation

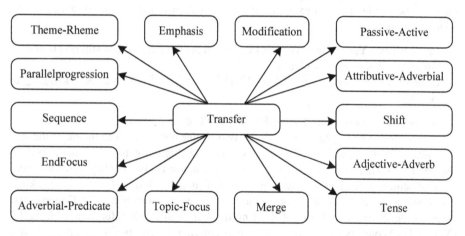

Fig. 2. Knowledge network with the tag-word "Transfer" as projecting node

The connection between different tag-words as illustrated in Fig. 1 can be exemplified by various combinations of several tag-words in specific data annotation. In other words, data annotation is constructed on the basis of the interconnection of tag-words. While the system of 198 tag-words covers the language and cultural phenomena as well as translation methods in the textual data and forms the theoretical framework for data annotation in the platform, the tag-word combination discloses the interrelation between different languages and cultural phenomena and translation methods, and illustrates this interrelation through data annotation, which is supposed to strengthen learners' sensitivity to language and cultural phenomena and translation methods in teaching and self-learning. The core of this teaching concept is as follows: the tag-words, through the dynamic interrelation between one another, provide a cognitive basis for specific textual phenomena, and the understanding of texts is based on the network composed of the tag-words. Therefore, it is safe to say that the system of tag-words is the theoretical foundation of this online teaching/self-learning platform. The integration and interaction of the modules, data annotation, exercises, topical boards, etc., are also driven by the interconnection embodied in the tag-word system.

3.2   Annotations as Learning Instructions in Knowledge Management Model

The possible tag-word combinations in tag-word definitions are a theoretically conceived scenario, which needs examples in authentic data annotation. New combinations might be discovered in the process of annotation. The tag-word combination usually has one key tag-word with other related tag-words centering on it as subordinate points to aid the annotation. The key tag-word and other related tag-words are integrated and form a miniature annotation of specific text data. For a particular piece of translation or bilingual textual data, regardless of whether it is a word, phrase, clause, sentence, paragraph or text, the annotation will proceed from the tag-word combination and formulate comprehensive analysis of the text design, stylistic feature, text function and effects. The following is an example of the annotation based on the knowledge management model.

> English Text: Yeung Hau Wong is the deity worshipped. There is still no consensus amongst scholars on his identity.
> Chinese Translation: 侯王宫供奉的是杨侯王，至于他究竟是何人，现时还是众说纷纭。

Tag-word Combination: Theme-Rheme, EndFocus, Emphasis

Annotation: The English text includes two simple sentences. The theme of the first sentence is "YeungHau Wong", a piece of new information which does not appear in the previous text. The EndFocus of the second sentence is "his identify" deriving from the first sentence, with "his" referring back to YeungHau Wong. Relatively speaking, "no consensus" is the new information in the second sentence. The Chinese text reverses the theme and rheme of the English text. Thus, new information "杨侯王" (YeungHau Wong) is placed as the rheme, occupying the end position of the sentence and emphasized as the EndFocus, its prominent position enhanced again by "shi" (是)-structure. The information "no consensus" in the English text is moved to the end of the sentence and translated into "众说纷纭", becoming the highlighted EndFocus. Moreover, in the Chinese text, the theme "侯王宫" of the first sentence has appeared in the first paragraph. Therefore, this information is added here as the starting pointing of the ensuing information presentation and contributes to textual cohesion. The pronoun "他" (he) closely follows the noun "杨侯王" it refers to and continues the topic about the identity of this person, until arriving at the focus "众说纷纭". Through information restructuring, the Chinese text achieves the movement from given information to new information, and strengthens the connection between sentences.

The annotation above functions as a piece of learning instruction, providing learners with key knowledge nodes through tag-words and detailed explanations of translation methods used in this case to help them build up knowledge network concerned in the learning process. Such annotations not only describe how the textual phenomena come into being and how the translation methods are realized, but also explain why the textual phenomena exist and why the translation methods are employed, in order to avoid value judgment, inadequate annotation and over-interpretation.

4 Application of Knowledge Management Model in MTI Programs

The knowledge management model has been applied in the teaching of such courses as Practical Translation and Literary Translation in MTI programs at Hefei University of Technology and Guangdong University of Foreign Studies. The following shows our observation of learners' mostly focused knowledge nodes in their learning of Practical Translation course at Hefei University of Technology. There are altogether 32 students from the Master of Translation and Interpreting Program enrolled in Practical Translation course in the first semester of 2017-2018 Calendar Year. Apart from the 64 class hours of normal teaching in the whole semester, learners are required to conduct online learning facilitated by the ClinkNotes Online Platform for at least two hours per week. Since the historical performance module of the Platform records learners' learning pathways, including the frequency of tag-words, annotations, texts and exercises they have visited in this online Platform, learners' performance can be observed quite clearly.

Statistics has been provided to figure out the top 15 mostly focused knowledge nodes of the whole class, in order to testify the pedagogical hypothesis of translation teaching and learning. The top 15 knowledge nodes as indicated in the relevant tag-words are as follows: (1) Allusion; (2) Intertextuality; (3) Active-Passive; (4) Four-character Words; (5) Adjective-Adverbial; (6) Perspective; (7) Background Knowledge; (8) Image; (9) Metaphor; (10) Noun-Verb; (11) Theme; (12) Rhythm; (13) Linear Thematic Progression; (14) Backward Thematic Progression; (15) Collocation.

To further analyze the features of the 15 mostly focused knowledge nodes, we may find that these 15 tag-words fall into the following categories, listed in descending order according to their popularity: (1) cultural background knowledge; (2) idiomatic usage; (3) grammar; (4) rhetoric; (5) sentence information distribution; (6) intra-paragraph development.

This result reveals the following features of learners' focus on knowledge nodes:

(1) Cultural background knowledge becomes the main focus of learners in their learning of translation, which far exceeds other categories of knowledge according to the frequency of visit on the online Platform.
(2) The categories of idiomatic usage and grammar, the foundation of bilingual competence, are also receiving great attention from learners, which testifies the conventional pedagogical focus of translation teaching and learning.

(3) Categories related to textual development such as sentence information distribution and intra-paragraph development also receive much attention from learners, which are supposed to be difficult parts of translation teaching and learning.

These above-mentioned findings show that, according to our observation of MTI students, while conventional pedagogical focus of idiomatic usage and grammar still take an important role in knowledge management model, more attention has been given to the category of knowledge nodes related to cultural background knowledge. However, the focus on cultural background knowledge in translation learning was not so widely recognized by our learners before the adoption of knowledge management model, according to a follow-up after-class interview with learners, some of whom spent too much time practicing grammar and idiomatic usage but little time learning cultural background knowledge in both source and target culture. Moreover, learners need more efforts on categories related to textual development such as sentence information distribution and intra-paragraph development. Our knowledge management model provides learners with a theory-informed and systematic understanding of knowledge network for translation learning.

5   Conclusion

The knowledge management model supported by a theory-informed tag-word system and annotations sheds new light on translator training and the construction of corpora for the purpose of translation studies, which will hopefully counteract the subjective and impressionistic practice in traditional translation teaching. Learners may build up their own knowledge network with the help of our knowledge management model. This model also attempts to set up an efficiency-motivated, theory-informed pattern for translation teaching, to counteract the labor-intensive, time-consuming and space-constrained teaching of translation. Hopefully, the knowledge management model will provide a ground-breaking and cost-effective educational paradigm for the teaching/(self-)learning of English-Chinese bilingual text-production in classroom/web-based settings to alleviate the pressure on language/translation courses.

Acknowledgements. The work was substantially supported by Anhui Provincial Education Commission (Project No. SK2017A0062).

References

1. Rosenblum, J.: American Translators Association surpasses 10,000 members (2017). http://www.bokorlang.com/journal/43ata.htm
2. Zhu, C., Wang, H.: A corpus-based, machine-aided mode of translator training: ClinkNotes and beyond. Interpret. Transl. Train. 5(2), 269–291 (2011). https://doi.org/10.1080/13556509.2011.10798821
3. Liao, Q.: Structure of translator training programs and the development of translation studies (学科设置与翻译学的发展). Chin. Transl. J. 25(3), 36–37 (2004)

4. Bosseaux, C.: A study of the translator's voice and style in the French translations of Virginia Woolf's the Waves. In: Olohan, M. (ed.) CTIS Occasional Papers, vol. 1, pp. 55–75. The University of Manchester, Manchester (2001)
5. Bowker, L., Pearson, J.: Working with Specialized Language: A Practical Guide to Using Corpora. Routledge, London and New York (2002)
6. Colominas, C., Badia, T.: The real use of corpora in teaching and research contexts. In: Rodrigo, E.Y. (ed.) Topics in Language Resources for Translation and Localisation, vol. 79, pp. 71–88. John Benjamins, Amsterdam and Philadelphia (2008). https://doi.org/10.1075/btl.79.06col
7. Stewart, D.: Safeguarding the lexicogrammatical environment: translating semantic prosody. In: Beefy, A., Inés, P.R., Gijon, P.S. (eds.) Corpus Use and Translating: Corpus Use for Learning to Translate and Learning Corpus Use to Translate, vol. 82, pp. 29–46. John Benjamins, Amsterdam and Philadelphia (2009). https://doi.org/10.1075/btl.82.04ste
8. Inés, P.R.: Evaluating the process and not just the product when using corpora in translator education. In: Beefy, A., Inés, P.R., Gijon, P.S. (eds.) Corpus Use and Translating: Corpus Use for Learning to Translate and Learning Corpus Use to Translate, vol. 82, pp. 129–149. John Benjamins, Amsterdam and Philadelphia (2009). https://doi.org/10.1075/btl.82.09rod
9. Cook, G.: Discourse and Literature: The Interplay of Form and Mind. Oxford University Press/Shanghai Foreign Language Education Press, Oxford/Shanghai (1994/1999)

Designing a Platform-Facilitated and Corpus-Assisted Translation Class

Lu Tian[1,2], Yuanyuan Mu[3(✉)], and Wenting Yang[3]

[1] School of Interpreting and Translation Studies, Guangdong University of Foreign Studies, Guangzhou, China
[2] Center for Translation Studies, Guangdong University of Foreign Studies, Guangzhou, China
[3] School of Foreign Studies, Hefei University of Technology, Hefei, China
390842884@qq.com

Abstract. An effective translation class relies on both clear and accurate instruction from the teacher as well as motivated and guided self-discovery by the learner. Various emerging technologies have made education as such possible and feasible. Taking the translation of reporting clauses as a case in point, this paper introduces the design and teaching procedure of a translation class which combines the adoption of an online platform for teaching and self-learning of English-Chinese translation and an online English-Chinese Parallel Corpus to facilitate effective teaching and learning. A platform-facilitated and corpus-assisted translation class as such demonstrates a new approach to translator training relying on emerging technologies. It not only enhances overall comprehension and digestion of knowledge but also encourages and inspires exploration spirit in learners.

Keywords: Online platform · Parallel corpus · Translation class
Reporting clause

1 Introduction

An effective translation class relies on both clear and accurate instruction from the teacher as well as motivated and guided self-discovery by the learner. Various emerging technologies have made education as such possible and feasible. This paper elaborates on the design and teaching procedure of a translation class which combines the adoption of an online platform for teaching and self-learning and an online English-Chinese Parallel Corpus to facilitate effective teaching and learning of reporting clause in English-Chinese translation.

Reporting clause, also known as reporting speech, refers to the clause that introduces speech or thought either in the form of direct speech or indirect speech. "It specifies the speaker or thinker, the addressee (sometimes), the type of act, and frequently also the mode of the act" [1]. Reporting clause widely exists in academic writings [2–4], news reports [5] and other ESP fields [6–8] thus deserves attention on its representation in translation. Therefore, it is worthwhile to carry out a systemic and intensive exploration of reporting clause from a comparative perspective in translation class.

© Springer Nature Switzerland AG 2018
T. Hao et al. (Eds.): SETE 2018, LNCS 11284, pp. 208–217, 2018.
https://doi.org/10.1007/978-3-030-03580-8_22

The translation class under discussion is a compulsory course for the first year MTI (Master of Translation and Interpreting) students in a Chinese university. All the students are native speakers of Chinese with English as their second language.

2   Methodology

Two emerging technologies are particularly integrated into the translation class — an online translation teaching and (self-)learning platform and an online parallel corpus.

The Online Platform for Computer-Aided Teaching and Learning of Bilingual Writing and Translating in/between English and Chinese, constructed by a research group of the City University of Hong Kong, features in its in-depth annotated texts and exercises with detailed explanation on various translation skills and textual features [9]. With its scientific and systematic knowledge management model, the platform facilitates translation teaching and learning by combining theories with language reality, text learning with exercises, thus not only helping consolidate students' knowledge in language and translation but increasing their textual awareness [10].

Constructed upon authentic data and facilitated by retrieval tools, parallel corpus enables convenient contrastive observation of the source language and target language texts and has been widely used in translation studies and translation teaching [11–13]. The corpus adopted in the present study is the Babel English-Chinese Parallel Corpus, which consists of 327 English articles and their translations in Chinese. The texts were collected from the *World of English* and *Time* of 2000 and 2001. The corpus contains a total of 544,095 words (253,633 English words and 287,462 Chinese tokens).

3   Class Design and Teaching Procedure

3.1   Before Class Preparation: An Overview of the Topic

A couple of theoretical and empirical studies can be found on reporting clause. Students are firstly provided with a list of references and asked to do a literature review on the topic so they can obtain a better understanding of the concept and raise awareness of its similarities and differences in different languages. From the given references, they should be able to discover the following findings.

Jia [14] categorized reporting clause into three different levels, i.e. formal, semantic and pragmatic. His study classifies and demonstrates the pragmatic functions of reporting clause in both Chinese and English languages. Zhang's [15–17] series of studies on reporting reveal that reporting verbs have quotative and discourse functions.

Following Ardekani's classification of reporting verbs, Liu and Hong [18] compared reporting verbs in *Hong Lou Meng* and its translations with an aim to investigate linguistic differences between the two languages. They found that Chinese literary narration is liable to combine reporting verbs with adverbs of manner while English translation tends to replace reporting verbs with explanatory or explicit expressions.

The rise of corpus linguistics sees researchers conduct studies based on large corpora of data. Biber et al. [1] analyzed the similarities and differences of reporting clause in fiction and news in terms of position, expansion, inversion, etc. Baker [19] initiated a new methodology to investigate the style of literary translators by focusing on the frequency and patterning of "say" in the translated texts and the use of optional "that" in reporting structures.

3.2   In-Class Teaching and Learning: Platform-Facilitated Instruction

On the translation teaching and learning platform, an authentic system of tag-words serves as "nodes" connecting related texts, annotation and exercises (Fig. 1). They also function as "signposts" guiding class instruction and self-learning in a systematic and informed manner. As far as reporting is concerned, the tag-word "quotation" is in close and direct relevance. Definition of "quotation" can be found on the platform, which reads "to quote words of others (or oneself) or resources in writing in order to achieve different purposes for demonstration". Clicking the retrieved entries, one will find the English and Chinese sentences involving quotation highlighted in the parallel texts with a floating window giving detailed explanation of the textual functions and effects in language transfer (Fig. 2). At this stage, the platform functions as a well-achived repository as well as the teacher's toolkit facilitating class instruction and discussion.

Fig. 1. List of tag-words on the platform

By now, students have been equipped with the basic knowledge about reporting and have accumulated certain knowledge about its actual use in real contexts. Then it is time that students consolidated what they have learned by doing exercises on the platform. Via the tag-word "quotation", relevant exercises will be sorted out (Fig. 3).

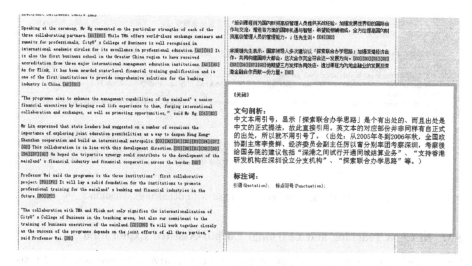

Fig. 2. Parallel texts with annotation

After finishing a set of three exercises, students can submit their answers. Feedbacks will then be provided together with the reference answers and detailed explanations (Fig. 4). All the learning history, including both text learning and exercise practicing, is automatically recorded, which helps with the monitoring and supervision by the teacher as well as the self-monitoring by the learner.

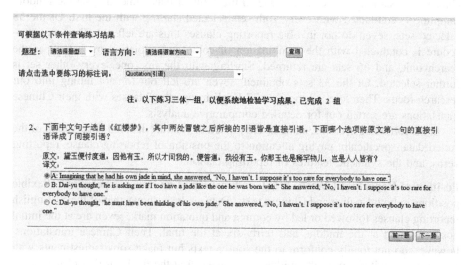

Fig. 3. Example of exercises

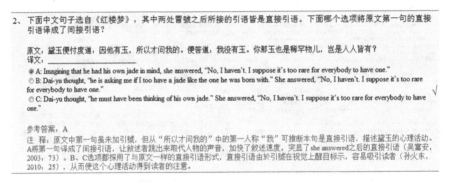

Fig. 4. Reference answer to exercise with detailed explanation

3.3   In-Class Teaching and Learning: Corpus-Assisted Exploration

Large data of online parallel corpus compensate the relatively limited annotated texts and exercises on the platform and provide learners with an opportunity to observe the sorted data, thus making meaningful discoveries.

Data Extraction. Data extraction has been done by the teacher before class, and the extracting method is explained and demonstrated in class. For the convenience of extraction, only reporting clauses which introduce direct speech are collected from the Babel English-Chinese Parallel Corpus. With the combination of comma and quotation mark (, ") as the key word for search, 571 matched English sentences with their Chinese translations are returned. Due to the limit of class time, a systemic random sampling is conducted with every 10th sets selected starting with the first. Of the 58 selected sets, seven do not involve reporting clauses thus are left out. The same procedure is conducted with the combination of colon and quotation mark (: ") as the search unit, and 66 sets are returned. Starting with the first one, every other set is further selected. Of the 33 sets obtained, seven are left out for not falling into our research focus. Therefore, all together 77 English reporting clauses with their Chinese translations are sorted out for detailed comparative analysis.

In the following sections, students are guided to conduct detailed observation of the sorted data, specifically paying attention to the position of reporting clause, reporting verbs, and the syntactic features of reporting clause.

Position of Reporting Clause. It is found that reporting clause appears with flexible positions in both English and Chinese texts. Data analysis shows that of the 51 English reporting clauses followed or led by comma and quotation mark, seven are at the initial position, eight at the middle, and thirty-six at the final. Their Chinese translations, however, do not totally conform to the source texts but make some adjustments with twenty-six at initial, six in the middle, and nineteen at the final position (Table 1).

While it is common to place reporting clause at the final position in English [1], in Chinese reporting clause seems to appear more before the reported speech. This is further proved by the discovery that all the 26 initial-placed English reporting clauses sorted by colon and quotation are kept at the same position in their Chinese

Table 1. Position of reporting clause

	Initial	Middle	Final	Total
English	7 (13.7%)	8 (15.7%)	36 (70.6%)	51
Chinese	26 (50.9%)	6 (11.8%)	19 (37.3%)	51

translations. Generally speaking, the Chinese translations show some flexibility in dealing with the position of reporting clause in order to meet the norms of the target language and make the translated texts more readable.

Such difference in preference of the position of reporting clause might be interpreted by the convention that in English the content of reporting is usually foregrounded by marking it at the beginning of a sentence whereas in Chinese it is commoner to retain it till the end and create an end focus. This also reflects different ways in information presentence and focalization between the two languages.

Reporting Verbs. The data of the study further prove Baker's previous assertion that *say* is "the most frequent reporting verb in English" [18]. With its inflectional variations (*says*, *said*), *say* appears 42 times in the sorted data, taking up more than a half of the total of 77 report clauses under analysis. Its obvious translation in Chinese, *shuo* 說, also appears conspicuously with a total occurrence of 49 times.

Apart from the generalized superordinates such as *say* and *tell*, a variety of reporting verbs indicating the function of utterance are also employed in the English texts. Such verbs include *ask, answer, begin, recall, continue, greet, explain, warn, note, admit, advise*, etc. Moreover, some reporting verbs such as *shout, stammer, exclaim*, etc. contain semantic component of the manner of utterance. In the translated Chinese texts, on the one hand, a part of these words could be rendered by equivalent words and expressions for instance *wen* 問 (ask), *gaojie* 告誡 (warn), *tanyan* 坦言 (admit), *zhichu* 指出 (note), *dazhaohu* 打招呼 (greet), *yishi yuse* 一時語塞 (stammer), etc. On the other, it is also noted that a couple of Chinese reporting verbs are compound words composed of modifier plus head word which in most cases turn to be the superordinates *shuo* 說 and *dao* 道. Examples of such words include *houdao* 吼道 (shout and say), *dadao* 答道 (answer and say), *huiyishuo* 回憶說 (recall and say), *jieshishuo* 解釋說 (explain and say), etc. It shows that while most of these English reporting verbs could independently express the meaning of "saying", their Chinese counterparts have to rely on an explicit *shuo* or *dao* to function as reporting verbs. In other words, lexically the meaning of saying is more explicitly expressed in Chinese.

Syntactic Features of Reporting Clause. When the English reporting clause appears at the middle position of a sentence, it is usually very brief in the simplest pattern of SV (e.g. *Bell said*) or SVO (e.g. *I told myself*). When placed at the final position, the order of the clause is usually inverted. It is discovered that more than one third of such reporting clauses are followed by an appositive specifying the identity of the speaker. In contrast, in the Chinese texts, these appositives are usually placed in front of the agents.

Eg. 1. "It's not the health objectives that will keep people doing things, frankly," says Judith C Young, director of the National Association for Sport and Physical Education in Reston, outside Washington.

"坦率地說，並不是那些健康目標使人們參加運動，"設在華盛頓城外賴斯頓的國家體育與運動協會主任朱迪思·C·揚說。

To depict a more vivid picture of the manner of speaking, an adverb might be adopted to modify the reporting verb (Eg. 2 & Eg. 3). Adverbial modifier can also be served by a present participle (Eg. 4) or an adverbial clause (Eg. 5). Their Chinese renditions also employ similar devices to express equivalent idea.

Eg. 2. ···he **modestly** answered···他**謙虛地**回答

Eg. 3. He greeted us **politely**···他**禮貌地**同我們打招呼

Eg. 4. Driving this economic transformation is the combination of shrinking computers and expanding communications, he says, **adding**: "We have seen only the beginnings of the anxiety, loss, excitement, and gains that many people will experience as our world shifts to a new highly technical planetary economy."

他說，正是日益縮小的電腦與不斷壯大的通訊業的結合在推動著這種經濟變革。他**還補充**說："我們已看到的僅僅是我們的世界向一個新的高科技全球經濟轉變時許多人將體驗到的焦慮、失落、激動與成就的開端。"

Eg. 5. "I'm glad they got those casinos," says Rock **as he reflects on the injustices endured by Native Americans**.
我對他們得到那些賭博娛樂場感到高興，羅克**在指責土著美國人所遭受的不公正待遇時**如是表白。

A unique feature discovered in Chinese reporting clause is that the pronoun *zheyang* 這樣 can be applied for reference, sometimes referring to the reference forward (Eg. 6), sometimes backward (Eg. 7), filling the semantic gap in the reporting clause.

Eg. 6. "School districts spend 90% of funds on new equipment, 10% on teacher training," says Charles Piller, the Macworld editor who conducted his magazine's study.

"學區花費90％的資金添置新設備，可花在教師培訓上的資金只有10％。"《邁科沃爾德》雜誌進行這方面研究的編輯查爾斯·皮勒**這樣**說。

Eg. 7. At another time he thus expressed his method of study: "I keep the subject continually before me, and wait till the first dawnings open slowly by little and little into a full and clear light."

在另一次，他**這樣**表述他的研究方法："我連續不斷地思考問題，一直等到最初的曙光慢慢一點一點地發展成完全明晰的亮光。"

In addition, nominalization is also found in both English and Chinese reporting clauses (Eg. 8 & Eg. 9). Sometimes, reporting clause is reduced to a nominal phrase (Eg. 10) or simply the name of the speaker (Eg. 11).

Eg. 8. The newlywed has made a public **appeal**: "If anyone has them, please give them back.

> 這對新婚夫婦向大眾**呼籲**：如果誰拿走了它們，請物歸原主。

Eg. 9. The **question** from Abby to her readers which sparked the greatest response was when she asked readers: "Where were you when President John F. Kennedy was shot?"

> 艾比引起讀者最大反響的**問題**是"約翰‧F‧肯尼迪總統遇刺時，你在哪裡？"

Eg. 10. His **answer**: "We will handle the employment issue carefully."
> 他的**回答**是：我們會慎重處理僱員問題。

Eg. 11. **Sally**: "Are they the same age?"
> **薩莉**："他們年齡一樣大嗎？"

Close scrutiny into the contexts of Eg. 10 and Eg. 11 shows that such simplified reporting clause tends to be used within conversations so the coherence of discourse can be better achieved.

3.4 After Class Reflection: Group Discussions

After a comprehensive learning of reporting, students are asked to work in groups and summarize their findings in the form of a report. Below are some extracts from students' reports.

Reporting clause in both English and Chinese is flexible in position. What is more, adverbial modifiers are widely adopted in the reporting clause of both languages.

The generalized superordinates, "say" in English and "shuo" and "dao" in Chinese, are the most frequently used reporting verbs complemented with a variety of more specific ones. In rendering the original English texts, Chinese may employ expressions in more variety to convey equivalent meanings.

On the lexical level, some English reporting verbs do not have equivalent words in Chinese but have to be expressed by a combination of modifier plus head word of "shuo" or "dao". Syntactically, final position is most preferred in English whereas in Chinese reporting clause is more placed at the initial position. In addition, Chinese sometimes applies referencing to reporting clause, a phenomenon which is not discovered in the English data.

An after-class assignment as such gives students an opportunity to reflect on and consolidate what they have learned in class. Their findings could be directly applied to their translation practice. Moreover, through working in groups, their capacities for critical thinking and teamwork spirit are also enhanced.

4   Conclusion

In this paper, we give a detailed account of the design and teaching procedure of a platform-facilitated and corpus-assisted translation class of reporting clause in English and Chinese from a comparative translational perspective. The platform-facilitated instruction familiarizes and equips translation learners with the basic knowledge about reporting. Featured in its in-depth annotated texts and exercises, the platform provides guidance on organized instructions in key issues, phenomena, and strategies in translation. In the corpus-assisted teaching and learning phase, abundant parallel data and the retrieval function of the online corpus provide possibility and opportunity for translation learners to explore specific usage and translation of reporting clauses in English and Chinese and figure out their similarities and differences on the lexical, syntactical and textual levels. This translation class demonstrates a new approach to translator training relying on emerging technologies. It not only facilitates overall comprehension and digestion of knowledge but also encourages and inspires exploration spirit in learners.

References

1. Biber, D., et al.: Longman Grammar of Spoken and Written English. Pearson Education Limited, Harlow (1999)
2. Tarone, E., Dwyer, S., Gillette, S., Icke, V.: On the use of the passive in two astrophysics journal papers. ESP J. 1(2), 123–140 (1981). https://doi.org/10.1016/0272-2380(81)90004-4
3. Swales, J.: Genre Analysis: English in Academic and Research Settings. Cambridge University Press, Cambridge (1990)
4. Thompson, G., Ye, Y.: Evaluation in the reporting verbs used in academic papers. Appl. Linguist. 12(4), 365–382 (1991). https://doi.org/10.1093/applin/12.4.365
5. Xin, B.: A comparative analysis of the reporting verbs in China Daily and the New York Times (汉英新闻语篇中转述动词的比较分析——以《中国日报》和《纽约时报》为例). J. Sichuan Int. Stud. Univ. 24(125), 61–65 (2008)
6. Bergler, S.: Semantic dimensions in the field of reporting verbs. In: Proceedings of the Ninth Annual Conference of the UW Centre for the New OED and Text Research, pp. 44–56. CiteseerX, Oxford (1993)
7. Baynham, M.: Direct speech: what's it doing in non-narrative discourse? J. Pragmat. 25(1), 61–81 (1996). https://doi.org/10.1016/0378-2166(94)00074-3
8. Charles, M.: Phraseological patterns in reporting speech used in citation: a corpus-based study of these in two disciplines. Engl. Specif. Purp. 25(3), 310–331 (2006). https://doi.org/10.1016/j.esp.2005.05.003
9. Zhu, C.S., Mu, Y.Y.: Towards a textual accountability-driven mode of teaching and (self-) learning for translation and bilingual writing: with special reference to a CityU on-line teaching platform (以文本解释力为导向的语料库翻译教学——香港城大翻译与双语写作在线教学/自学平台的设计与试用分析). Chin. Transl. J. 2, 56–62 (2013)
10. Mu, Y.Y., Zhu, C.S.: In-depth data processing in constructing an online platform for teaching/self-learning of E-C translation and bilingual writing (在线翻译与双语写作教学/自学平台建设中的语料精加工). Contemp. Transl. Stud. 1, 56–62 (2013)

11. Baker, M.: Corpus linguistics and translation studies. Implication and application. In: Baker, M., Francis, G., Tognini-Bonelli, E. (eds.) Text and Technology: In Honor of John Sinclair, pp. 233–250. John Benjamins, Amsterdam (1993)
12. Laviosa, S.: Corpus-based translation studies: Where does it come from? Where is it going? Lang. Matters **35**(1), 6–27 (2004). https://doi.org/10.1080/10228190408566201
13. Hu, K.B.: Introducing Corpus-Based Translation Studies. Springer/Shanghai Jiao Tong University Press, Heidelberg/Shanghai (2016). https://doi.org/10.1007/978-3-662-48218-6
14. Jia, Z.H.: The reporting speech and its pragmatic functions (转述语及其语用功能初探). J. Foreign Lang. **2**, 35–41 (2000)
15. Zhang, R.J.: On the quotative and discourse function of reporting verbs (管领词的引述功能与话语功能). J. Foreign Lang. **1**, 48–52 (1998)
16. Zhang, R.J.: English reporting verbs: a functional study. J. Foreign Lang. **1**, 66–76 (2000)
17. Zhang, R.J.: A multi-angled analysis of English reported speech. J. Chongqing Norm. Univ. **2**, 103–107 (2007)
18. Liu, Z., Hong, H.: A corpus-based study of reporting verbs in fictions: a translational perspective. US-China Foreign Lang. **2**(8), 48–54 (2004)
19. Baker, M.: Towards a methodology for investigating the style of a literary translator. Target **12**(2), 241–266 (2000). https://doi.org/10.1075/target.12.2.04bak

Users' Stickiness to English Vocabulary Learning APPs in China

Nana Jin[1], Zili Chen[2], and Jin Wang[1(✉)]

[1] School of Foreign Languages, Shenzhen University, Shenzhen, China
nanajin7@163.com, szuwangjin@163.com
[2] School of Professional Education and Executive Development, CPCE,
The Hong Kong Polytechnic University, Hong Kong, China
spczili@speed-polyu.edu.hk

Abstract. This study is based on mobile-assisted language learning APPs and specifically focuses on users' stickiness to them. Several popular vocabulary learning mobile APPs in China are chosen for the study: Baicizhan, Shanbei, Kaixincichang, Zhimi, etc. The participants for the study are from three different age groups: 19 junior high students, 22 senior high students and 33 college students. The survey results indicate that the users' stickiness to the APPs declines with age growing. Major reasons for stopping using the APPs are: the lack of intrinsic motivation, no interests after using it for a period of time, no time for it, easily forgetting about it. Three suggestions to optimize the vocabulary learning mobile APPs and to help users learn efficiently and wisely are proposed: offering a highly matched task-based reading plan for vocabulary leaning; recommending a personalized learning group for learners of similar language proficiency to join; developing specific course book-oriented vocabulary learning functions to coordinate with in-class teaching.

Keywords: Vocabulary learning mobile APPs · Users' stickiness
Study motivation

1 Introduction

Mobile assisted language leaning (hereafter, MALL) is becoming more and more popular than computer assisted language learning, and it attracts language learners due to its unique advantages: portability and immediacy. Various mobile APP stores offer a large number of free language learning practices to attract users, which have an increasing influence on language education and second language acquisition [1]. One essential part of the language learning APPs is vocabulary learning APP which is an active area for linguists and researchers [2]. Language learners' evaluations on word learning APPs show some highly valued features: enabling users to choose specific target groups of words, offering vivid visual aids, providing pronunciations, detailed and accurate definitions and examples, and allowing users to interact with other users [3]. Furthermore, a personalized learning is essential to learner engagement and learning effectiveness [4].

© Springer Nature Switzerland AG 2018
T. Hao et al. (Eds.): SETE 2018, LNCS 11284, pp. 218–226, 2018.
https://doi.org/10.1007/978-3-030-03580-8_23

In this research, we traced and recorded language learners' stickiness to English vocabulary learning APPs among three different age groups. The word 'stickiness' refers to the binding between users and products. Examples of this type of product usage would range from visiting the splash page of the product to actually playing the product itself. Users' stickiness is measured in this study by daily active time and how long users would keep using a product. Six popular vocabulary learning APPs for Chinese users were chosen for the study. Different age groups were asked to compare the APPs they have used, and to choose their favorite ones. They were also asked how long they have been using their favorite APPs and why they refused to continuously use some other APPs. Whether there are differences of APP preference due to age difference? If yes, what functional features are highly preferred in each age group? Moreover, the reasons of stopping using vocabulary learning APPs are discussed and analyzed. Additionally, a personalized and users' stickiness-oriented and task-based learning APP model for effective vocabulary learning is suggested.

2 Literature Review

On vocabulary learning researches, it is widely proved that game-based learning applications are effective tools for ESL (English as a Second Language) learners to learn new words [2, 5–8]. And thus many vocabulary learning Apps are created as game-based ones. The representation of words in those APPs offers a multimodal context (picture, sound, animation, color, interaction, exercise, game, etc.) to learn new words and to distinguish them from similar ones. In the game-based vocabulary APPs, once language learners advance in the game, their satisfaction and motivation are enhanced. The incentives such as rewards, points and top score lead boards provide intense motivation to players [9]. The extrinsic motivation and learners' learning satisfaction have a great influence on ESL learners' vocabulary acquisition [5]. These Apps offer a platform where you may choose to learn English words by yourself with a self-paced speed, or by groups with peers' competition.

The sources for ESL learners to choose suitable vocabulary learning APPs include the evaluation display from the third part online, introduction from peers, recommendation from teachers, online advertisements, etc. There are also comparison data of vocabulary learning APPs released on well-known websites. Most of the evaluation and comparison focuses on the following aspects: design features, visual pictures, pronunciation sounds, examples, exercises, games. All the results show that a number of vocabulary learning APPs have more users than others [2]. They are Baicizhan, Momo, Kaixincichang, Shanbei, etc. A brief comparison of the APPs is shown in Table 1.

Most of the vocabulary learning mobile Apps share the following functional features:

i. Allowing users to choose their vocabulary group, for example, vocabulary for Primary students (Grade 1–6), for Secondary school students, for college students, for IELTS, for TOEFL, for SAT etc.

Table 1. A comparison of features among six popular vocabulary learning mobile APPs

	Baicizhan	Bubeidanci	Kaixincichang	Momo	Shanbei	Zhimi
Affix analysis	√		√		√	√
Explanation in English	√	√			√	
Visual aid	√					√
Associated knowledge				√		
Sentences with sound	√	√	√	√	√	√
Synonyms	√					√
Related phrases				√	√	√
Multiple exercises	√	√	√	√	√	√
Personalized settings	√	√	√	√	√	√
Game-based competition	√		√		√	√
Award stimulus	√	√	√	√	√	√

ii. Allowing users to set the amount of words for daily study. Consequently the APPs will automatically calculate when to review the words.

iii. Learning words step by step with breaking through tasks. After learning a number of new words, related questions are automatically presented. Users are supposed to answer the questions correctly and then go to the next task. The questions usually include: multiple choices for word meanings, spelling words according to given sounds with provided letters, fill in blanks with provided words. Take the APP Kaixincichang as an example, once users couldn't answer a question correctly, they lose one life. Each task gives you 10 lives for answering 40 questions. When users finish the task and have 8–10 lives left, they gain 3 stars (the highest); if 5–7 lives left, gain 2 stars; and if less than 5, 1 star gained. If users lose all 10 lives, they need to do the same task once again.

Although new multimodal vocabulary learning APPs are emerging continuously on line, very little studies are cast on how long would language learners stick to them.

3 Methodology

A survey was conducted to describe ESL learners' stickiness to various vocabulary learning APPs. A pilot study had been taken before the survey. Several college students were invited to have a free talk about their English study. They are English majors, facing the challenges of enlarging their English vocabulary quickly, of taking Tests for English Majors or other English proficiency tests, such as IELTS, TOEFL. They memorize new words from their in-class course syllabus and find it far less than enough to meet their needs. Thus after class, they turned to extra-curriculum English materials, for example, novels, test materials, newspapers and online essays. However, they found reading comprehension training and learning new words were two different tasks and could not be done well at one time. Because reading materials are not tailored for word learning and language learners usually need to spend a lot of time in looking up new words in the dictionary by themselves. Thus many of them began to search for vocabulary learning mobile APPs. They usually download two or more APPs at a time and choose the suitable one after a comparison. The vocabulary learning mobile APPs chosen for the study are popular ones in China, suggested by many students, teachers and well-known websites.

In the research, students at different ages were invited to participate in the survey: 19 junior high school students (12–14 years old), 22 senior high school students (16–17 years old), and 33 college students (19–20 years old). These participants, aged between 12 years old and 20 years old, are the major group of students whose compulsory subjects at school include English. Students younger than 12 years old in China may haven't begun learning English, and the most important thing is that they might not have an access to mobile phones, let alone mobile-assisted language learning. For students who are older than 20 years old, English is no longer a compulsory subject and thus the extrinsic motivation to learn English declines, except for English major students. Therefore, this study chose the participants in two conditions: English subject is compulsory at school; have an access to mobile-phones. The participants were chosen randomly in two different high schools and one university. They were guided by their English teachers to finish a questionnaire, or answer the questions in a WeChat group (one of the most popular social media in China). Some of the questions in the questionnaire are shown in Table 2.

Table 2. A Survey on the use of vocabulary learning mobile APPs

1. Have you used any vocabulary learning mobile APPs?
2. If yes, please list the mobile APPs you've used
3. Do you enjoy the vocabulary competing part with peers or prefer memorizing words by yourself?
4. How long can you keep active in using the APPs on average?
5. What are the reasons of stopping using a vocabulary learning mobile APP?

In our pilot study talk, a noticeable fact is that most of the college students could not keep using the vocabulary learning mobile APPs for more than 2 months. Some of them would like to download other APPs to have another try, but still find it hard to be an active user. Therefore, it is worth investigating whether these vocabulary learning APPs have any common design flaws, or whether the massive users' dropouts result from students' personal reasons, such as weak motivation. In Table 2, Questions 4 and 5 are included as the key part to investigate the reasons for the dropouts.

4   Results

There are nineteen junior high school students participating in the survey and answering the questions in Table 2. The survey shows that about 70% of the teenage students at 12-14 years old used a vocabulary learning mobile APP. However, they had a very limited number of choices. 6 out of the total 19 students haven't tried any English vocabulary learning mobile APPs. For those 13 students who have vocabulary learning APP experience, almost everyone used the APP Baicizhan only, except for one student using Kouyu 100 APP. 10 of the 13 students were active users and were rather sticky to the APP Baicizhan, but they also found it hard to follow the study pace due to too much homework after school, too many new words in the APP to learn every day, low motivation, no time, no interests. Sometimes they simply forget about using the APP. Only 2 male students are still using the App regularly. This situation is similar to MOOC learning: massive registration at the beginning and many dropouts after a period of study. In the survey, 3 out of the 13 students said they liked the game-based competing part with peers on line and the self-learning part; 5 students prefer the competing part; 2 students prefer the self-learning part, and 3 prefer neither of them. The detail information of the survey is shown in Table 3.

Table 3. A survey of junior high school students' using English vocabulary learning mobile APPs

Students (gender, age)	Tried any APPs?	If yes, what are they?	Prefer competing part?	Prefer self-learning?	How long of using an APP?	What are the reasons of giving it up?
1 (male, 14)	Yes	Baicizhan	Yes	No	Everyday	—
2 (male, 12)	Yes	Baicizhan	Yes	No	20 min/day	—
3 (male, 13)	Yes	Baicizhan	Yes	Yes	10 min/day	No time; forget it sometimes
4 (male, 13)	No	—	—	—	—	—
5 (male, 13)	No	—	—	—	—	—
6 (male, 13)	No	—	—	—	—	—
7 (female, 13)	Yes	Baicizhan	No	No	5 min/day	Low motivation
8 (female, 13)	Yes	Baicizhan	Yes	No	Not regular	No time; forget it sometimes
9 (female, 13)	Yes	Baicizhan	Yes	No	5 months so far	Too much homework
10 (female, 13)	Yes	Baicizhan	Yes	Yes	3 months so far	Too much homework
11 (female, 13)	Yes	Baicizhan	No	Yes	5 months so far	No time for it
12 (female, 13)	Yes	Baicizhan	Yes	No	3 months so far	Can't follow the pace, too many words
13 (female, 14)	Yes	Baichizhan	No	No	Everyday	Too many words
14 (female, 12)	Yes	Baichizhan	Yes	Yes	3 months	Not willing to keep it
15 (female, 13)	Yes	Kouyu 100	No	Yes	2 weeks	Boring, time wasting, low efficiency
16 (female, 12)	Yes	Baicizhan	No	No	5 days	Troublesome (parents push)
17 (female, 12)	No	—	—	—	—	—
18 (female, 13)	No	—	—	—	—	—
19 (female, 13)	No	—	—	—	—	—

A second survey, taken among 22 senior high school students at 16-17 years old, shows similar findings. There are 19 out of the 22 students having the experience of using English vocabulary learning mobile APPs, such as Baicizhan, Youdao, Shanbei. The average period of using the APPs is one week, and the major reasons of giving it up are: the prohibition of using smartphones at school and home, interference from other mobile APPs, boring content of the vocabulary learning mobile APPs. However, most of them value highly on the words competing part with peers on line. Comparing the two surveys on junior high and senior high students, there are some noticeable differences. Firstly, senior high students have a broader view of choosing vocabulary learning mobile APPs than junior high students. They choose different APPs to meet their individual study needs. Secondly, senior high students are far less sticky to the APPs than junior high students, and their average using period is shorter than junior high students. It is believed that senior high students have more study pressure, more homework and less free time than junior high students, and thus they are very busy with in-class study and homework. It is also suggested that senior high students are more interested in some other mobile APPs while using a smartphone, and which interferes them from keeping using the vocabulary learning APPs regularly.

A third survey was conducted among 33 college English major students at the age of 19-20 years old, who have their smartphones. The survey questions were sent to them through the APP WeChat, and their answers could be concluded as follows. Firstly, all of them have tried at least two different kinds of English vocabulary learning mobile APPs, and the APPs include 8 kinds: Baicizhan, Shanbei, Kaixincichang, Zhimi, Momo, Bubeidanci, Keke, Vocabulary Builder, which are much more various than the choices of high school students. Secondly, more than half of them prefer self-learning part to the game-based word competing part on line, which shows that the older the students are, the less they are interested in learning new words through game playing. Thirdly, only 2 out of the 33 college students are regular users, and they are being active because of automatic reminder from the APPs. The other 31 students all have the same difficulty to be sticky to the APPs. They are irregular users and they found it hard to keep using the APPs for more than 3 continuous days at a time. Thus, they feel that the learning efficiency is quite low. Fourthly, 5 students mentioned that they were easily distracted by other mobile games while using vocabulary learning mobile APPs. Since college students feel free to use their smartphones, it is really hard to force them to focus on one APP only. As it was proved that even though the mobile APP WeChat could help teachers in in-classroom teaching, students might also be distracted by other information when using their smartphones [10]. Fifthly, one of the students suggested that they should join a word learning study group on line to remind them of using the APPs every day.

In conclusion, the reasons for the high rate of dropouts are: using vocabulary learning mobile APPs is not a compulsory task from teachers or parents, there is no compulsory check or test, the game-based vocabulary learning is not attractive to college students, the satisfaction gained from the APPs is not strong enough to keep them as active users.

A brief comparison of the three different age groups in using vocabulary learning mobile APPs is shown in Table 4.

Table 4. The comparison of three different age groups in using vocabulary learning mobile APPs

	Junior high students (12–14 years old)	Senior high students (16–17 years old)	College students (19–20 years old)
With APPs use experience	68%	86%	100%
Types of APPs in use	2	3	8
Preferring word competing part	62%	About 80%	About 33%
Preferring self-learning	38%	About 20%	About 67%
Average period of being active users	About 2 months	About one week	Less than one week, (irregular)
Major reasons for dropouts	No time for it; too much homework from school	Prohibition of using smartphones; interference from other APPs; boring content design	Low efficiency; distraction by other mobile games while learning words; weak motivation

The comparison shows that the older the students are, the less sticky they are in using vocabulary learning mobile APPs. The major reasons of dropouts vary among the three different age groups, but one thing is clear that the APPs are not attractive enough to keep them being active.

The comparison also raises a question: how can we use vocabulary learning mobile APPs wisely and efficiently? As it is presented in the previous part, the current vocabulary learning mobile APPs are not only multimodal and multifunctional (visual aid, sounds, movie clips, game-based exercise, etc.), but also smart (automatic reminder, personalized review plan). What the users need is a strong intrinsic motivation which most users lack, or a pressure to keep them going on. What users can do is to create such a motivation or build a short-term target, for example, building a personalized learning group on line, taking task-based word learning, being combined with in-class teaching.

Since primary students usually don't have their own smartphones, we had an interview with a 7 years old boy and an 11 years old girl who had been introduced to three different vocabulary learning mobile APPs: Baicizhan, Kaixincichang, and Momo. After two months' use experience of the APPs, they said they liked Kaixincichang App the most. Because it has game-based competition, various task-based exercises, signing up for earning virtual coins, joining a study team, and a dynamic study rank. They got enough satisfaction and found it interesting to compete with others on line. Joining a study team can encourage them to keep a daily study habit. The team leader will remind them to finish a task in time and correctly. Their performance in the tasks directly influences the team's place in the rank. That's to say, they are not only studying by themselves, but also fighting as a team. They become very sticky to the App. They sometimes sent a request to participate in a pair competition. Instantly the App will automatically find them a competitor whose English proficiency is more of less the same as theirs. In the game, they compete on word spelling accuracy and speed. By doing this, they earn stars. By doing this, they have a great satisfaction when winning a game, or a strong study motive when losing it.

To summarize, the vocabulary learning mobile APPs are designed age free. In fact, our study shows that they attract young users the most. The current users don't usually have a clear target, which results in their low efficiency and easy dropouts. To keep older users being sticky to the APPs, we propose three revisions for future development of vocabulary APPs:

i. Add a task-based reading plan function. Build a list of classified reading books for choosing, for example *Charlotte's Web, Little Women, Gone with the wind*. When users choose a novel as their reading target, match the words of the book with the proficiency of the user, and then extract new words as the vocabulary learning group. Suggest users to read the chosen target novel after learning the extracted words completely. While learning the words, it would be better to extract sentences from the target novel as example sentences.

ii. Add a personalized learning group function. Test users' language proficiency, and automatically suggest other users with the same proficiency as a study pair, or study group. Users in similar situations and in a stable group are usually quite willing to compete with each other while learning.

iii. Develop specific course-oriented or book-oriented vocabulary learning functions. Foreign Language Teaching and Research Press and Shanghai Foreign Language Education Press are the top two presses for English textbooks. Most of college English textbooks in use are offered from them. This new function may help college student users be more active to the APPs than before. Furthermore, the course-oriented or book-oriented vocabulary learning function would naturally be tasked-based and with strong extrinsic motivation.

5 Conclusion

This research initially investigates users' stickiness to vocabulary learning mobile APPs, which hasn't been studied yet. The users' stickiness is the binding between users and products, which is one of the key indicators to evaluate whether an APP is a good product. Furthermore, the research was taken among three different age groups, junior high, senior high, and college students, which helps investigate the relation between APP users' habits and age differences. The research findings show that: the APP

Baicizhan has the most users in every age group; the older the users are, the more they are willing to try new APPs, and the less they are sticky to the APPs; the average period of being an active user declines with age growing; and the attraction of game-based vocabulary learning strategies weakens gradually with time going on. Therefore, some suggestions to optimize vocabulary learning mobile APPs are proposed as follows: offering a highly matched task-based reading plan for vocabulary leaning; recommending a personalized learning group with the same language proficiency on line; developing specific course-oriented or book-oriented vocabulary learning functions to coordinate with in-class teaching. The research not only gives suggestions to APP developers, but also helps language learners use the APPs efficiently and wisely.

Limitations of this research include the small number of participants and questions in the survey, and the lack of detailed records of APPs usage time due to participants' rough answers. Future studies are suggested to have a deep investigation on the stickiest users and to keep a long-term observation on sticky users. The efficiency of the suggestions proposed in the study will also be a topic of future interest.

References

1. Chen, M.H., Tseng, W.T., Hsiao, T.Y.: The effectiveness of digital game-based vocabulary learning: a framework-based view of meta-analysis. Br. J. Educ. Technol. **49**(1), 69–77 (2018)
2. Zou, D.: A study of the components of the involvement load hypothesis: how involvement load should be allocated to "Search" and "Evaluation". Ph.D. dissertation, City University of Hong Kong, Hong Kong (2012)
3. Zou, D., Wang, F.L., Xie, H., Kohnke, L.: Game-based vocabulary learning in china and hong kong: students' evaluation of different word learning APPs. In: Cheung, S.K.S., Lam, J., Li, K.C., Au, O., Ma, W.W.K., Ho, W.S. (eds.) ICTE 2018. CCIS, vol. 843, pp. 44–55. Springer, Singapore (2018). https://doi.org/10.1007/978-981-13-0008-0_5
4. Zou, D., Xie, H.R.: Personalized word-learning based on technique feature analysis and learning analytics. J. Educ. Technol. Soc. **21**, 233–244 (2018)
5. Calvo-Ferrer, J.R.: Educational games as stand-alone learning tools and their motivational effect on L2 vocabulary acquisition and perceived learning gains. Br. J. Educ. Technol. **48** (2), 264–278 (2017)
6. Chen, C.M., Chung, C.J.: Personalized mobile English vocabulary learning system based on item response theory and learning memory cycle. Comput. Educ. **5**(2), 624–645 (2008)
7. Rankin, Y., Gold, R., Gooch, B.: 3D role-playing games as language learning tools. In: Gröller, E., Szirmay-Kalos, L. (eds.) Proceedings of EuroGraphics 2006, vol. 25, no. 3. ACM, New York (2006)
8. Uzun, L., Cetinavci, U.R., Korkmaz, S., Salihoglu, U.: Developing and applying foreign language vocabulary learning and practicing game: the effect of vocaword. Digit. Cult. Educ. **5**(1), 50–70 (2013)
9. Kapp, K.: The Gamification of Learning and Instruction: Game-Based Methods and Strategies for Training and Education. Wiley, Hoboken (2012)
10. Jin, N.: Mobile-assisted language learning: using wechat in an English reading class. In: Huang, T.-C., Lau, R., Huang, Y.-M., Spaniol, M., Yuen, C.-H. (eds.) SETE 2017. LNCS, vol. 10676, pp. 500–506. Springer, Cham (2017). https://doi.org/10.1007/978-3-319-71084-6_59

ETLTL (International Workshop on Educational Technology for Language and Translation Learning)

Website and Literature Teaching: Teaching Experiment of Literary Texts at the Beginning of German Studies in China

Weihua Du[(✉)]

Guangdong University of Foreign Studies,
Guangzhou 510420, Guangdong, China
nankaidu@126.com

Abstract. In German or in other language disciplines except English discipline of Chinese universities and colleges, literature teaching is now on the edge. More and more trained students in German discipline have no idea about the German literature. The author has tried to teach the Chinese students in German discipline, how to read and understand the literary texts in the courses in the first academic year, with the help of website. In this paper, the author does carry out the real situations and views of the students on literary texts at the beginning of their study. With the help of a questionnaire survey, the author does think: the students do not refuse literature, with the help of Internet, and they can learn more about the literary texts than in the textbooks. In the survey, we find that the reading of literary texts depends more on the education of the parents of the students, the kinds of Intelligentsia have found more enjoy on the reading of literary texts. What the teachers have to change is not the curriculum, but their positions, ideas and the methods to the teaching of literary texts.

Keywords: Literary texts · Chinese students · German discipline

1 Introduction

Manfred Lukas Schewe considers the literature teaching in the German studies in foreign countries is critical and argues that in this country, the literature teaching is associated [1]. In his opinion, there are no places for the German literature in the lessons where German is as a Foreign Language (DaF, Deutsch als Fremdsprache). So we need to discuss his point of view, how to teach literature in the German studies in foreign countries.

Many Chinese experts of German studies have the opinion that the students should be trained in communication skills, instead of reading of traditional literary texts. This is also showed in the *Framework for German Studies in Chinese Colleges and Universities*: the goal of the teaching is to train the students in the communication skills and the ability to promote the intercultural communication [2].

In the first and second bands of German textbooks for Chinese students *Grundstudium Deutsch* and *Studienweg Deutsch*, there are only grammatical texts and communication centered texts. Unfortunately, there is nothing about German literary

© Springer Nature Switzerland AG 2018
T. Hao et al. (Eds.): SETE 2018, LNCS 11284, pp. 229–233, 2018.
https://doi.org/10.1007/978-3-030-03580-8_24

texts. The design concept of these two German textbooks is based on the need of the labor market, not on the German discipline.

Then it comes to a question: have the teachers (former students) and students been presented with the beauty of the language and the fun in the understanding of literary texts? If not, then how and in which way the learners can experience the beauty and fun in the study? If so, then we can see which literary texts the students like.

2 Design and Implementation of the Teaching and Study

2.1 A Subsection Sample

All of these questions can only be answered by exact survey. The empirical research on this subject is rarely carried out in China. Prof. Krumme of the University Heidelberg wrote about the negligence of the Chinese colleagues to literature teaching in China [3]. Prof. Zhang Yushu from the Peking University also criticized this negligence many times in different conferences. Many young researchers and teachers in China also saw this problem: Prof. Jin Xiuli wrote an article on literature teaching for German discipline students in China. She tried to give the importance of literature in Chinese bachelor study [4].

To know the desire of students to the literature and the results of the literature teaching, in 2017, the author has chosen seven German literary texts for the course in the second semester at Nankai University. There are three poems and four short stories. The students should work in group and read more Chinese papers or comments on the Internet. Then the teacher tried to enjoy the beauty of language in the lessons and do some grammar practices (Table 1).

Table 1. Teaching plan.

Text name	Time in the lesson	Time before the lesson	Teaching goals
Ich will mit dem gehen, den ich liebe (Brecht)	30 min	1 h	1. Beauty of language 2. Grammar practice: wollen
Wanderers Nachtlied (Goethe)	1 h	2 h	1. Beauty of language 2. Comparison with chinese poetry: quiet night thought (li bai) 3. Comparison of different chinese translations
Heidenröslein (Goethe)	30 min	1 h	1. Beauty of language 2. Comparison with Wanderers Nachtlied
Die Bremer Stadtmusikanten (Grimm)	2 h	4 h	1. Beauty of language 2. Grammar practice: Präteritum
Ein Tisch ist ein Tisch (Bichsel)	2 h	4 h	1. Fun of understanding 2. Fun in language game
Das Brot (Borchert)	2 h	4 h	1. Beauty of language 2. Grammar practice: Präteritum 3. Fun of understanding
Vor dem Gesetz (Kafka)	2 h	4 h	1. Beauty of language 2. Grammar practice: Präteritum 3. Kafkas character in the text

After two weeks, there was a survey in Chinese language. In the survey, there are totally 30 questions to the seven texts, and also five questions to study the information of the learners. 28 of 30 questions should be answered by five degrees: very good, relatively good, so, relatively bad, and bad.

3 Analysis of the Survey

Totally 20 students participated in this survey, but only 18 (11 female student) have succeed. Two papers have almost the same choice to all 30 questions, which are clearly incorrect.

The First Part (5 Questions) of the Survey: Situations Before the Study
Most Chinese students like literature in the school, and this is also the first question. To the question "Do you like literary texts?", only two have a negative view. 15 like novels and short stories, four want fables and fairy tales, and nobody is interested in poem. This makes the author very disappointed, and also nobody cares theater.

Nine respondents admit that they know little of German literature, and more than half (9) like the works of Goethe, Kafka; one likes Schiller.

The Second Part (25 Questions): Assessment of the Teacher's Selected Texts
The students in the class showed strong commitment, perhaps under pressure from the teacher.

3.1 Assessment of Poems

The words in the Brecht's poem are very easy, so most of the students can read and understand it easily. It also sounds very nice, if you read it, but three boys do not like it.

Goethe's *Wanderers Nachtlied*: thirteen find the beauty of the language. They compared with the well-known Chinese poem *Thoughts in silent night* (jingye si) and so learned the internal mental peace. A girl does not like *Heidenröslein*, although it is well understood.

On the question "Would you like later to read German poetry?", only two say with "probably not," on the other hand, nine with absolutely yes.

3.2 Evaluation to Fairy Tale

The teacher did this text with grammar practice, and this task falls the students a little heavy. Many words are still stranger, seven cannot understand fairy tale well. If there is another choice, like *Schneewittchen* (snow white), then everything could be in order.

All respondents will read in the future further German fairy tales, Grimm's fairy tales is already a brand in China.

3.3   Analysis of Short Stories

Bichsels *ein Tisch ist ein Tisch* (a table is a table): four cannot understand well. Five people do like *das Brot* (the bread), and four of them cannot understand it well.

3.4   Assessment to Kafka's Text

One third of the respondents like Kafka, but eight find, the text is hard. In classes it has been discussed almost in all directions, and the students have found too many interpretations from the internet. Six students answer with "yes" to the question "Can you explain the meaning of the text?"

3.5   Assessment in General

Four answer with "sure" to the question "Are you later to read German short stories?", six "probably", and other five with "maybe." As a result, we have to seriously take the learners in the field of literature like short stories in German.

Only a boy does not like this teaching method. Four do not accept the grammar exercises by the reading. To the question "Will you find the background of the popular texts after class?", only a boy says "probably not."

Two thirds will in future research German literature if they later choice German teacher as work.

4   Relationship Between Private Information and the Choices

Gender plays a role in the choice of literature types. On the second question, "Which types do you like?" 55% of the female students answer with "short stories and fairy tales", however, 50% of the male students put great value on novels. About a fifth of each female and male respondents do not like short stories and fairy tales selected by the teacher.

The educational level of the parents has also an influence on the choice of students. 11 Students have not read German literature in the school, for their parents do not have a university degree. 5 female students, whose mothers ever studied literature, all like literature.

Town and country are very different, especially on the cultural life. Nine students come from country and village. A boy from country do not like German poems, and a girl from the city do not like the short story. The differences are not as large as we thought, in terms of town and country, because China had a unified general education system and the socialization of young people is similar.

All students find that the website is very helpful for the reading of the text. But one student thinks that much information on the internet is similar.

5   Conclusion

In the survey, the students have learnt about 2000 German words. So the teachers can already do many to lead the students to find the beauty of literary texts. In the two textbooks, there are no literary texts, but the teacher can try, through their own efforts, so as to give students the opportunity as much as possible. Therefore, the students can enjoy the beauty of literary texts and the fun of understanding. In this process, the website is very helpful for the students, when they want to find more information and give a discussion.

This survey shows that the internet can help the Chinese students to read German poems, German fairy tales and fables, and German short stories. After the students have experienced the beauty of the German language and the fun of understanding, most of them would want to read more literary texts, and the self-learning can go to the website.

Therefore, the teachers themselves must have knowledge of the German literature and also the ability to evaluate good literary texts for the students at the beginning of their studies.

References

1. Schewe, M.L.: Literaturvermittlung in der Auslandsgermanistik (Literature teaching in German studies outside of German-speaking countries). In: DAAD (Hrsg.) Germanistiktreffen Deutschland-Großbritannien, Ireland, 30 September–3 October 2004, pp. 93–112. Dokumentation der Tagungsbeiträge, Köln (2005)
2. Commission for Foreign Languages in Chinese Colleges and Universities: papers about German teaching in China (zhongguo deyu jiaoxue lunwenji). FLTRP, Beijing (2000)
3. Krumme, P.: Wozu Literatur und Interpretation? (why literature and interpretation?). Wir lernen Deutsch (4), 15–19 (2001)
4. Jin, X.: Die Bedeutung der deutschen Literatur im chinesischen Bachelorstudium der Germanistik. Eine Untersuchung zur Problemlage (The importance of German literature in the chinese bachelor study on German studies. a study on the problems). In: Bialek, E., Lipinski, C., Tomiczek, E. (Hrsg.) Orbis Linguarum, vol. 32, pp. 195–203. Oficyna Wydawnicza ATUT, Breslau (Wroclaw) (2007)

Use Corpus Keywords to Design Activities in Business English Instruction

Lidan Chen[(✉)] [ID]

Guangdong University of Foreign Studies, Guangzhou 510420, China
cld4teaching@126.com

Abstract. Corpus keywords have been found to be useful indicators of "aboutness" of a text and are extensively applied to explore specialized corpora. However, little research has been conducted to apply keywords analysis into ESP teaching, especially in Business English instruction, which entails both acquisition of language and mastery of subject-matter knowledge. This study extracts keywords and KW clusters from Business English Textbook Corpus by use of *WordSmith 6.0* and designs engagement activities to facilitate learners' reading comprehension of an individual text, to develop their subject-matter knowledge and help them acquire domain-specific keywords deeply.

Keywords: Corpus keywords · KW clusters · Business English instruction

1 Introduction

Corpus keywords are the "words which are significantly more frequent in one corpus than another" [1] and can be extracted automatically by the corpus concordancer *WordSmith*. They have been used as a useful starting point in investigating a specialized corpus in that it can distinguish technical or domain-specific words from general words. What's more, those keywords create a dense network of intercollocation, including both continuous and discontinuous phraseological patterns, which would contribute to an identification of "aboutness" or discourse topic of a text [2, 3]. In other words, corpus keywords are often studied through their typical co-occurrence with each other. To explore how they construct meaning, KW cluster [4], keywords linkage [5] and keywords network were proposed and constructed [6].

In view of their function as markers of "aboutness" and style of a text [5], corpus keywords have been studied extensively in domain-specific text analysis to unveil the subject-matter, styles and even stance, thus providing insights for ESP teaching. The relevant studies include keywords analysis in political speeches [7], engineering discourse [8], traveling writing corpus [9], press releases [10], and telecommunication discourses [11], to name just a few. Meanwhile, research perspectives have shifted onto cross-cultural [12], cross-disciplinary [13] and cross-register [14] analysis of keywords. A highly relevant and enlightening study among these is Rizzo and Péréz [11]'s article on keywords analysis of a specialized telecommunication English corpus which implies a considerable advantage of mastering keywords in Content and Language Integrated Learning program. Despite its inspiration on great potential of keyword analysis in ESP

© Springer Nature Switzerland AG 2018

T. Hao et al. (Eds.): SETE 2018, LNCS 11284, pp. 234–243, 2018.
https://doi.org/10.1007/978-3-030-03580-8_25

teaching, this study just focused on analysis of single keywords without demo of teaching activities. The other two relevant studies demonstrated effective application of keywords analysis into in-depth English reading teaching in Chinese setting [15, 16]. These two researches present how keyword list, keywords concordance plot and keywords concordance lines could facilitate in-depth English reading teaching of a single text regarding its topic identification, sub-topics elaboration, development of topic and writing style. The clear instructions fully reveal keywords' function in constructing meaning in a text. All the above-mentioned exploratory applications of keywords analysis into language teaching are based on corpus keywords' recurrent exposure to content of the subject. However, little empirical study has been conducted on use of keywords analysis in Business English instruction to enhance both subject-matter knowledge acquisition and English learning. What's more, as introduced earlier, keywords can be extended into KW clusters, two or more keywords which are found repeated near each other [4], which indicates that co-occurring keywords could construct meaning in a more specific way. But no research has been found to present how KW clusters could be used in Business English instruction.

Based on this research gap, the present article aims to present how to extract corpus keywords and KW clusters in a single text and a theme-based corpus and then incorporate them into three engagement activities in Business English Course with a focus on reading instruction. The purposes of these activities are to facilitate learners' comprehension of main idea and major specifics of individual reading text on keywords and KW clusters, to construct learners' subject-matter knowledge with KW clusters as building blocks and to help learners acquire deep knowledge of domain-specific keywords on concordance analysis.

2 Research Method and Procedures

2.1 Construction of Specialized Textbook Corpus

Four series of textbooks on business or Business English composed Business English Textbook Corpus (BETC). It is specialized not only as it represents a specific text-type and addresses a specific domain, but also because it is created for specific teaching and learning purpose. Table 1 lists out its composition.

Table 1. Composition of BETC

Textbook title	Publication information	Size
Business English: A Comprehensive Course (1st Edition, Book 1 to 4)	Higher Education Press, 2009	379,030
Business Essentials (9th Edition)	Pearson Publications, 2013	231,373
Market Leader (3rd Edition, Book 1 to 5)	Higher Education Press & Pearson Publications, 2012	329,122
Intelligent Business (1st Edition)	Foreign Language Teaching and Research Press & Pearson Publications, 2016	25,844

BETC is split into several sub-corpora on different business themes when used as extended teaching resources in theme-based Business English teaching. For example, all the book chapters on "Money & Banking" were extracted to construct Money & Banking Textbook Sub-corpus (MBTS). The individual reading text titled "Inflation, Banking & Economic Growth" in the textbook *Business English: A Comprehensive Course* on "Money & Banking" composed a micro corpus ITC. Table 2 is an overview of all the corpora used in the present article.

Table 2. Overview of corpora in the present study

Corpus name	Resources	Size
Business English Textbook Corpus (BETC)	4 Business English textbooks	965,369
Money & Banking Textbook Sub-corpus (MBTS)	Textbook chapters on "Money & Banking" in BETC	19,757
Inflation, Banking & Economic Growth Text Corpus (ITC)	Close reading text in "Money & Banking" theme-based teaching	1,634

2.2   Pedagogical Processing of Corpora

This section, taking the theme "Money & Banking" as an example, demonstrates the stepwise procedures of processing the corpora in Table 2.

Step 1: *WordSmith 6.0* was used to extract keyword list of ITC with BETC the reference corpus (Fig. 1). After lemmatizing, 33 keywords were developed. Deducting the only functional word "that", the other 32 keywords are semantically categorized[1] into 6 sub-topics (Table 3). In view of keywords' indication of "aboutness" of individual texts [5], they have great potential to demonstrate main idea and key specifics of the text. From the grouped keywords, a vague idea about the text could be developed: it might be about inflation, banks loans and economy since most of the keywords are related to them semantically. But this kind of "guess" is neither sure nor complete.

Table 3. Grouped keywords in ITC

Business concepts	Business people & entities	Business measurement	Business analysis	Business description	Business action
Inflation	Bank	Rate	Theory	Economic	Lend
Return	Sector	Ratio	Impact	Nominal	Ration
Credit	Country	Percent	Quartile	Real	Rise
Loan	Economist		Median	Intermediary	Growth
Interest	Borrower		Empirical		
Friction			Negatively		
gdp			Associate		
Profitability					
Activity					

---

[1] The author draws on ideas about semantic categorization from Nelson [17].

Step 2: 35 KW clusters of ITC were extracted by *WordSmith 6.0* (Fig. 2). Technical terms like "inflation rate", and "N + V" and "V + N" patterns like "inflation rises" and "ration credit" are selected manually. Incomplete clusters with potential to compose a semantically complete phrase can be integrated. Figure 3 demonstrates how KW clusters within the same semantic pattern are incorporated. Then all together 12 phrases retrieved or developed from the 35 KW clusters composed the KW cluster list. They are *inflation rate, banking sector, real economic activity, nominal interest rates, real rate of return, ratio of bank lending to GDP, media rate of inflation, bank lending, bank profitability, interest rate, inflation rises,* and *ration credit.* Those KW clusters could more effectively and specifically indicate main idea of the text: inflation affects economic growth through banking sector, maybe through bank lending measured by the ratio of bank lending to GDP; Bank profitability measured by real rate of return might be a consideration. Although this kind of connecting ideas is still kind of guess work, they could be more informative in presenting conceptual structure of the text.

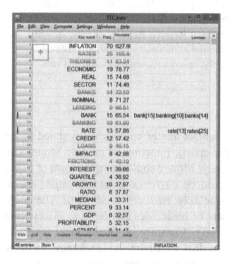

Fig. 1. Keywords of ITC

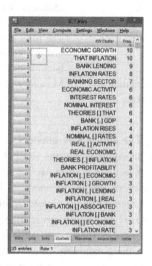

Fig. 2. KW clusters of ITC

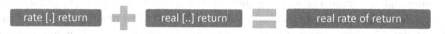

Fig. 3. Integration of auto-extracted clusters into complete phrases (One dot in brackets ([.]) means one unlisted word is used between two keywords; Two dots means two unlisted words between two keywords.)

Step 3: Likewise, keywords and KW clusters of MBTS were extracted by *WordSmith 6.0*. What is different in handling them in this step from that in Step 2 is that semantic categorization is conducted on KW clusters instead of on individual keywords for two reasons. First, KW clusters can construct a more specific and complete picture of meaning as suggested in Step 2; second, compared to a large size of keywords of MBTS, KW clusters can be combined into a much smaller and meaning-focused sum. Finally, the author transformed all the 256 KW clusters into 29 in 5 semantic categories in Table 4.

Table 4. Semantically categorized KW clusters of MBTS

Sub-topics	KW cluster
Function of money	Medium [.] exchange
Form of money	Paper money, electronic money, currency (cash), paper check
Commercial bank	Commercial bank, bank account, pay interest, borrow money, currency exchange, bank [.] hold, bank [.] pay, credit card, debit card, bank profitability, real rate [.] return, ration credit
Central bank	The fdic, financial system, Federal Reserve Bank, economic stability, nation's economic growth, the fed's, monetary policy, government's bank, control the money supply, reserve requirement, interest rate
International banking	Monetary fund

The above KW clusters could construct subject-matter knowledge as stated in the following propositions (with KW clusters italicized). Function of money: Money can work as a *medium of exchange*. Forms of money: Money could be in the form of *paper money* or *electronic money*. The former could be *currency (cash)* or *paper check*. Commercial bank: *Commercial bank*s can issue *debit card* and *credit card*. They *hold deposits* and *pay interest* for them. Consumers or businesses can *borrow money* from commercial banks and *pay interest* accordingly. Commercial banks make payment from the consumers' *bank account*. They also deal with *currency exchange* business. *Bank profitability* can be measured by the *real rate of return* of assets. Commercial banks will *ration credit* if the *real rate of return* of assets decreases. Central bank: *The FDIC* supervises *commercial bank*s. *The Fed* acts as US *government's bank*. It *controls the money supply* and conducts US *monetary policy*, i.e. management of *economic stability* and the *nation's economic growth* by managing the money supply and *interest rates*. *Reserve requirements* and *interest rate* controls are two major tools of *the Fed*. International banking: *International Monetary Fund* is an international organization to finance international trade.

Step 4: Concordance lines of sample keyword "INFLATION" in MBTS were extracted by *WordSmith 6.0* (Fig. 4). It was selected as the sample not only for its high Keyness and Frequency in ITC and MBTS[2], but also because it is the theme of the text.

---

[2] INFLATION ranks 1 in both Keyness and Frequency in ITC, and ranks 6 in Keyness and 7 in Frequency in MBTS.

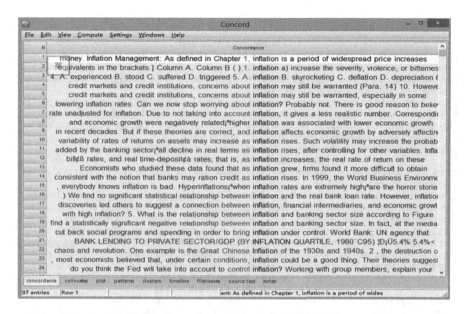

Fig. 4. Part of concordance of INFLATION

3   Classroom Activities Demo

Based on the above pedagogical processing of corpora, this section demonstrates three engagement activities in "Money & Banking" theme-based teaching, to aid reading instruction of an economic commentary titled "Inflation, Banking and Economic Growth" which reports theoretical discussion and empirical findings on inflation's negative impact on economic growth. These activities were embedded into Business English Course, a reading & writing-based course open to undergraduate in Guangdong University of Foreign Studies to develop English proficiency and consolidate business knowledge. Theme-based teaching is adopted in this course.

3.1   KW and KW Cluster Gap-Filling: Text Reading Comprehension

After learners skim the text, teacher presents the classified keywords (Table 3) and KW cluster list (Step 2 in Sect. 2.2) of the text, and asks learners to fill in the gaps in the following text structure and paragraph summary with appropriate keywords (underlined) or KW clusters (double underlined). The initial letters are given as a clue.

Introduction (Para. 1-4)

Para .1: Hyperinflation is a bad thing, and even moderate inflation rate of 5%-10% is also harmful.

Para. 2: In the mid-1990s, evidence started to emerge supporting the claim that across countries, inflation and economic growth were negatively related, i.e. higher inflation was associated with lower economic growth, with findings provided by Robert J. Barro.

Para. 3: Meanwhile, other economists suggested the essential role that financial intermediaries play in economic development. Therefore, a connection between inflation, financial intermediaries and economic growth is suggested. Specifically, it is speculated that the way inflation hurt economic growth was by interfering with the role financial intermediaries play in an economy.

Para. 4: This article aims to discuss the theories and present new empirical findings.

Theoretical insights into inflation (Para. 5-7)

Para. 5: Inflation will exacerbate frictions in credit markets, which poses an obstacle for banks to adjust the nominal interest rate.

Para. 6: Inflation might affect economic growth through the banking sector by rationing credit to business-es. The story chain begins with decreased real rate of return on assets, which encourages borrowing. In turn, new borrowers with higher default risks flood into credit market. To reduce the risk, banks react by ration-ing credit, which lowers the investment in the economy. In this sense, lowers real economic activity.

Para. 7: However, beneath some threshold, higher inflation might actually lead to increased real economic activity. When inflation rate and interest rate are both low, moderate inflation allows banks to raise nominal interest rates, encouraging bank lending. Thus higher investment results in increased economic activity.

Empirical findings (Para. 8-13)

Impact of inflation on bank lending

Para. 8: High inflation rates lead to inefficiently small banking sectors and equity markets.

Para. 9 &10: An analysis in the sample period of 1980-1995 suggests that ratio of banking lending to GDP declines with inflation. What's more, inflation affects bank lending even at a relatively low median infla-tion rate.

Para. 11: There's a statistically significant negative relationship between inflation and banking sector size.

Impact of inflation on asset returns and bank profitability

Para. 12: The findings from the data support that inflation is negatively associated with the real return on assets, measured in the instruments like real money market rates, real treasury bill rates, and real time-deposit rates.

Para. 13: In addition, inflation does appear to have a negative impact on bank profitability measures, like net interest margins, net profits, rate of return on equity, and value added by the banking sector.

Conclusion (Para. 14-18)

Para. 14: Concerns about inflation still exists because theories predict that inflation above some moderate amount can harm the banking sector, and in turn economic growth.

Para. 15: Another prediction is that the variability of rates of returns on assets may increase as inflation rises.

Para. 16: The question of the exact rate at which inflation becomes destructive still remains.

Para 17: For some countries the threshold is 5 percent or 10 percent. So inflation above that level should be reduced so as to have a beneficial impact on real economic activity.

As stated earlier, keywords and KW clusters can reveal "aboutness" of the text, thus playing an essential role in constructing conceptual structure of a single text. This could be demonstrated by the intensive distribution of keywords and KW clusters across the text. As Gavioli [18] stated, a major contribution of corpora in language teaching is that it changes the way of language description and thus indicates what should be taught. In this activity, keywords and KW clusters of an individual text are highlighted as missing words and phrases, and required to be "noticed" and "mastered" in text comprehension.

3.2   KW Clusters Grouping and Connecting: Subject-Matter Knowledge Building

After text analysis, learners are asked to develop business knowledge on "money & banking". Teacher presents Table 5, which rearranges KW clusters in Step 3 of

Sect. 2.2 on grammatical pattern. Apart from proper nouns, all the other KW clusters could be put into five grammatical patterns. The first three patterns are mostly business concepts or entities, while the last two describe business actions, activities or functions.

Table 5. KW Clusters presented to learners

Pattern	KW cluster
Proper nouns	Federal Reserve Bank, the FDIC, the Fed, International Monetary Fund[a]
N + of + N	Medium of exchange, real rate of return
N + N	Credit card, debit card, bank account, bank profitability, reserve requirement, interest rate, paper money, currency (cash), paper check, currency exchange
A + N	Monetary policy, financial system, economic stability, nation's economic growth, government's bank, commercial bank, electronic money
N + V	Bank hold, bank pay
V + N	Pay interest, borrow money, ration credit, control the money supply

[a]The original KW cluster extracted automatically is "monetary fund", which was further developed into the proper noun "International Monetary Fund" for a complete idea.

Learners, working in pairs, are first encouraged to put the above clusters into 5 sub-topics addressed previously in Table 4, i.e. function of money, form of money, commercial bank, central bank, and international banking. And then they are required to connect grouped clusters into complete propositions. An example is given on the first sub-topic "function of money": Money can work as a medium of exchange. The previously-suggested propositions in Step 2 of Sect. 2.2 could work as reference answers.

This 2-step KW cluster-based activity aims to construct learners' subject-matter knowledge within the given frame of subtopics. Treating KW clusters from grammatical pattern and semantic grouping is an intellectually challenging but rewarding task to construct knowledge both in subject-matter (money & banking) and language (co-occurring pattern of keywords). With grouped KW clusters as building blocks and scaffolding, connecting key concepts into propositions is constructing the building of subject-matter knowledge.

3.3   Concordance Analysis: Key Concept and Its Lexical Pattern

Teacher demonstrates the concordance of INFLATION (Fig. 4), and asks learners to observe and discuss the following questions:

(1) What types of words co-occur with INFLATION immediately?
(2) What is prominent lexical-grammatical pattern of INFLATION?
(3) Do INFLATION's co-occurring words in the neighborhood have a certain semantic preference? If yes, what is it?
(4) Do INFLATION's co-occurring words imply certain kind of attitudinal stance? If yes, what is it?

First, a quick look at the concordance can give learners some idea about INFLATION's immediate collocates. The words before INFLATION could be Verb (control, avoid, manage, beat, etc.) and Adj (current, extreme, high, spiraling, etc.). The words after it could be Verb (affect, rise, lower, damage, etc.), and Noun (rate, quartile, issue, etc.). Second, accordingly INFLATION's prominent lexical-semantic structures include "as inflation + V (meaning "changes")", "V (meaning "deal with") + inflation", "inflation + V (meaning "affect") + by V-ing". Those patterns are mostly used to convey semantic functions of description of inflation, analyses on its impact and countermeasures against it. Third, phrases like "economic growth", "interest rate" and "banking sector (central bank, bank lending, etc.)" usually occur in its neighborhood, which means inflation is probably addressed and discussed as an economic issue affecting banking sector. Last but not least, extending the span of observation, learners may find that negative words (concern, worry, negative, destructive, harmful, etc.) frequently co-occur with INFLATION, while positive words like good, beneficial, and favorable have only 5 occurrences. So it is safe to conclude that INFLATION tends to convey negative meaning.

The co-selection analysis of keywords concordance in theme-specific corpus provides learners with rich language resources to discover deep knowledge of the target keyword from lexical, grammatical, semantic and pragmatic perspectives and dig out really important business knowledge about the key concept.

4   Concluding Remarks

This exploratory study employed keywords analysis to design engagement activities in Business English classroom in view of keywords' function to indicate "aboutness" of a text. Keywords and KW clusters extracted from a single text have been found to be important in constructing main idea and major details and thus were highlighted in text analysis; meanwhile, categorized KW clusters of theme-specific textbook corpus were found to be important building blocks of the subject-matter knowledge, so categorization and connection of KW clusters were designed to develop learners' subject-matter knowledge; lastly, a co-selection analysis of keywords concordance with guiding questions from lexical, grammatical, semantic and pragmatic perspectives was conducted for in-depth lexical teaching, which not only encourages deep learning of language, but also elicits really important and deep knowledge about the key concept it conveys. The three classroom activities demonstrated could be implicative for ESP pedagogy.

However, a brief assessment of both the research procedures and classroom activity designs render some limitations of the present study. First, the pedagogical processing of corpora is time-consuming. Therefore, a more effective alternative to analyze how keywords co-occur to construct meaning is expected. Second, the feedback and effectiveness of the engagement activities are to be evaluated in further studies.

References

1. Hunston, S.: Corpora in Applied Linguistics. Cambridge University Press, Cambridge (2002)
2. Bondi, M.: Perspectives on keywords and keyness: an introduction. In: Bondi, M., Scott, M. (eds.) Keyness in Texts, pp. 1–18. John Benjamins Publishing Company, Amsterdam (2010)
3. Tyrkkö, J.: Hyperlinks: keywords or key words. In: Bondi, M., Scott, M. (eds.) Keyness in Texts, pp. 79–91. John Benjamins Publishing Company, Amsterdam (2010)
4. Scott, M.: WordSmith Tools Manual (Version 6.0). Lexical Analysis Software Ltd., Liverpool (2013)
5. Scott, M., Tribble, C.: Textual Patterns: Keyword and Corpus Analysis in Language Education. John Benjamins Publishing Company, Amsterdam (2006)
6. Lahiri, S., Chouudhury, S., Caragea, C.: Keyword and keyphrase extraction using centrality measures on collocation networks. Comput. Sci. **26**(1), 1–16 (2014)
7. Milizia, D.: Keywords and phrases in political speeches. In: Bondi, M., Scott, M. (eds.) Keyness in Texts, pp. 127–145. John Benjamins Publishing Company, Amsterdam (2010)
8. Warren, M.: Identifying aboutgrams in engineering texts. In: Bondi, M., Scott, M. (eds.) Keyness in Texts, pp. 113–126. John Benjamins Publishing Company, Amsterdam (2010)
9. Gerbig, A.: Key words and key phrases in a corpus of travel writing: from early modern english literature to contemporary "block". In: Bondi, M., Scott, M. (eds.) Keyness in Texts, pp. 147–168. John Benjamins Publishing Company, Amsterdam (2010)
10. Philip, G.: Metaphorical keyness in specialized corpora. In: Bondi, M., Scott, M. (eds.) Keyness in Texts, pp. 185–203. John Benjamins Publishing Company, Amsterdam (2010)
11. Rizzo, C., Pérez, M.: A key perspective on specialized lexis: keywords in telecommunication engineering for CLIL. In: 7th International Conference on Corpus Linguistics: Current Work in Corpus Linguistics: Working with Traditionally-Conceived Corpora and Beyond. Procedia-Social and Behavioral Sciences, vol. 198, pp. 386–396 (2015)
12. Sznajder, H.: A comparative study of keywords in English-language corporate press release. Discourse Interact. **9**(1), 49–64 (2016)
13. Malavasi, D., Mazzi, D.: History v. marketing: keywords as a clue to disciplinary epistemology. In: Bondi, M., Scott, M. (eds.) Keyness in Texts, pp. 169–184. John Benjamins Publishing Company, Amsterdam (2010)
14. Grabowski, L.: Keywords and lexical bundles within English pharmaceutical discourse: a corpus-driven description. Engl. Specif. Purp. **38**, 23–33 (2015)
15. He, A.P., Xu, M.F.: Text keywords and advanced reading teaching. In: He, A.P. (ed.) Corpus Phraseology and its Pedagogical Processing, pp. 136–146. Guangdong Higher Education Press, Guangzhou (2013)
16. Xu, M.F., He, A.P.: Corpus technology aided English in-depth reading teaching. China Educ. Technol. **12**, 87–90 (2016)
17. Nelson, M.: A corpus-based study of Business English and Business English teaching materials. Unpublished Ph.D. thesis, University of Nottingham (2000)
18. Gavioli, L.: Exploring Corpora for ESP Learning. John Benjamins Publishing Company, Amsterdam (2005)

Towards an Electronic Portfolio for Translation Teaching Aligned with China's Standards of English Language Ability

Dongyun Sun[✉] [iD]

Fudan University, Shanghai 200433, China
dysunfd@126.com

Abstract. The paper proposes a new electronic portfolio for translation teaching to College English students in China to contribute to formative assessment. With the self-assessment grid aligned with the translation ability module of China's Standards of English Language Ability and the distinction between the process portfolio and the product portfolio, it can serve both diagnostic and pedagogical purposes. This e-portfolio builds upon the existing Moodle course center of Fudan University and is complemented by local and cloud storage devices to facilitate the functionalities of learner corpora. A pedagogical design for the implementation of the e-portfolio is also proposed, incorporating the use of corpus tools as well as online resources, and stressing the need for self-assessment, feedback, learner diaries and peer revision. It is envisaged that such an e-portfolio will be well customized to the needs of College English students, making them active learners who understand their own pace of progress and march proactively towards their own objectives.

Keywords: E-portfolio · Translation teaching
China's Standards of English Language Ability · Self-assessment

1 Introduction

1.1 Background

Notwithstanding a multitude of voices on translator training at the undergraduate and graduate levels and the Master of Translation and Interpreting (MTI) programs in China, the course of English-Chinese translation for College English students, viz, non-English majors is a much less fertile soil for the pursuit of teaching methodologies and best practices. The distinction between "translator training" for the former and "translation teaching" for the latter echoes the dichotomy between "translation pedagogy" and "pedagogical translation" [1]. The course of translation for College English students is thus perfectly compatible with the objectives of "pedagogical translation" as "a mode of translation practiced as an exercise for the purpose of learning a foreign language" [1].

In the context of English-Chinese translation as an optional course for College English students in Fudan University, this paper seeks an effective tool for enhancing translation teaching within a highly compact course design. Cai Jigang points out the

© Springer Nature Switzerland AG 2018
T. Hao et al. (Eds.): SETE 2018, LNCS 11284, pp. 244–253, 2018.
https://doi.org/10.1007/978-3-030-03580-8_26

feasibility of offering this optional course at the fourth semester by citing the "3 + 1" model of Fudan University, in which College English constitutes a three-semester module for English training and complemented by one semester of optional courses [2], including English-Chinese translation. However, a two-credit course spanning one semester offers very limited room for hands-on practice, and learners often end up knowing much about translation but doing little to improve their skills. In view of this, the author proposes an e-portfolio for translation teaching with its assessment grid aligned with that of China's Standards of English Language Ability.

1.2   E-portfolio and Translation Teaching

A portfolio can be defined as "[a] purposeful collection of student work that exhibits the student's efforts, progress and achievements in one or more areas. The collection must include student participation in selecting contents, the criteria for selection, the criteria for judging merit and evidence of student self-reflection" [3]. It can be divided into the **process portfolio** and the **product portfolio** [4]. The process portfolio mainly collects all the materials displayed by students in different time periods, in order to reveal the growth track of students. The product portfolio mainly collects students' representative excellent works and reflects their best abilities. The e-portfolio is the extension and development of portfolio as an evaluation tool.

The portfolio approach contributes to learner autonomy and can be adapted to translation teaching. Bowker and Bennison [5] collect electronic documents of students' translation assignments with tagged information and incorporate them into a "student translation archive", and develop a student translation tracking system that can be retrieved in multiple ways. Wen, Wang and Wang [6] capture the progress of students' translation competence through continuous collection and reflection on translation assignments. Wang [7] builds upon Mahara an e-portfolio tool that integrates translation theories and techniques in his portfolio approach, but does not specifically introduce the modules of his e-portfolio. Kelly [8] proposes the use of e-portfolio as an alternative approach to assessment in translation teaching. Rico [9] discusses the practice of incorporating digital portfolio into translator training in the context of the European Higher Education Area, citing the module of translation technology as a case study.

To sum up, these active explorations, however pioneering, are not directly transferrable to translation courses for College English students. The most recent study by Galán-Mañas [10] introduces a portfolio for translator training consisting of the following modules:

- Diagnostic assessment (questionnaire, translation)
- Self-assessment (diagnostic questionnaire report, self-assessment reports)
- Usefulness of (electronic) resources for translation purposes (templates)
- Translations and reports on translations
- Revised versions of translations
- Report on a forum
- Summaries of two public lectures
- Contrastive aspects of language

This comprehensive portfolio sheds light on the author's current study towards e-portfolio for College English translation teaching. It also partly coincides with her course design but the latter incorporates more translation-specific components.

1.3 Translation Ability Scales in China's Standards of English Language Ability

The celebrated Common European Framework of Reference (CEFR) project undertaken by the Council of Europe is widely credited for the subsequent European Language Portfolio (ELP), a "tandem" to the celebrated CEFR project and widely piloted across Europe [11–13]. It consists of three components, namely, a language passport, a language biography, and a dossier. The language passport is a self-assessment grid based on CEFR; the language biography is an account of user's language experience; and the dossier is a collection of all supporting documents or certificates substantiating the self-assessed language competence. This e-portfolio also inspired the author's project China Plurilingual Portfolio (CPP), a learner's e-portfolio supported by the Ministry of Education of China, of which the current e-portfolio for translation teaching being one of the components. CPP seeks to develop an e-portfolio of multiple languages for diagnostic and pedagogical purposes of college students in China. It is thus proper to align her CPP with CEFR to achieve better compatibility.

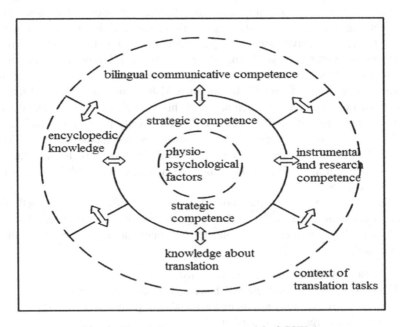

Fig. 1. Translation competence model of CSELA

In April 2018, the Ministry of Education of China officially launched *China's Standards of English Language Ability* (CSELA) (No. GF0018-2018), a national standard comprising a comprehensive assessment grid built upon CEFR but thoroughly expanded to contextualize the English learners in China, covering English listening, reading, speaking, pragmatic knowledge, language knowledge and interpreting/ translation abilities. The CSELA team proposed a translation competence diagram as follows (Fig. 1):

A five-level grid (Level 5 to Level 9) of six categories, namely, translating written narration, translating written description, translating written exposition, translating written argumentation, translating written instruction and translating written interaction (CSELA 6.5.3) is prepared in line with the communicative functions of different text types that range from politics, commerce, technology, tourism, journalism, academe, law to ancient classics [14]. The strategic competence of translation is divided into three categories, namely, planning, implementation, and evaluation/compensation, while knowledge about translation is divided into knowledge about translation theories, knowledge about translation practice and knowledge about the translation industry [14]. These issues, however, are considered of little relevance to translation teaching, a training course for further enhancing language skills of students. Thus only the six categories of text types are combined into a five-level grid in the current e-portfolio, serving both as a module for assessment, with implications on the arrangement of text types in the translation course modules. The following chart provides a general scale of translation ability in SCELA (Table 1):

Table 1. A general scale of translation ability in SCELA

Level 9	Ability to translate a variety of professional texts with a wide range of topics and complex languages. The translations are accurate, complete, standardized and authentic
	Ability to translate literary texts with abstract themes and complex structures, reproducing the original style and connotation with accurate diction
Level 8	Ability to translate expository texts with complex language and profound topics, such as literary criticism articles, academic dissertations and writings, etc. With prominent targets and good logic, the translation basically conforms in style to the source text
	Ability to translate professional texts for practical purposes, such as various product operation instructions, survey reports, etc., and to build a glossary or termbase in related fields as required, with concise and clear language and appropriate terminology
	Ability to translate descriptive texts rich in rhetorical devices such as character and scenes, reproducing the rhetorical devices and style of the source text
Level 7	Ability to translate narrative texts with complex syntactic structures, such as non-literary texts like case or event statements, narrative essays, complex plots, etc., with complete translations, language features, and styles close to the original text
	Ability to translate commentary articles, such as social science reviews and comments on current affairs, reproducing the logical relationship of the original text and conforming to the standards of the genre of the target language
	Ability to translate directive texts of familiar fields such as experimental procedures, daily product manuals, etc., with accurate terminology and compliance with industrial standards

(*continued*)

Table 1. (*continued*)

Level 6	Ability to translate the argumentative texts of familiar fields, such as general arguments, social and life commentaries, etc., with good faithfulness and accuracy while reproducing the views and attitudes of the source text
	Ability to translate narrative texts of popular content, such as anecdotes of celebrities or short stories of popular social life, accurately conveying the main information of the source text with a variety of sentence structures and smooth expressions
	Ability to translate regular communicative texts, such as cover letters, recommendation letters, and formal invitations with good accuracy and completeness
Level 5	Ability to translate short and easy texts of daily life, reproducing the general idea of the source text
	Ability to translate texts that describe the space, location and the natural environment faithfully and accurately
	Ability to translate general directive texts, such as signs and event schedules, with complete translation information and clarification

This assessment grid for translation ability is incorporated into the e-portfolio for use during a pilot test, with the expectation that this grid scale can accurately reflect the actual translation competence of College English students.

2 Design of an Electronic Portfolio for Translation Teaching

2.1 ELP-Inspired E-portfolio for Translation Teaching

Inspired by the ELP project, the author proposes that the dossier in ELP should be perfectly compatible with the product portfolio while the abovementioned assessment grid aligned with CSELA constitutes a key component of the process portfolio. The part of language biography is not considered an integral part in the current e-portfolio because, unlike the case in Europe, the language experiences of most College English students tend to be homogenous. The process portfolio is enriched with integral components for formative assessment, including all possible written assignments or revisions involved during the learning process. The product portfolio (or the dossier) is classified into all supporting documents to attest the final achievements of learners. As reflection plays a pivotal role in portfolio assessment, learner diaries are incorporated as an integral component in this e-portfolio.

Hence, the author proposes the following model of e-portfolio, identifying all possible components as listed in the left column, each of which corresponding to its expected function(s) as shown in the right column:

The Table 2 shows that this model seeks to combine all possible components into portfolio analysis, with the expectation of achieving a comprehensive and formative assessment based on evidence thus collected. A major difference between this localized model of ELP and the traditional ELP is the emphasis on the pedagogical functions, specifically the portfolio modules that facilitate formative assessment as well as the technological leverage towards technology-enhanced learning.

Table 2. Components of an e-portfolio for translation teaching

Components of the e-portfolio	Expected functions	
Process portfolio	*Formative assessment*	
Assignments	Feedback; corpus building	
Teacher revision	Teacher assessment	
Peer revision	Peer assessment	Learner autonomy
Learner diaries	Reflection	
Videos and reports of group presentation	Peer learning	
Assessment grid of translation ability of CSELA	Self-assessment	
Product portfolio	*Dossiers*	
Final exam papers	Summative assessment	
Course papers		
Self-regulated translation exercises	Additional practice	Learner autonomy
Translator qualification certificates	Third-party attestation/assessment	
Certificates of translation contests		

It is expected that this learner-centered e-portfolio will contribute to technology-enhanced learning by incorporating the following technical modules:

- **Learner corpus.** A learner corpus can be monolingual in format, compiled by collecting certain translated works of learners selected by a certain principle of sampling. Granger [15] mentions an EFL translation corpus from German undergraduate students of translation; Popescu [16] discusses the error patterns produced by EFL students in translation tasks; Kunilovskaya, Morgoun and Pariy [17] compare the lexical profiles between learner translation and professional translation by building learner corpora. With students submitting assignments electronically, teachers can compile them into an on-going learner corpus to be examined with corpus tools such as WordSmith or AntConc, and available for comparison against a corpus of professional translations or a corpus of written materials by native speakers of the target language. Findings of such research can identify common errors and styles of learners, shedding light on action-oriented pedagogical designs.
- **Online dictionaries and corpora.** In her translation class, the author always requires students to conduct careful research of terminology and phraseology through the use of a variety of online resources, including bilingual dictionaries, parallel corpora, parallel texts, and other search engine skills. For instance, the author has incorporated BCC, a monolingual Chinese corpus in her translation teaching, requiring students to retrieve useful information on word collocation, diachronic changes of terms, and word choice in the mother language of Chinese [18]. In her translation class, students are required to delve deep into the nuances and subtlety of language by scrutinizing every word in the source text with the aid of online dictionaries and corpora [19]. Each assignment should be submitted alongside with a lengthy learner diary explaining the process of researching with

online resources. Thus, these resources and skills are integrated into the current e-portfolio, specifically in the module of learner diaries but also permeating the whole process of implementation.

2.2 Class Design for the Implementation of E-portfolio for Translation Teaching

The e-portfolio can be implemented in the following stages:

- **The preparatory stage.** The preparatory stage involves an orientation activity for new students to acquaint them with the design of the e-portfolio and the grading policy therewith, the objectives of the course as well as principles of self-assessment. A pre-assessment of translation ability not only serves for comparison with results of post-assessment but also enables students to identify areas of particular interest and importance.
- **The learning stage.** The teacher adopts a bottom-up approach to translation teaching, starting with a basic primer on translation (Unit 1) and followed by a hierarchy of translation skills ranging from the word level to the text level (Units 2–6), and subsequently translation strategies of each text type (Units 7–14) punctuated by two translation mini-project presentations. Instead of the teacher-centered approach to classroom teaching, each class session revolves around the discussion of language data harvested from real-world materials, modulated by the teacher but preferably dominated by students, who are expected to utilize all technologies and tools available for research, reflection and revision. A typical cycle of class design can be illustrated by the following diagram (Fig. 2):

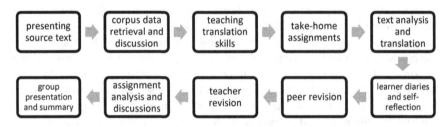

Fig. 2. Implementation of e-portfolio for translation teaching in classroom teaching

As shown in the diagram, a diverse set of activities permeate each unit of teaching, thereby requiring students to invest additional time and efforts in both online and offline team collaboration. Peer revision as a form of peer assessment that "emphasizes skills, encourages involvement, focuses on learning, establishes a reference, promotes excellence, provides increased feedback, fosters attendance, and teaches responsibility" [20] can be facilitated by a dedicated course site built upon Moodle.

- **The review stage.** Towards the end of the semester, after students fulfill all necessary learning tasks, the course culminates in a routine exam and a collection of all credentials of achievements available. Students are rated not only by how well they perform in the final exam but also by how well they have achieved throughout the whole semester, while those presenting certificates of distinguished achievements merit additional grades in proportion to their dedication and diligence.

2.3 Technological Tools for Implementation

Notwithstanding a number of e-portfolio tools (non)commercially available to teachers, this paper argues for a convenience-based blending of existing tools that are readily accessible to most teachers:

- **Moodle.** Assignments, learner diaries, teacher revisions and peer revisions can be performed on Moodle-based course sites. With built-in functions such as teacher feedback, peer feedback, polling, homework management and forums, Moodle is an open-source e-learning toolkit that is widely used for building course sites in schools and universities across the world. The Moodle toolkit of Fudan University can enable teachers to build and maintain their own course sites easily, with its built-in modules supporting these aforementioned functions.
- **Shared local or cloud storage.** As Moodle cannot be easily customized to enable translation-specific functionalities, students are also required to submit their assignments and learner diaries by email or file storage/transfer services simultaneously. These assignments are revised by the teacher with Microsoft Word, of which the rich word-processing functions makes this student-teacher unidirectional communication a good complement to the cross-revision functions enabled by Moodle. All materials involved throughout the whole learning process can be stored in dedicated folders that are subsequently shared on local, compact or cloud storages between teachers and students.
- **Corpus tools.** The assignments submitted can also be easily converted into plain text format for use as data of an ongoing learner corpus with which teachers can identify common errors of learners and provide remedial suggestions accordingly. A variety of corpus tools, including AntConc, ParaConc and WordSmith, are available for conducting corpus analysis, a lengthy topic that does not merit further elaboration in this paper.
- **Online collaborative writing tools.** The online writing tools such as Google Docs, Tencent Docs or Youdao Cloud Notes boast the merits of both Moodle modules and MS-Word, the former exceling in teacher-student online interactions while the latter preferred for word-processing and annotation, a function especially prized by translation teachers. While these tools are usually recommended for teachers of extraordinary computer literacy, it is advisable to make it more readily available to a greater audience as a tool for collaborative scaffolding.

3 Conclusion

This paper proposes a dedicated e-portfolio for translation teaching to College English students. A noteworthy feature that differs this e-portfolio from other general-purpose e-portfolio toolkits is the self-assessment grid that is adapted from CSELA, the latest and the most authoritative assessment scale for English language ability in China. This e-portfolio is also enriched by corpus tools and a learner corpus. Corpus tools, online or offline, provides hard evidence of language that enables students and teachers to give due attention to the fine shades and subtlety of words, retrieve reliable translation equivalents or terms, and identify problems in learner corpora.

A practical solution to the technical aspects of the e-portfolio is proposed by utilizing different existing tools and resources, depending on the availability of tools and the computer literacy of teachers and students. Anyway, a portfolio approach to learning should highlight the feasibility for implementation rather than the integrity of technical solution toolkits.

An earlier version of the e-portfolio has been piloted in the author's English-Chinese translation classes for two consecutive semesters, achieving satisfying results. The current version as an integral part of China Plurilingual Portfolio is an updated version, incorporating the five-level grid of translation ability of CSELA. A new pilot test is expected to launch thereafter to be reported in follow-up research papers.

Acknowledgements. This work is supported in part by a grant from the Ministry of Education of China (15YJC740071).

References

1. Delisle, J., Lee-Jahnke, H., Cormier, M.C. (eds.): Terminologie de la Traduction: Translation Terminology. Terminología de la Traducción. Terminologie der Übersetzung, vol. 1. John Benjamins Publishing, Amsterdam (1999)
2. Cai, J.: Emphasizing college English translation teaching and enhancing practical English competences of students. Chin. Transl. J. **1**, 65–68 (2003)
3. Paulson, F.L., Paulson, P.R., Meyer, C.A.: What makes a portfolio. Educ. Leadersh. **48**(5), 60–63 (1991)
4. Belanoff, P., Dickson, M. (eds.): Portfolios: Process and Product. Boynton/Cook, Portsmouth (1991)
5. Bowker, L., Bennison, P.: Student translation archive: design, development and application. In: Zanettin, F., et al. (eds.) Corpora in Translator Education, pp. 103–117 (2003)
6. Wen, J., Wang, D., Wang, L.: An experimental study of portfolio assessment of translation course. Foreign Lang. China (6), 50–54 (2006)
7. Wang, F.: Design and implementation of a Mahara-based electronic portfolio for course of translation. (MS thesis). Shanghai international Studies University (2012)
8. Kelly, D.: A Handbook for Translator Trainers. St. Jerome Publishing, London (2005)
9. Rico, C.: Translator training in the European higher education area: curriculum design for the Bologna Process A case study. Interpret. Transl. Train. **4**(1), 89–114 (2010)
10. Galán-Mañas, A.: Learning portfolio in translator training: the tool of choice for competence development and assessment. Interpret. Transl. Train. **10**(2), 161–182 (2016)
11. Little, D.: The European Language Portfolio: structure, origins, implementation and challenges. Lang. Teach. **35**(3), 182–189 (2002)
12. Little, D.: The Common European Framework and the European Language Portfolio: involving learners and their judgements in the assessment process. Lang. Test. **22**(3), 321–336 (2005)

13. Little, D., Goullier, F., Hughes, G.: The European Language Portfolio: the story so far (1991–2011). Council of Europe, Strasbourg (2011)
14. Bai, L., Feng, L., Yan, M.: Conceptualization and principles of translation ability scale of China's standards of English language ability. Mod. Foreign Lang. **41**(1), 10–15 (2018)
15. Granger, S.: A bird's-eye view of learner corpus research. In: Computer Learner Corpora, Second Language Acquisition and Foreign Language Teaching, no. 6, pp. 3–33 (2002)
16. Popescu, T.: A corpus-based approach to translation error analysis. A case-study of Romanian EFL learners. Procedia-Soc. Behav. Sci. **83**, 242–247 (2013)
17. Kunilovskaya, M., Morgoun, N., Pariy, A.: Learner vs professional translations into Russian: lexical profiles. Transl. Interpret. **10**(1), 33–52 (2018)
18. Sun, D.: The Application of BCC Chinese Corpus in English-Chinese Translation Teaching. Foreign Language Teaching Theory and Practice (2018, forthcoming)
19. Li, C.: Ensuring adequate results with the "Due Process": the role of translator's notes in translation teaching. Chin. Transl. J. **27**(3), 49–52 (2006)
20. Weaver, R.L., Cotrell, H.W.: Peer evaluation: a case study. Innov. High. Educ. **11**(1), 25–39 (1986)

Author Index